1999

THE THIRTY YEARS WAR

European History in Perspective
General Editor: Jeremy Black

Published
Benjamin Arnold *Medieval Germany*
Ronald Asch *The Thirty Years War*
Christopher Bartlett *Peace, War and the European Powers, 1814–1914*
Mark Galeotti *Gorbachev and His Revolution*
Peter Waldron *The End of Imperial Russia, 1855–1917*

Forthcoming
Nigel Aston *The French Revolution*
N. J. Atkin *The Fifth French Republic*
Ross Balzaretti *Medieval Italy: A Cultural History*
Robert Bireley *The Counter Reformation*
Donna Bohanan *Crown and Nobility in Early Modern France*
Robin Brown *Warfare in Twentieth Century Europe*
Patricia Clavin *The Great Depression, 1929–39*
Roger Collins *Charlemagne*
Geoff Cubitt *Politics in France, 1814–1876*
John Foot *The Creation of Modern Italy*
Alexander Grab *Napoleon and the Transformation of Europe*
O. P. Grell *The European Reformation*
Nicholas Henshall *The Zenith of Absolute Monarchy, 1650–1750*
Colin Imber *The Ottoman Empire, 1300–1481*
Martin Johnson *The Dreyfus Affair*
Timothy Kirk *Germany and the Third Reich*
Peter Linehan *Medieval Spain, 589–1492*
Marisa Linton *The Causes of the French Revolution*
Simon Lloyd *The Crusading Movement*
William S. Maltby *The Reign of Charles V*
David Moon *Peter the Great's Russia*
Peter Musgrave *The Early Modern European Economy*
Kevin Passmore *The French Third Republic, 1870–1940*
J. L. Price *The Dutch Republic in the Seventeenth Century*
Roger Price *1848: A Year of Revolution*
A. W. Purdue *The Second World War*
Maria Quine *A Social History of Fascist Italy*
Martyn Rady *The Habsburg Monarchy, 1848–1918*
Francisco J. Romero-Salvado *A History of Contemporary Spain*
Richard Sakwa *Twentieth Century Russia*
Thomas J. Schaeper *The Enlightenment*
Brendan Simms *A History of Germany, 1779–1850*
Graeme Small *Later Medieval France*
David Sturdy *Louis XIV*
Hunt Tooley *The Western Front*

THE THIRTY YEARS WAR
The Holy Roman Empire and Europe, 1618–1648

Ronald G. Asch
Professor of Early Modern History
University of Osnabrück

First published 1997 by
MACMILLAN PRESS LTD
Houndmills, Basingstoke, Hampshire RG21 6XS
and London
Companies and representatives
throughout the world

ISBN 0–333–62694–X hardcover
ISBN 0–333–62695–8 paperback

A catalogue record for this book is available
from the British Library.

This book is printed on paper suitable for recycling and made from fully
managed and sustained forest sources.

10   9   8   7   6   5   4   3   2   1
06 05 04 03 02 01 00 99 98 97

Typeset by EXPO Holdings, Malaysia
Printed in Hong Kong

Published in the United States of America 1997 by
ST. MARTIN'S PRESS, INC.,
Scholarly and Reference Division
175 Fifth Avenue, New York, N.Y. 10010

ISBN 0–312–16584–6 (cloth)
ISBN 0–312–16585–4 (paperback)

Für Brigitte

CONTENTS

940.24
A812

PREFACE

This is a brief introduction to a vast subject. Undoubtedly
many readers will feel that important aspects have been neglected or treated too superficially, or they will think that the
work of certain historians should have been referred to more
extensively in the notes. However, in writing a book of this sort
one inevitably has to sacrifice completeness to brevity and to
the aim of presenting one's arguments clearly and neatly.
Moreover, the Thirty Years War is a particularly difficult
subject to deal with, as each nation which took part in the war
has its own distinct historiographical tradition of presenting
and analysing the period from 1618 to 1648. In fact, if I have
let myself be persuaded by the general editor of this series,
Jeremy Black, to write this book, it is because I am convinced
that we must, now more than ever, make an effort to bridge
the gulf separating the different national traditions of scholar-
ship in Europe. I hope that the following pages will make a
modest contribution to achieving this objective. My own perspective is, admittedly, that of a German historian, though, I
hope, one not entirely unfamiliar with research and debates in
other European countries and Great Britain in particular. In
writing this book I have incurred many debts. I am particularly
grateful to Simon Adams, Johannes Arndt, Heinz Duchhardt,
Mia Rodríguez-Saldago, Georg Schmidt and Gregor
Horstkemper for their advice, suggestions and criticism.
Special thanks go to Angela Davies for transforming my at
times perhaps somewhat Germanic style of writing in a language which is not originally my own into readable English.

Westfälische Wilhelms-Universität Münster
Ronald G. Asch

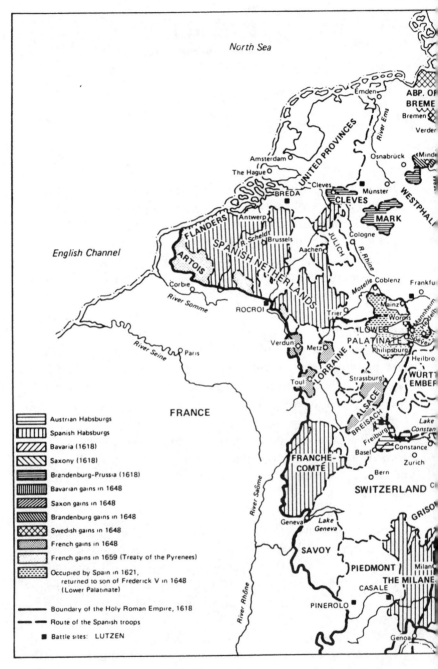

Map 1   The Holy Roman Empire during the Thirty Years War

Legend:

- Austrian Habsburgs
- Spanish Habsburgs
- Bavaria (1618)
- Saxony (1618)
- Brandenburg-Prussia (1618)
- Bavarian gains in 1648
- Saxon gains in 1648
- Brandenburg gains in 1648
- Swedish gains in 1648
- French gains in 1648
- French gains in 1659 (Treaty of the Pyrenees)
- Occupied by Spain in 1621, returned to son of Frederick V in 1648 (Lower Palatinate)
- Boundary of the Holy Roman Empire, 1618
- Route of the Spanish troops
- Battle sites: LUTZEN

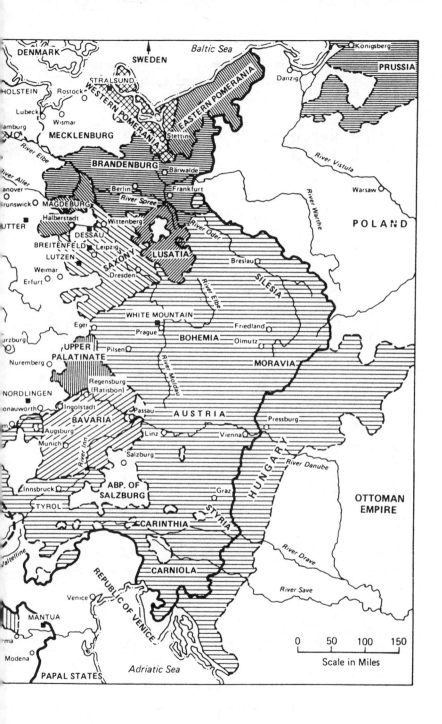

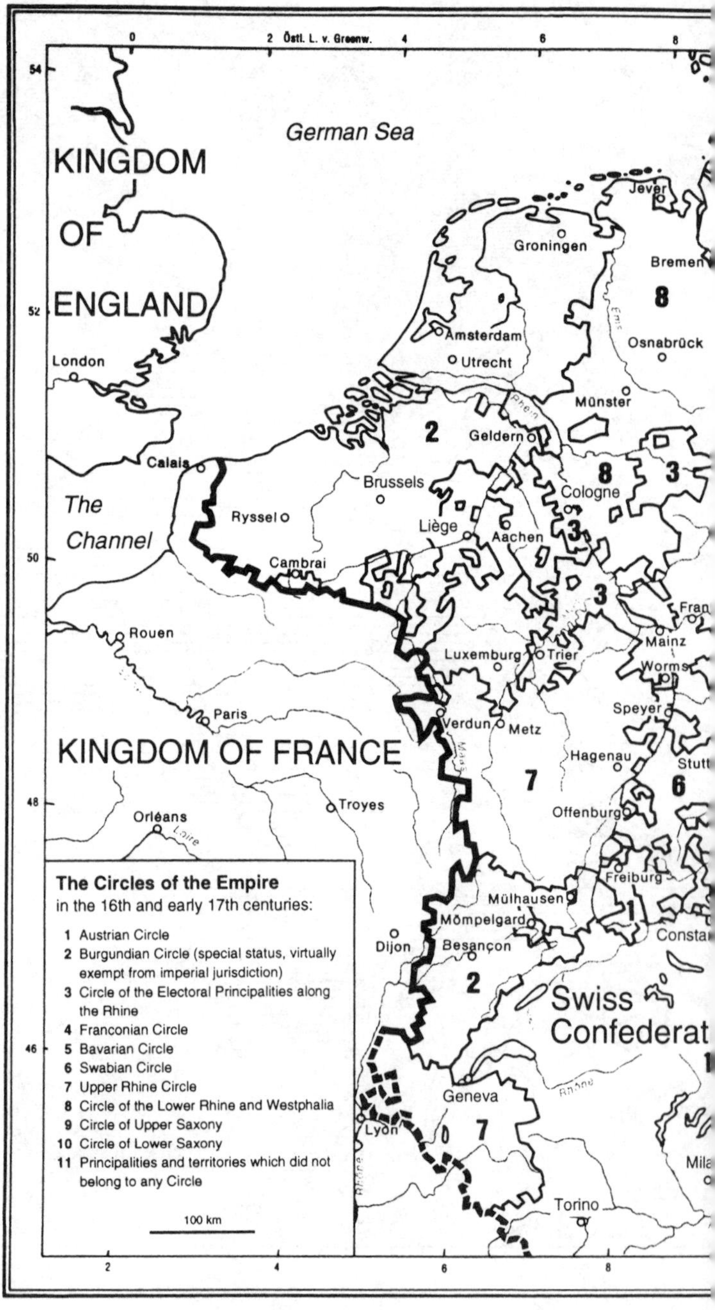
Östl. L. v. Greenw.
German Sea
KINGDOM OF ENGLAND
London
The Channel
Calais
Ryssel
Cambrai
Brussels
Liège
Aachen
Amsterdam
Utrecht
Groningen
Jever
Bremen
Osnabrück
Münster
Geldern
Cologne
Mainz
Worms
Speyer
Trier
Luxemburg
Verdun
Metz
Hagenau
Offenburg
Freiburg
Mülhausen
Mömpelgard
Besançon
Rouen
Paris
KINGDOM OF FRANCE
Troyes
Orléans
Loire
Dijon
Geneva
Lyon
Torino
Swiss Confederat
Rhône
Rhein
Ems
Maas
The Circles of the Empire
in the 16th and early 17th centuries:
1 Austrian Circle
2 Burgundian Circle (special status, virtually exempt from imperial jurisdiction)
3 Circle of the Electoral Principalities along the Rhine
4 Franconian Circle
5 Bavarian Circle
6 Swabian Circle
7 Upper Rhine Circle
8 Circle of the Lower Rhine and Westphalia
9 Circle of Upper Saxony
10 Circle of Lower Saxony
11 Principalities and territories which did not belong to any Circle
100 km

LIST OF ABBREVIATIONS

APW   *Acta Pacis Westphalicae* (see Bibliography)
BA NS   *Briefe und Akten zur Geschichte des Dreißigjährigen Krieges.* New Series (see Bibliography)
EDG   *Enzyklopädie Deutscher Geschichte*
EHR   *English Historical Review*
ESR   *European Studies Review*
HZ   *Historische Zeitschrift*
IPM   Instrumentum Pacis Monasteriense (Peace of Münster)
IPO   Instrumentum Pacis Osnabrugense (Peace of Osnabrück)
JMH   *Journal of Modern History*
VSWG   *Vierteljahresschrift für Sozial- und Wirtschaftsgeschichte*
ZHF   *Zeitschrift für Historische Forschung*

INTRODUCTION

A fifth bucket is the contemplation of Germany which is now become a Golgotha, a place of dead mens skuls; and an Aceldama, a field of blood. Some nations are chastised with the sword, others with famine, others with the man-destroying plague. But poor Germany hath been sorely whipped with all these three iron whips at the same time and that for above twenty yeers space. Oh let us make use of this bucket and draw out water and power it out before the Lord this day.

Edmund Calamy, *England's Looking Glass*, 1641.[1]

In a century which has seen the death of millions of soldiers and civilians in two world wars, the horrors of warfare three and a half centuries ago may have lost some of their vividness. For many contemporaries, however, the war ravaging central Europe between 1618 and 1648 was a traumatic experience. Even men and women in countries not immediately affected by warfare looked with horror upon the slaughter and the political and religious upheaval, as Edmund Calamy's sermon quoted above and many other documents testify. In fact, as late as 1651 the divine John Durie circulated in Britain an English translation of a German tract which tried to prove that the events of the years 1618–48 were leading directly to the Final Judgement of the world which was predicted for 1655. In the opinion of the German author of the original pamphlet, the Silesian Protestant mystic Abraham von Frankenberg, the suppression of Protestantism in the Habsburg dominions, starting in the late 1590s, completed after 1620 and now confirmed by the Westphalian Peace, was a portent and precursor of the imminent apocalyptic struggle between the forces of light and darkness.[2] Of course, even in the early seventeenth century, what was for some an essentially religious

1

conflict with eschatological dimensions was for others a struggle for political power in which the two principal contestants were the Spanish and Austrian Habsburgs on the one hand and the French Bourbons on the other, and in which religion was little more than a cloak for much more secular ambitions. Cardinal Richelieu, for example, the leading French statesman of the late 1620s and the 1630s, certainly saw Spanish policy in this light.[3]

Like contemporaries, modern historians have disagreed about the causes and principal issues of the Thirty Years War. For some historians even the name Thirty Years War itself is a misnomer. Thus as recently as 1992 Nicola Sutherland stated that the 'Thirty Years War is a largely factitious conception which has nevertheless become an indestructable myth'. For her, the war is at best a mere episode or phase in an almost interminable struggle between the Habsburgs and the French royal dynasty, the Valois, and their successors, the Bourbons. In her view this struggle went back ultimately to the 1490s if not, as one might argue, to 1477, when the last Duke of Burgundy died without a male heir (his inheritance was claimed by both the Habsburgs and the Valois), and did not come to an end until 1715.[4]

The significance of the dates 1618 and 1648 for the political history of Europe can indeed *prima facie* be impugned. Depending on one's perspective, the Thirty Years War may seem to dissolve into a series of individual conflicts with different issues – with no real common denominator – and different participants, without any clear beginning or end. Thus France only became a full participant in the war in 1635, after earlier briefer and more limited interventions, and was to fight on against Spain until 1659, well beyond the Peace of Westphalia. Poland on the other hand fought Sweden, with several intermissions of various length, from 1600 until 1629 and again during the years 1655–60. Thus for a number of years the military contest between Sweden and Poland coincided with the Thirty Years War in which Sweden undoubtedly played a prominent part from 1630 onwards.

The Swedish–Polish war is only one example of a number of conflicts which were to some extent connected with the events in central Europe, but which cannot easily be integrated into the traditional framework of interpretation for which the term 'Thirty Years War' stands. Must it therefore really be abandoned as Nicola Sutherland suggests? This is hardly convincing. It would be very difficult to prove, and Sutherland certainly does not manage to do so, that the elements of coherence and continuity in the alleged more than 200 years of conflict between the Habsburgs and France are greater than those in the 30 years of warfare from 1618 to 1648. In fact there is less continuity between the great European wars of the 1580s and 1590s and the Thirty Years War than is sometimes claimed (see below, pp. 34–6). Moreover, such attempts to discard well-established conventional terms of historiography are rarely successful because they tend to be indispensable in practice – a fact which is only thinly disguised by putting them into inverted commas. Finally, the expression 'Thirty Years War' is in fact a contemporary one commonly employed by authors who had already spoken of a 'fifteen years war' in 1633 and a 'twenty years war' in 1638 (and so on). This has been conclusively demonstrated by Konrad Repgen in a number of articles unfortunately ignored by Sutherland.[5]

In fact, there was one central issue justifying the contemporary judgement that the Thirty Years War was a contest with a definite beginning and a definite end and with a structure giving coherence to the various military campaigns, not just an amorphous and haphazard series of individual wars: the constitution of the Holy Roman Empire and – inseparable from this question – the balance of political and religious forces in central Europe. Of course, looking at the events of the early seventeenth century from the purely national perspective of, for example, Portuguese or Polish or, more problematically, even English or French history, the notion of the Thirty Years War as an interpretative framework may possibly be rejected as irrelevant. However, once this framework is accepted, it can make sense only if events in the Empire are seen as the central issue, otherwise we are indeed left with a chaos of individual political and military conflicts. If, therefore, our analysis focuses again and again on the course of the war in

Germany, this is a necessary consequence of accepting the notion of a Thirty Years War as such. Here in the Holy Roman Empire the war did have a clear beginning and a clear end, although the frontlines of the contest determining the allegiance of the individual states and princes were by no means the same in 1646 as in 1636 or in 1620.

This, of course, is not to deny that the war, which early on had a second focus on the periphery of the Empire in the Low Countries, was increasingly internationalised from the later 1620s onwards. What had started as a conflict in central Europe was in the end to engulf almost the entire European world, with repercussions as far away as the Iberian Peninsula, where Catalonia and Portugal rose against the King of Spain in 1640. In fact, the Thirty Years War was very much a European civil war as well as a contest between dynasties, princes and republics. As one of most important recent interpretations of the war, Johannes Burkhardt's *Der Dreißigjährige Krieg*, a brilliantly written and thought-provoking intellectual *tour de force*, has emphasised, the states of the early seventeenth century were by no means 'closed' political systems. The right and the capacity to wage war and to achieve political objectives by force of arms, in inter-state or domestic contests, was not yet the exclusive privilege of fully sovereign princes (or for that matter republics).

In fact, the distinction between 'states' and 'estates', 'Staaten' and 'Stände', or 'l'état' and 'les états' was not yet as clearly drawn as it was to become later, in western Europe at least. The Estates and their assemblies or parliaments still claimed the right, on certain occasions, to act as more or less independent agents in European politics and to wage war, if necessary, on their own. In doing so the Dutch 'States General' were indeed singularly successful, becoming fully sovereign themselves in 1648, and the German princes, the Estates of the Empire, also ultimately managed to frustrate all attempts by the Emperor to monopolise the right to wage war and to regulate and control diplomatic relations with other European powers. Strikingly less successful were the Estates of Bohemia, and the noble magnates, as well as the Protestant cities and noblemen, in France.

They were reduced to the status of mere subjects in a domestically demilitarised state in the seventeenth century, either during the course of the war itself or in the decades following the Peace of Westphalia. The war was thus an important phase in the process of European state formation.[6]

In 1618 this process, clearly distinguishing 'states' from 'estates', was far from complete, which to a large extent accounts for the fact that there was a constant interaction between 'international' and domestic conflict between 1618 and 1648. It would have been far less close had the coherence of the European monarchies been greater. The close linkage between inter-state and domestic conflicts was at least partly responsible not only for the outbreak of the war but also for its escalation and prolongation. In some cases domestic confrontations caused or at least triggered war between European states – as in Bohemia in 1618. In other cases the pressure which the international power struggle exerted on state and society opened fissures in the political structure, and caused provincial rebellions or open civil war, as in France in the 1620s and again from 1648 to 1653 during the Fronde, or in the Iberian peninsula in the early 1640s, or even, it could be argued, in neutral England at about the same time, as a belated response to the Stuart monarchy's disastrous involvement in the war from 1625 to 1629.

It needs to be emphasised that military finance was a crucial problem in this context. Only very few countries were able to finance their armies (and navies) either by pressing allies and occupied provinces into paying for them, like Sweden in the 1630s and 1640s, or by actually raising the necessary taxes at home in a way which neither destroyed political consensus nor disrupted economic life, as the Dutch Republic did. In most other cases the costs of warfare were so staggering that they caused either bankruptcy or domestic rebellion or both, as in France and Spain, unless a ruler decided to delegate the business of waging war with all its financial risks to a more or less independent private military entrepreneur. This could, however, entail a dangerous loss of control over military operations, as the career of the imperial general Wallenstein was to show. In any case, the problems of war finance, which will be analysed in greater depth in this survey (below, pp. 150–77), are an important key to the interaction between inter-state and domestic conflicts during the war.

The other key is, of course, religion. Confessional tensions were a decisive factor linking internal and domestic disputes. This is obvious in the case of the Bohemian rising of 1618–19 but also holds true for the later stages of the war. At no stage was the Thirty Years War an exclusively religious contest, though there were phases when the confessional issue became more or less dominant, at least in the Empire (for example, during the late 1620s and early 1630s). Nevertheless, large sections of the political and social elites in the various European countries perceived the war as a confessional struggle – as probably did many humbler men and women who had to foot the bill in the form of higher taxes, or as victims of plunder, epidemics and military atrocities as well.

This was important because the war which had erupted in 1618 with serious implications for the religious balance of power in the Empire tended to undermine the stability of religious peace in other European countries where different confessional groups were competing for power or just fighting for survival too. Issues which had seemingly been settled by compromise in the preceding years or decades were reopened. Thus in France the Catholic extremists, the *dévots*, could hope that the Catholic advance in the Empire would at least indirectly strengthen their own position and enable them to undo the French religious settlement of 1598, the Edict of Nantes, with its concession of toleration to Protestants. The total victory which had rather narrowly escaped the pro-Spanish *dévots* in the 1590s now once more seemed within reach. The French Protestants themselves were understandably worried by this prospect, and their decision to defend their privileges by force of arms, ultimately taking recourse to foreign (in particular, English) support, must be seen in the context of a European political scenario which was apparently becoming bleaker and bleaker for Protestants nearly everywhere.

Moreover, and not just in France, foreign policy decisions, even if it was only the decision to stay neutral, had implications for the confessional identity of the countries concerned. Could a French kingdom which was allied with Protestant princes, as it was in the 1630s and 1640s, be a truly Catholic country? Or could an English king who preferred to stay neutral in the great European war after 1630 be a truly Protestant monarch governing a truly Protestant kingdom? These were explosive questions linking domestic tensions to the conflict between the European states.

The competition for power and, ultimately, sovereignty between princes and Estates, religious tensions, and the social and political issues raised by the enormous costs of warfare were structural problems which were permanent features of the entire war. Nevertheless, no exclusively or, indeed, primarily structural approach can do justice to the complicated process of political decision-making which must be understood if the war itself is not to become incomprehensible. Without giving undue prominence to high politics, it must be stressed that ultimately the history of political 'events' cannot be reduced to structural history. Events such as the outbreak of the war in 1618 or the imperial decision to ratify the Edict of Restitution in 1629 cannot be deduced with a sufficient degree of certainty from structural models, while the Thirty Years War is itself the best example of a political 'event' which profoundly changed political and social structures, and perhaps even collective mentalities (though this is a field as yet largely unexplored).

On the other hand, this survey does not and, indeed, cannot aim to provide the reader with a comprehensive and detailed history of the entire war. Rather, it will concentrate on the long-term preconditions for the outbreak of hostilities and on four key dates. The war will be analysed looking forward – and backward – from these key dates. Two of them are, of course, 1618 and 1648, the beginning and the end of the war; the two others are 1629 and 1635.

Both 1629 and 1635 were turning points in the war, when a final settlement of the conflict, at least within the Empire, seemed possible – in 1629 a settlement imposed by the Emperor on his opponents, and in 1635 a compromise between the Emperor and the Catholic princes on the one hand and the moderate Lutheran Protestants of eastern and northern Germany on the other. In both cases attempts to reach a settlement failed, and in both cases the subsequent years witnessed a continuing escalation of warfare as well as a further 'internationalisation' of the conflict in the Empire.

With the Edict of Restitution passed in 1629 the militant Counter-Reformation in the Empire reached its climax. Six years later, in 1635, the Peace of Prague, though failing to end the war, at least defused a number of the confessional issues. During the last phase of the conflict these played a less prominent role than before, not least because France's co-operation with Sweden and a minority of Germany's Protestant princes put paid to any attempts to interpret the war in exclusively religious terms, even for propaganda purposes. Nevertheless, under the surface of a contest between two multi- or bi-confessional alliances – after 1635 many Lutheran princes and Estates actively supported the Emperor for a number of years – the confessional issues which had figured so prominently in the earlier phases of the war simmered on. In fact they were to re-emerge during the peace conference at Osnabrück in the late 1640s. Thus in this as in many other areas, there was an underlying continuity of problems and issues throughout the entire length of the war. They were not resolved until the Peace of Westphalia was signed in 1648. Though failing to achieve a lasting settlement for Europe, it managed to a surprisingly large degree to bring internal peace to the Holy Roman Empire.

1

THE ORIGINS OF THE CONFLICT

Religion, Law and Politics in the Holy Roman Empire

With the benefit of hindsight it is easy to consider the outbreak of the Thirty Years War in 1618 as inevitable. Indeed, as
we shall see, there was no lack of combustible material in the
Holy Roman Empire before 1618. However, the Empire had
successfully avoided the disasters of religious war in the later
sixteenth century. France, so often depicted as the paradigm
of the successful modern state, was rent by an almost interminable series of wars and feuds motivated by aristocratic rivalries and political and social tensions as much as by the
hatred between Catholics and Huguenots from the 1560s to
the 1590s, whereas the seemingly much more old-fashioned
political commonwealth of the Holy Roman Empire had
managed to defuse the religious tensions of the post-
Reformation years. The Religious Peace of Augsburg (1555),
one of the fundamental laws of the Empire, had officially
recognised Protestantism as defined by the *Confessio Augustana*
(1530) as one of the two religions which could legally be
practised in Germany, the other being, of course, Roman
Catholicism.[1] The principle of religious toleration was thus
officially established.

Of course, toleration as defined by the Peace of Augsburg
was not the same as the freedom of conscience and worship
that modern constitutional charters grant to individual

citizens. Essentially it was the princes and Estates of the Empire who benefited from toleration, not their subjects. These had to accept the religious decisions and predilections of their rulers. To choose one of the two confessions permitted in the Empire for themselves and their subjects was, indeed, one of the main prerogatives of the princes after 1555. Later, at the end of the sixteenth century, Protestant lawyers coined the phrase *cuius regio, eius religio*: he who rules a territory is entitled to dictate its religion. This phrase only summed up what the jurisdiction of the Chamber Court of the Empire (Reichskammergericht) had identified as the core of the agreement reached in Augsburg during the years after 1555, namely that the *ius refomandi*, the right to reform the Church, was essentially a prerogative of the princes and rulers of the Empire like any other regalian right. Those who had signed the Peace of Augsburg, however, did not yet see this principle as the essence of the settlement as clearly as the lawyers interpreting the peace later were to do; for they had not yet given up the hope of re-establishing some sort of religious unity.

As it was, after 1555 the inhabitants of the various principalities had the choice of accepting the ruler's confessional decision or emigrating. Only in some of the free cities of the Empire (the *Reichsstädte*) was genuine toleration with equal rights for both churches established, at least in theory. Elsewhere the *ius emigrandi*, the right to leave towns and villages where one could not practise one's own religion freely, was, at least legally, guaranteed to every person in the Holy Roman Empire down to the humblest peasant by the peace of 1555. In normal legal practice, however, being forced to leave one's country was one of the severest punishments a court of law could impose. The *ius emigrandi* was, therefore, a privilege of dubious character and the majority of Protestant legal scholars did, in fact, argue that somebody who had the right to emigrate should *a fortiori* be allowed to stay in his country, as the benefits of the Peace of Augsburg could hardly be meant as a punishment.[2]

Whatever its imperfections – and there were many – the Peace of Augsburg spared Germany the fate of France in the later sixteenth century. This is in many ways quite surprising, for most of the various Estates of the Empire – the secular and ecclesiastical princes, the counts of the Empire (*Reichsgrafen*), even the free and imperial cities, and, though to a markedly lesser extent, the knights of the Empire (*Reichsritter*) – had the means to pursue whatever legal and political claims they had by force of arms. Although the Ewige Landfriede (Perpetual Peace) of 1495 had declared such feuds illegal, it is remarkable that open warfare of this sort was indeed a comparatively rare event after 1555, and remained limited in extent when it did occur. Princes and other rulers had become accustomed to settling their conflicts by litigation in the courts of law of the Empire, the Reichskammergericht in Speyer and the Reichshofrat (Imperial Aulic Council) at the imperial residence in Prague and later in Vienna.

It could, of course, be argued that the settlement of 1555 did not really solve the religious and political conflicts undermining the stability of the Empire. In the last resort both sides, Protestants and Catholics, remained convinced that their own religion was the only true one, and that the concessions made to the other side were no more than a temporary expedient. On the one hand, Catholics considered the toleration granted to Protestants as at best an irregularity, and at worst as absolutely incompatible with canon law and the principles of the Catholic faith. Protestants, on the other hand, were still confident in 1555 and for many years longer that the Peace of Augsburg had opened the way for a further erosion of the Catholic position, already much weakened. To some extent the less than sincere compromise of 1555 can be compared with the fudged religious settlement in Elizabethan England after 1558. In both cases a great many questions were left unresolved, and while the generation born during the years of the Reformation managed to achieve relative confessional peace, the conflicts which they had successfully set aside returned to plague their descendants in the seventeenth century.

What were the principal problems of the settlement achieved in 1555 in Germany? The attempt to confine religious conflicts to the level of internal territorial affairs could only work if the domestic disputes of individual territories could be clearly separated from the political problems of the Empire. If this was difficult for the secular principalities, it was all but impossible for the ecclesiastical ones, where secular authority was exercised by bishops and prelates. (As experience was to show, it was equally impossible for the hereditary lands ruled by the imperial dynasty.) Did ecclesiastical rulers enjoy the same same *ius reformandi* as the secular princes? What was to happen if a prince-bishop decided to embrace Protestantism? These were crucial questions for the political future of the Empire. Not only did ecclesiastical princes rule vast territories, in particular along the Rhine and in Franconia but also in parts of northern Germany, they also had about half, if not more, of the votes in the second of the three councils (or *curiae*) of the Diet of the Empire (Reichstag), the Council of Princes (Fürstenrat). Moreover, three of the seven electors of the Empire were ecclesiastical dignitaries (the Archbishops of Mainz, Cologne and Trier). However, a special clause, the *reservatum ecclesiasticum*, had been added without the consent of the Protestant Estates to the resolution of the Diet of 1555 which established the Religious Peace. This clause required ecclesiastical princes who converted to Protestantism to resign all their offices and benefices, thus ensuring the survival of the various episcopal territories as Catholic ecclesiastical principalities.

The Protestants never really accepted the validity of the *reservatum ecclesiasticum*. In practice a number of prince-bishops did convert to Protestantism, or at least cathedral chapters elected Protestants as prince-bishops when a vacancy occurred. In particular, in northern and eastern Germany quite a few ecclesiastical territories were thus gradually secularised, for example the important Archbishopric of Magdeburg. The Catholics considered these secularisations illegal and in a number of cases they were able to maintain their position. If necessary they resorted to force, as in Cologne where the Archbishop, who had become a Protestant, was driven into exile and eventually forced to resign after an intervention by

Spanish and Bavarian troops in the 1580s. Thus the guiding principle of the Peace of Augsburg, the religious autonomy of every prince, nobleman or corporation who was the Emperor's immediate subject and owed obedience to no other lord, could never be applied consistently because it was in many ways incompatible with the special character of the ecclesiastical territories. This incompatibility was underlined not only by the *reservatum ecclesiasticum* but also by a special concession which Ferdinand I had made to the Protestants in 1555. In a declaration, whose legal validity was, however, uncertain, he had granted the noblemen and cities under the rule of ecclesiastical princes the right to remain Protestants if they had been so before 1555 (*declaratio Ferdinandea*).

The status of ecclesiastical possessions within the Protestant principalities was also a problem. Did the princes' *ius reformandi* include the right to confiscate or otherwise secularise the estates and goods of monasteries and other ecclesiastical corporations which were normally dissolved once the separation from Rome had taken place? If Catholics were prepared to accept such measures at all, then it was only if they had taken place before 1555, or rather 1552 when the preliminary treaty on which the peace of 1555 was based had been signed (Treaty of Passau).[3] But of course the confesssional status of many territories and their rulers had been unclear in the 1550s and was only subsequently clarified. Conflicts were thus unavoidable.

Both sides appealed to the law courts of the Empire to resolve these conflicts, but with the passage of years the judgements of these courts became more and more a cause of controversy and were rejected by many princes and Estates. In Protestant eyes both the Imperial Aulic Council – under the control of the Emperor – and the Chamber Court in Speyer, where the judges apart from the presiding chief justice were appointed by the Estates or Circles of the Empire, favoured the Catholics in their decisions. In Speyer, not to mention Prague, the seat of the Aulic Council, the Catholics were over-represented among the judges. Admittedly, the settlement of 1555 provided for an equal number of Protestants and

Catholics to take part in the deliberations and decisions of the Chamber Court (but not of the Aulic Council) concerning religious questions.[4] However, even the Protestant lawyers serving in Speyer were often inclined to favour a cautious, conservative interpretation of the Peace of Augsburg which was difficult to accept for those Protestants who saw the Reformation in Germany as something still to be completed.

Among the latter the followers of the Reformed confession, the Calvinists, played a prominent role. Their status was complicated enough anyhow. Officially the *Confessio Augustana* of 1530 was the only legal Protestant creed in the Empire. Unless they could demonstrate that their faith was compatible with the *Confessio*, the Reformed Protestants, who looked to Zurich and Geneva for theological guidance, were in purely legal terms outlaws. In practice, however, the Calvinists claimed that they were as much adherents of the *Confessio Augustana* as the Lutherans, and thus entitled to enjoy the protection of the peace of 1555. They got away with this, partly because some of the most prominent Lutheran theologians, in particular Melanchthon, had indeed favoured an interpretation of the 1530 confession of faith which was not too far removed from the tenets of the more moderate Reformed Protestants. Even more important was the fact that most Lutheran princes were reluctant to call the bluff of Reformed rulers such as the Elector Palatine in the years after 1555. They were far too valuable as allies, for the time being at least.

However, tensions between Reformed Protestants, by now mostly Calvinists, and Lutherans grew when in the late 1570s strict Lutheran theologians drew up the Formula of Concord (1577–78), a rigidly anti-Calvinist confession of faith, which made compromise between the two principal groups in German Protestantism impossible once and for all.[5] Not all Lutheran princes and independent cities signed the *Formula Concordiae* but in the years before the outbreak of the Thirty Years War theologians in some Lutheran regions, such as Saxony, for example, considered the Calvinists worse enemies than the Catholics. On the other hand, the comparative isolation of the Calvinists only encouraged a relentless political activism in the years before 1618 and a search for allies outside Germany, in the Netherlands, in England or among the French Huguenots.

Thus the mere existence of Reformed Protestants in the Empire, something which was unforeseen or ignored in 1555, helped to undermine the stability of the constitutional arrangements agreed in Augsburg. Initially not many princes embraced Calvinism, but the conversion of the Elector of Brandenburg to the Reformed faith in 1613 meant that two of the prince electors were Calvinists. In addition to the Hohenzollern Prince of Brandenburg and the Elector Palatine, the Landgrave of Hesse-Kassel and a number of counts also favoured the Reformed faith. Some of these counts, in particular those who held territories in the area around Frankfurt (Wetterau), had supported the Dutch revolt against Spain in the later sixteenth century or even, like the counts of Nassau, taken a leading part in it.[6]

The emergence of Reformed Protestantism as a separate church in the later sixteenth century was in itself a sign that the frontlines between the various religious groups had become more clearly defined. For the 1550s, when the Peace of Augsburg was signed, it could still be argued that the adherents of the old faith were united more by their loyalty to Rome and their determination to be faithful to the traditions of medieval piety than by any positive programme. It was the Council of Trent, completed in 1563, which provided them with such a programme. However, even then it was a long time before this programme was implemented and before a Catholic reform of the manifold abuses which had crept in during the later Middle Ages – or of what were now seen as abuses – prepared the ground for an active Counter-Reformation directed against Protestantism in all its forms. Catholic reform was certainly more than a mere reaction to the threat of Protestantism, but at the same time repressive measures against Protestants – the Counter-Reformation in the strict sense of the word – were seen by nearly all Catholic reformers as a necessary complement to the spiritual and administrative renewal of the Roman Church.[7]

When the Peace of Augsburg was passed, there was still something like a middle ground between the confessions, in spite of all the theologians railing at the heresies and abominations of their opponents. At least in some regions of Germany – along the lower Rhine, for example, and in many ecclesiastical principalities where the ruling princes were either unwilling or unable to enforce strictly one of the religious options available – confessional development remained in a sort of limbo. Religious practice, probably more than official theological doctrine, remained linked to some extent to an older pre-confessional piety. In fact, the peace still anticipated the eventual re-unification of the Church by a general council, or within the Empire by political negotiations, though not in the immediate future.[8] This may have been just a token commitment in 1555 and hardly realistic even then, but 30 years later it was a mere pipe-dream. In 1555 it was probably still possible for a sincerely religious man or woman to avoid a final and irrevocable commitment to one of the contending religious movements and churches. Indeed, the prince who ruled the Empire from 1564 to 1576, Maximilian II, provides a good example of such an ambivalent attitude,[9] and during this period it was not yet uncommon for Protestant councillors to serve Catholic princes or, perhaps more rarely, for adherents of the old faith to act as officeholders for Protestant rulers.

Gradually, however, the competing churches defined their positions ever more precisely and, what is even more important, they adapted to the challenge of permanent confessional conflict. The division of Christianity had to be accepted as a reality for the immediate future; theologians now became specialists in the permanent intellectual warfare which this division made inevitable. They made it their principal task – in Lutheran orthodoxy as much as in Counter-Reformation theology, not to mention Calvinism – to define the tenets of their own confessional community as clearly as possible and to distinguish them from those of their rivals. In line with theological doctrine, specific religious practices which had already developed before the 1550s became entrenched, giving each confession its special culture and mentality. The different forms of celebrating the eucharist for example, the cult of saints and of the Virgin Mary in Catholicism, or a specific tradition of sacred music in Lutheranism were all features distinguishing the various confessions.

The growing rigidity of confessional structures and of religious attitudes, which crystallised into fixed mentalities, was part of a wider process of 'confessionalisation' (*Konfessionalisierung*), a term prominent in recent German research. It refers to the influence of confessional structures and conflicts on all spheres of life – education, culture, politics and constitutional law – and also implies that the intensification of government activity in the territories was closely connected with the imposition of a uniform faith by secular authorities.[10]

Confessionalisation as such may not have made the co-existence of different religious communities in the Empire impossible. But religious controversies were deeply interwoven with political conflicts. Not the least of these conflicts were those which arose from debates about the Emperor's constitutional position. To work properly the settlement of 1555 would have required, ideally at least, a neutral authority supervising its implementation. But the Emperor, the highest authority in the Reich, was far from neutral. If Maximilian II still had some sympathy for Protestantism, his succcessor Rudolf II (1576–1612) gave his support, though perhaps somewhat reluctanctly, to the Counter-Reformation, at least during the later phases of his reign and in his own hereditary lands which he governed as King of Bohemia and Archduke of Austria. Although his personal religious tastes were rather unorthodox – given a choice he preferred experiments in alchemy to the celebration of mass during his later years – he saw no reason to grant his subjects the freedom to choose from as wide a range of religious options as he himself did.[11] But could a monarch bent on suppressing Protestantisn in his own kingdoms and principalities rule an Empire which was *de iure* bi-confessional and *de facto* tri-confessional?

17

The extent of the Emperor's powers had never been exactly defined, all attempts by the princes of the Empire to do so notwithstanding. Now under the conditions of permanent religious conflict, the debate on the Emperor's constitutional position was inevitably linked with the confessional issues. Naturally enough, the Catholics were inclined to stress the Emperor's personal authority. They declared his interpretation of the imperial statutes and of the peace of 1555 authentic and binding, although they were rarely friends of imperial 'absolutism' as such – in any case an anachronistic term for this period of German history. The majority of the Catholic princes were ecclesiastical rulers who had a long tradition of looking to the Emperor for protection; the only major secular Catholic rulers apart from the members of the House of Habsburg were the Duke of Bavaria, the Duke of Lorraine (whose status as a member of the Empire was uncertain) and the Duke of Jülich, Cleves and Berg. The heads of the latter dynasty were Catholics but neither able – the last two dukes before the extinction of the male line of the ducal dynasty in 1609 were mentally incapitated for most of their adult life – nor truly willing to ban Protestantism in their dominions.

It would, however, be a mistake to assume that the Protestant princes and their legal advisers simply rejected the Emperor's authority. The Lutherans, at least, were firmly committed not only to the Empire and its institutions, such as the Reichstag, but also to the Emperor as their liege lord and as the symbol of the Empire's unity.[12] By no means all Lutheran princes went as far as Landgrave Ludwig of Hesse-Darmstadt, one of the Emperor's most loyal supporters, who as late as 1625 admonished his sons in his will never, under any circumstances, to take up arms against the Emperor or the House of Austria but to respect the Emperor all their lives as their natural ruler and highest lord ('ordentliche Obrigkeit unnd daß höchste Oberhaubt').[13] None the less, had they been accused before 1618 of undermining the Emperor's authority, most of them would have sincerely and indignantly rejected any such insinuation.

But how could this loyalty to a Catholic Emperor be combined with a defence of those rights which Protestants – Lutherans as well as Calvinists – considered essential for their political survival? It was this question which forced Protestant political theorists and lawyers to reflect more deeply on the nature of political authority and on the constitution of the Empire. When the institutions which had so far made the peaceful settlement of conflicts possible, the Chamber Court as well as the Diet of the Empire, gradually disintegrated or lost their efficiency from the 1590s onwards, the search for theoretical solutions to these serious questions became even more urgent. Furthermore, German legal scholars found provocative the accounts which political theorists in western Europe gave of the Empire's constitution. In Jean Bodin's opinion, for example, the Empire was a mere aristocracy not a monarchy, while other theorists outside Germany even saw the princes as the real sovereigns and the Empire as a mere alliance of virtually independent rulers. But if Germany was not a true monarchy, it could hardly be the successor of the ancient Roman Empire, the last of the four universal monarchies prophesied by Daniel in the Old Testament. The status of the Holy Roman Empire as the most eminent of the European monarchies was therefore in danger.[14]

In the heated discussion of the constitution of the Empire which got underway around the turn of the century, most theorists therefore continued to affirm the character of the Empire as a monarchy, although they also tended to stress the limitations to which the Emperor's power was subjected; in the final resort they saw the constitution of the Empire as a mixture between aristocracy and monarchy. Those who rejected this interpretation of the existing political structure as a mixed constitution and emphasised the exclusively monarchical character of authority in the Empire, like the Lutheran scholar Theodor Reinking, could still defend the princes' inherited privileges by allowing for a right of resistance against acts of tyranny. According to Reinking, everyone who exercised political authority – even if subject to an overlord – possessed this inalienable right of resistance.[15] By confirming the nature of the Empire as a genuine monarchy while at the same time appealing to a theory of a mixed constitution or a natural right of resistance, legal theorists were able to present the Empire as a true state, not too different from the great monarchies of western Europe, without denying the privileges and autonomy of the princes of the Empire.

It needs to the stressed that the new science of *ius publicum* (public law) which formed the framework for these theories of government, was more the work of Protestant legal scholars than of Catholics during the two or three decades preceding the outbreak of the war.[16] Catholics were inclined to appeal to the personal authority of the Emperor whom they knew to support their case. Lutherans, while underlining their loyalty to the Emperor, nevertheless tended to distinguish between the Emperor as a person and the *maiestas* (sovereignty) of the Empire as a body politic founded on law, custom, privileges and statutes. At a time when their position was clearly under threat, the rule of law was more attractive than ever as an ideal to Protestants, or at least to those among them, the Lutherans, who could expect to be protected by the existing legal structures. Politically now increasingly weaker than their opponents, the Lutherans felt that the security which the statutes and fundamental constitutions of the Empire offered were the best they could hope for.

These new political theories and legal concepts must be seen in a wider context. As a number of historians have pointed out, their emergence was part of a process which had been under way since the later sixteenth century, and by which political conflict and political thought were 'juridified'.[17] The new language of public law seemed to offer a chance to find an idiom which both sides, Catholics as well as Protestants, could use, whereas the various theological concepts had become so incompatible that they seemed to rule out any sort of meaningful communication between the confessions. Even though the jurisdictional structure of the Empire ceased to function effectively after the 1590s, the rule of law still seemed to offer the best opportunity to overcome the political impasse in the Empire. The 'juridification' of political thought and politics itself was certainly not a phenomenon unique to Germany during this period. The role which the common law played in England as the dominant idiom of politics between 1600 and 1640 offers an obvious parallel.[18] But in Germany, the legal concepts developed before 1618 and during the Thirty Years War itself to master the political crisis were to remain influential in the later seventeenth century and beyond. Political debate in the Empire, probably more than in most other European countries, continued to be conducted in the language of law, in the sense of a specifically German *ius publicum*, even in the later seventeenth and in the eighteenth centuries.

Of course, as far as the situation before 1618 was concerned, the juridification of the religious and political conflicts in the Empire was deeply ambivalent. On the one hand, after theological communication had largely broken down Protestant and Catholics now had a common language again. On the other hand, legal concepts were as least as much a weapon to be used in a 'cold' war, as a means of communication.[19] As both sides articulated their claims in ever more inflexible terms, informal compromise became increasingly impossible. In fact, when open war broke out it was very much a war about the interpretation of law. None of the warring parties within Germany consistently denied the validity of the existing statutes and fundamental constitutions of the Empire, especially the Peace of Augsburg, or really tried to abrogate them as such, whatever the mental reservations of the Catholics in particular may have been in theory. What was at stake between 1618 and 1648 was their interpretation.[20]

Of course, the religious conflict between Catholics, Lutherans and Calvinists in its various theological, legal and politial forms was not the only cause of the breakdown of the Empire's constitution before 1618 and thus of the war. The religious question can, however, be considered the focus of all other issues, be it the dispute about the authority of the Emperor or the purely dynastic rivalries between the various territorial princes, which often went back to pre-Reformation times. The religious antagonism created political options which would not have existed otherwise. To pursue a radical confessional policy was made worthwhile, or could seem to be so, in particular for those princes who were, for various reasons, dissatisfied with the *status quo* in the Empire and the position and authority assigned to them within the existing political framework. Both the Palatinate and Bavaria offer examples of such a policy.[21]

The Duke of Bavaria was potentially one of the most powerful rulers in the Empire and one of the few who could count on a regular surplus in his duchy's budget before 1618, but in southern Germany, a region which he could normally hope to dominate, his position was overshadowed by the Habsburgs. They held both the imperial crown and vast territorial possessions to the east and south of Bavaria and in south-western Germany (in Upper Swabia, the Breisgau and Alsace). Not only were the Habsburg neighbours too close for comfort, but Bavaria's status in the Imperial Diet was also unsatisfactory. Bavaria did not belong to the exclusive circle of prince electors, and thus remained a second-rate power according to the offical hierarchical order. However, if Maximilian of Bavaria (1598–1651) could manage, by taking a radical Catholic stance, to become the spokesman for all those, mostly ecclesiastical, Catholic princes who either felt threatened by their Protestant neighbours or were inclined to call for a Catholic 'roll-back', his influence would greatly increase. As head of a Catholic alliance Maximilian could become the Emperor's most important and virtually indispensable partner, and perhaps even be able to dictate his policies, as he in fact largely succeeded in doing after 1618.[22]

The case of the Electorate of the Palatinate was different, but again a radical confessional policy could look like the best option. In the fifteenth century the Elector Palatine had been one of the most powerful German princes, thanks not only to his control of key positions along the river Rhine but also to his extensive network of clients in the Palatinate region outside the borders of the electoral principality itself. Most of the smaller – generally ecclesiastical – princes and lesser noblemen along the lower course of the Neckar and west of the Rhine between Strassburg and Mainz had been the Elector's clients, attending his court or taking a seat in his council and supporting him in war. During the sixteenth century, however, this network had largely fallen apart, partly for confessional reasons (Catholic princes and noblemen were not prepared to live under the protection and tutelage of a Protestant ruler), and partly because the institutions of the Empire – strengthened in 1495 and at the beginning of the sixteenth century – offered the smaller Estates of the Empire (*Reichsstände*) a greater chance to maintain their independence.[23] However, if the Elector Palatine were to form a confessional alliance under his own leadership, this could compensate for his loss of influence and power. By pursuing a more radical policy, he could even hope to oust the Prince Elector of Saxony, who was widely considered the born leader of the Protestants in Germany,[24] from his position at the head of the Protestant camp.

Thus the formation of the great confessional alliances, Liga and Union, after 1607 must also be seen in the light of quite traditional dynastic policies, although they did assume a different character in the light of the battle between 'Antichrist and the Godly' or between the 'one, all embracing, true church and heresy'. In any case a distinct religious policy – even one less radical than in Bavaria or the Palatinate – governing domestic affairs as much as relations with other princes or the Empire, was certainly one way for territorial rulers to increase the coherence of their principality as well as to boost their autonomy within the Empire. Ecclesiastical policy, an area in which Emperor and Reichstag alike were forced to abdicate direct responsibility in 1552–55, was an ideal field in which the territorial rulers could develop their authority to its full extent and emancipate themselves from imperial control. But at the same time, the conflict between Protestant and Catholic princes and the legal disputes to which the controversial interpretation of the 1555 peace settlement gave rise could give the Emperor a key position as arbiter between the warring factions. He could exploit the religious conflict to enhance his own authority, as he was in fact to do in the 1620s. The confessional conflict was a force driving the Estates of the Empire apart as much as a potential catalyst for developments which strengthened the Emperor's influence.[25] Whichever perspective one takes, it is not surprising that it was the confrontation between the three great confessional groups which brought the struggle over the future structure of the Empire to a head: were the territorial princes to be mere *Estates* in a monarchy, or rulers governing their own *states* belonging to a greater confederation?[26]

This leaves us with the question of whether other factors, in particular social and economic developments, also contributed to a heightening of political tensions in the Empire before 1618. Can the war be seen as part of a more general crisis of the seventeenth century, perhaps even a crisis of 'feudalism', understood as the traditional social system dominated by a nobility living on the rents and services which a dependent peasantry had to provide?[27] To be sure, around 1600 there were signs of crisis in Germany as much as in other countries. There had been continuous demographic growth between 1500 and 1600. Whereas in 1500 Germany had had a population of about 12 million people, this figure had grown to at least 15 million a century later, while other estimates even assume that as many as 18 million people were living in Germany in 1618. This figure is further increased to about 21 million if the non-German speaking areas of the Empire and the Habsburg kingdoms and principalities such as Bohemia are included.[28] Agricultural production had certainly also grown during the same period, but not enough to prevent an increasing imbalance between demand and supply and a corresponding rise in grain prices. Available data show that in Germany as in other European countries the income of large sections of the population had fallen drastically in real terms during the century before 1618.[29]

In villages, the proportion of the population which owned no land or very little had grown. While noble landlords had initially been among the victims of the inflation of prices, they later tried to recoup their losses and indeed to benefit from the favourable economic situation by demanding higher rents and payments in kind, or by extending the forced labour services of the peasants. They were not successful everywhere. In particular, in the western parts of Germany the territorial rulers tended to defend the peasantry against the nobility because they wanted to raise taxes themselves.[30] In many areas east of the river Elbe, however, as well as in Austria and Bohemia, the landlords definitely put more pressure on the peasantry, and the economic and social position of the rural population deteriorated correspondingly. This was bound to lead to social conflicts, if not to rural riots. Such open conflicts were particularly frequent in the Habsburg dominions, where the 1590s saw major peasant risings in the Archduchies of Upper and Lower Austria.[31] Nor were the German towns – imperial cities as well as towns subject to a territorial ruler – spared similar trouble. The four decades before 1618 saw a wave of urban unrest, partly socially and partly politically motivated.[32]

Despite the population growth of the preceding decades, there were also signs of an incipient agricultural 'depression' in some areas of Germany where the trend towards ever-increasing grain prices was broken in the 1590s.[33] But of course we can only speculate what the course of economic development would have been had the war not broken out. Moreover, it can be doubted – for Germany in particular – whether all the economic problems mentioned really amounted to a profound crisis of the whole social and economic system before 1618. Equal caution is required with regard to the alleged decline of the German towns as centres of trade during the period under discussion.[34]

Whatever our assessment of the general economic and social trends of the early seventeenth century, it is very difficult to establish a clear correlation between these developments and the political crisis in Germany which led to the outbreak of war; outside Germany the Spanish and Dutch case may be to some extent different, though hardly less complex (see below, pp. 42–6).[35] If any such correlation between political events and social problems can be established, then perhaps this can be done most easily for Austria and Bohemia. Here, however, the correlation is a negative one. The tensions between landlords and peasants must have dampened the revolutionary ardour of the rebellious nobility in 1618 and earlier, thereby far from favouring the uprising in Bohemia and in the neighbouring principalities, actually contributing to their defeat (see below, pp. 55–6, 65–6). This is not to say that once the war had started it did not in itself precipitate social tensions (not only in the Empire but also outside it). Thus the Thirty Years War may indeed have 'exported disorder to the whole of Europe'. But if this was the case, it was far more likely the cause of a 'general crisis' affecting the political and social order of most European countries than its consequence.[36]

The Empire in Crisis 1607–1618

The preceding section has stressed the tensions which undermined political stability in Germany in the early seventeenth century. Were the last years before 1618 therefore a highroad to war? They have certainly often been depicted as such. Even before 1600 the Chamber Court of the Empire had already passed a number of highly controversial judgements restoring to the Catholic Church secularised estates which had once belonged to ecclesiastical corporations.[37] Normally a committee of the Imperial Diet was entrusted with the task of revising the judgements of the Chamber Court, but this committee became inoperative in 1588 because the Catholic princes were not prepared to admit the Bishopric of Magdeburg's delegate. Magdeburg, an important prince-bishopric, was governed by a Protestant administrator, whom the Catholic Estates of the Empire did not recognise. Twelve years later the Deputationstag (a smaller version of the Imperial Diet, in a manner of speaking, with a more restricted membership, which had taken over the task of supervising and revising the jurisdiction of the Reichskammergericht) was also paralysed. This time it was the Elector Palatine and a number of other Protestants princes who refused to co-operate any longer because they saw no chance of gaining a majority for their own views among the members of the committee, which was numerically dominated by Catholics.

Thus the Chamber Court in Speyer largely ceased to function as an effective agent of law enforcement in conflicts in which the great political and religious issues of the day were at stake, although it continued to adjudge many minor cases quite successfully. There was, of course, a second law court in the Empire, the Aulic Council in Prague, but its judges tended to favour the Catholic cause even more strongly than their colleagues in Speyer. This tendency found its most spectacular expression in the occupation of Donauwörth, an imperial free city with a largely Protestant town council, in 1607. Though governed by Protestants, Donauwörth had a Catholic minority. Catholics and Protestants had long been engaged in a sort of war of attrition by disrupting each other's religious ceremonies and by similar measures. After another Catholic procession had been interrupted by Protestants, the Aulic Council imposed the Imperial Ban on the town council of Donauwörth and the Emperor authorised Bavaria to execute the verdict against the city. This was against the normal legal rules, for Donauwörth belonged to the Imperial Circle of Swabia, not to the Bavarian Circle (the princes and Estates of each of the eight, or with Austria and Burgundy ten, Circles of the Empire were responsible for maintaining peace within their confines).

Protestants in the Empire were even more scandalised when Maximilian of Bavaria not only sent troops to Donauwörth, but occupied the town permanently and took measures to suppress Protestantism altogether. Clearly the protection which the statutes of the Empire had granted to Protestants could no longer be relied upon. Under the leadership of the Elector Palatine, those Protestant princes and towns which felt most acutely threatened formed an alliance, the Union, in 1608. The Elector Palatine and some of the more militant Protestant princes had been seeking such a confessional alliance for some time, but without the Donauwörth affair it would not have been possible to find sufficient support for these plans.

By no means all Protestant princes joined the alliance. Electoral Saxony, for example, was conspicuous by its absence and the new alliance's centre of gravity clearly lay in south-western and central Germany (Hesse, Franconia). The following year, in 1609, a similar Catholic organisation, the Liga, was founded in response to the creation of the Protestant alliance. The Liga was led by Bavaria. Initially comprising mainly the prelates of southern Germany in addition to the Duchy of Bavaria, it was subsequently also joined by the three ecclesiastical electors whose territories lay along the Rhine.

With the increasing polarisation of the religious alliances, the deliberations of the Imperial Diet were bound to be disrupted, though Electoral Saxony and some conservative Lutheran princes still tried to steer a middle course and to maintain co-operation with the Emperor.[38] The more radical Protestants, resenting the structural majority which the Catholics enjoyed in the Diet, in particular in the second *curia*, the Council of Princes, had always been reluctant to accept majority decisions on matters which, they felt, concerned religious problems in any way.[39] In 1608 they walked out of the meeting of the Diet (in Regensburg) in protest when their objections to the Catholic interpretation of the Peace of Augsburg, to all intents and purposes supported by the Emperor and the Empire's courts of law, remained unanswered. The Diet found itself unable to pass any statute or resolution. Behind the uncompromising attitude of the Protestant Estates lay anger about the recent occupation of Donauwörth. Moreover, in earlier years the war against the Sultan's troops in Hungary and the threat from the Turks had ensured Protestant co-operation with the Emperor's policy – after all the imperial hereditary lands were the most important bulwark protecting central Europe against the attacks of the infidels – but this was now no longer the case. For in 1606 Archduke Matthias, in the name of the entire House of Habsburg, had signed the Peace of Zsitvatorok with the Sultan. The treaty was intended to run for 20 years. It did, in fact, defuse conflict with the Ottoman Empire for even longer, although the danger of large-scale warfare in Hungary was never entirely absent and more limited military conflicts remained frequent after 1606.

The truce, however, removed the main justification for levying new taxes on the princes and cities for the defence of the Empire and inevitably made the religious question the main topic of discussion in the Diet, which might otherwise have concentrated on the war against the Turks. Five years later, in 1613, when the Diet met again, chances of finding a compromise seemed to have improved. Betweeen 1608 and 1612 the internal crisis of the Habsburg monarchy, culminating in the confrontation between the Emperor Rudolf II and his brother Matthias, had reached its climax. Rudolf was politically paralysed as head of the Empire during those years.[40] With Rudolf II now dead and a slow and gradual recovery of Habsburg power in Bohemia and Austria already under way in 1613, chances for finding a solution to the problems eroding political stability in the Empire seemed slightly better than before. In fact, Rudolf's successor, Matthias, left politics mostly to his advisor Cardinal Klesl. Though he had been an ardent adherent of the Counter-Reformation in earlier years, Klesl now tried to restabilise the Empire's political system, partly because he realised that open conflict in the Empire was likely to undermine the position of the Habsburgs in their hereditary lands too.[41] However, tensions between Protestants and Catholics remained as strong as ever. The majority in the Imperial Diet did pass a final resolution this time but the more radical Protestants refused to accept it and walked out once more. The Diet was to remain paralysed for 27 years, and the next meeting did not take place until 1640.

The Empire had already come to the brink of open war between the Diet's meetings in 1608 and 1613. In 1609 the mentally incapacitated last Duke of Jülich, Berg and Cleves died. His principalities occupied a strategic position on the lower Rhine, bordering on the Dutch Republic and the Spanish Netherlands, and troops of both powers had repeatedly occupied parts of the duchies in the past. The inheritance was claimed by a number of pretenders. The Elector of Saxony based his claim on an old treaty with the ducal house of Jülich-

Cleves. The two other principal pretenders were the Prince Elector Johann Sigismund of Brandenburg and the Count Palatine Philipp Ludwig of Pfalz-Neuburg, or rather his son, Wolfgang Wilhelm. These princes based their claims on the rights of inheritance enjoyed respectively by Marie Eleonore and Anna of Jülich-Cleves, two of the last Duke's four sisters.[42] Brandenburg and Pfalz-Neuburg decided to occupy the contested territories, and came to an arrangement to govern them jointly for the time being (Treaty of Dortmund, June 1609). However, Rudolf II was not prepared to accept this; he favoured other claimants to the duchies, among them the Elector of Saxony. Open conflict seemed unavoidable. In July 1609 Archduke Leopold, Bishop of Strassburg and Passau, had already occupied the town of Jülich, an important fortress, with the Emperor's authority. He continued to raise troops in his Bishopric of Strassburg not far from the borders of the Palatinate.

Brandenburg and Pfalz-Neuburg, on the other hand, both Lutheran Protestants, enjoyed the support not only of the Union but also of the Dutch and of King Henry IV of France, who feared that the Habsburgs would gain control of the duchies (see below, p. 38) However, in May 1610 Henry IV was murdered by a Catholic fanatic, Ravaillac. Although the Union's troops still managed to reconquer the fortress of Jülich with French help and successfully attacked Archduke Leopold's position in Alsace, the Union had now lost the impetus and the resources for a full-scale offensive against the forces of Catholicism. For the time being things could be patched up. But then the two main pretenders, Brandenburg and Pfalz-Neuburg, fell out among themselves. Alarmed at the prospect of being ousted from his position in the Rhenish duchies by the much more powerful Elector of Brandenburg, the Neuburg pretender joined the Catholics. Wolfgang Wilhelm of Neuburg married Princess Magdalena of Bavaria (a sister of Duke Maximilian) in November 1613, having secretly converted to Catholicism shortly before the wedding. He revealed his conversion in May 1614, thereby gaining access to Bavarian, imperial and Spanish support. At about the same time, 1613, Johann Sigismund of Brandenburg embraced Calvinism, thus strengthening his ties with the Palatinate and the Dutch Republic, although it needs to be stressed that for quite some time the Elector had been under the influence of advisers and relations who were Reformed Protestants.[43]

On the lower Rhine an armed confrontation between the two pretenders and their protectors, Spain and the Dutch Republic, seemed to be inevitable. Spanish and Dutch troops did indeed intervene and the Dutch occupied the important fortified town of Jülich in 1614, whereas the Spanish took Wesel in the Duchy of Cleves. But neither power was really interested in a major war before the 12-year truce they had signed in 1609 had expired. A new settlement of sorts was achieved with the mediation of France and England in November 1614 (Treaty of Xanten). Brandenburg took control of Cleves and the Counties of Mark and Ravensberg, while Wolfgang Wilhelm of Neuburg was to administer the Duchies of Jülich and Berg with the capital Düsseldorf. On balance Spain and the Catholic Estates of the Empire had now gained an important, though limited, victory after their initial defeat in 1610, and the conversion of Wolfgang Wilhelm to Catholicism, by no means the last conversion of a Protestant prince during the seventeenth century, showed that solidarity of Protestant rulers against the Counter-Reformation could no longer be taken for granted, even at the most elementary level – an alarming prospect for all Protestants.

Nevertheless, the great conflagration which had seemed imminent during the years 1610–14 had at least been postponed. But what was the outlook for the future? The confrontation during the struggle for the succession in the duchies on the Lower Rhine had certainly increased the already considerable mistrust on both sides. None the less, the front lines between the hostile camps were not entirely inflexible. None other but the highest ranking ecclesiastical prince of the Empire, the Archbishop of Mainz, Johann Schweikhard von Cronberg, tried in 1610–11 to gain Protestant Electoral Saxony as a member of the Catholic Liga.[44] Though tempted to intensify his co-operation with the Catholic federation in order to strengthen his position in the Jülich-Cleves succession crisis, the Elector of Saxony in the end preferred to maintain an independent position. However, the mere fact that such a proposal could seriously be discussed shows that the confessional antagonism was not yet all-pervasive, at least not as far as relations between Lutherans and Catholics were concerned.

For Saxony, as Axel Gotthard has recently shown, its special relationship with the Emperor – going back ultimately to the War of Schmalkalden of 1546–47 when Moritz of Saxony had fought on Charles V's side[45] – was more important than solidarity between all Protestant princes of the Empire.[46] This special relationship had been reinforced in the 1590s when Saxony's Lutherans had regained their undisputed ascendancy after the brief interlude of the 'crypto-Calvinist' reign of Prince Elector Christian I (1586–91), and had taken revenge, with Rudolf II's support, on theologians and politicans who had allegedly tried to lead Saxony into the Calvinist camp.[47] Unfortunately, the electoral councillors in Dresden had no real ideas of their own for resolving the problems paralysing the Empire. In the final resort, the policy pursued by Saxony was too cautious and unimaginative to anticipate, let alone to prevent, the crisis which broke out in 1618.

Attempts to transform the Liga into an alliance controlled or led by the Emperor, and supporting his policy and not just the interests of the Catholic princes, were potentially more promising. The influential Archbishop of Mainz, who held an important position as official head of the imperial chancellery, by no means a mere sinecure during this period, gave some support to such a transformation in 1612–13. In 1613 the princes of the Liga accepted the Grandmaster of the Teutonic Order, Archduke Maximilian, a member of the imperial dynasty who also ruled Tyrol and the so-called *Vorlande* (the Habsburg dominions between the Arlberg and the Vosges), as a member and as head of a new *directorate* comprising Swabia. The result of this decison was ultimately that the Liga lost its coherence. Maximilian of Bavaria, who resented Habsburg and imperial influence in the Liga, went his own way and formed a sort of sub-alliance uniting Bavaria and a number of bishoprics and prelacies in its immediate vicinity in southern Germany. Bavaria thus maintained its dominant position in its special sphere of influence but the Liga, outside this sphere, had all but broken down.

The Protestant Union did not fare much better. Though strengthened by treaties of assistance with England (1612) and the Dutch Republic (1613), its position in Germany was gradually eroded. In 1617, when the alliance was extended, some of the princes and especially the cities insisted on limiting the life-span of the new confederation to three years after the expiry of the original treaty. Without a further extension, the Union initially founded for ten years in 1608 would thus expire in May 1621. Given that the Dutch–Spanish truce would also expire in 1621, which made a major international crisis likely in that year, this was a very short time indeed.[48]

A final assessment of the situation before 1618 is not easy. In various ways both sides, Protestants as well as Catholics, felt threatened. During the final agony of Rudolf II's reign before his death in 1612, the position of the Habsburgs in their own principalities seemed to be about to collapse. Of course, this would have affected the Empire as well, and the Catholics were rightly nervous about the consequences of Habsburg decline. In 1618 a revival of Habsburg power was already under way, but still everything seemed to be possible: a Catholic–Habsburg offensive led by Ferdinand of Styria, the successor designate of the Emperor Matthias, in the hereditary lands as well as the Empire, or a further deterioration in the Habsburg position, which was still far from secure. Thus the policy of the Palatinate in particular was motivated as much by fear of a general Catholic conspiracy to undermine the safeguards which the constitution of the Empire granted to Protestants, as by the hope that determined and decisive action at the right moment could tip the balance in favour of the Protestants and quash the Catholic threat once and for all.

The attitude of Catholic extremists, on the other hand, may have been equally ambivalent. Those who favoured a military solution were not necessarily motivated by the wish to eliminate Protestantism as such, although this wish was certainly not absent from the Catholic camp. However, the dominant feeling was probably fear that the alternative would fatally undermine the Catholic position. The alternative was a new compromise based on the Peace of Augsburg, but more comprehensive in scope, this time including the Calvinists in some way and solving the problem of secularised church property. Thus one of the most aggressive Catholic polemicists, Kaspar Schoppe, declared in 1619 during the Bohemian crisis, that in spite of its shortcomings the Peace of Augsburg was to be observed. But on no account was the Catholic cause to be betrayed by a new compromise, a *nova compositio*, with the Calvinists and those Protestants who had violated the terms of the peace, which admittedly Schoppe interpreted from a strictly Catholic point of view unacceptable to most Protestants.[49]

What settled the matter was in the last resort the combination of the mounting political and religious tensions in the Empire with a crisis in the dominions of the German Habsburgs going back to the decade 1600–10 and culminating in 1618–19 and with the expiry of the truce between Spain and the Netherlands in 1621.

European Politics and the Origins of the War

For Germany it clearly makes sense to consider the outbreak of hostilities in 1618–19 as a decisive event, marking the end of an era. But what about the rest of Europe, in particular western Europe? Here the date of 1618 seems much less significant. Hostilities between the Dutch and the Spanish did not break out until 1621 and war between France and Spain, after the comparatively brief war over Mantua in 1629–31 (see below, pp. 79–80), did not commence in earnest until 1635, but then lasted until 1659. Moreover, whereas Germany had enjoyed peace, with only limited disturbances, from 1552 to 1618, this was clearly not the case in western Europe. As early as the 1560s, a rebellion had shaken Spanish rule in the

Netherlands. The subsequent war between Spain and the re-bellious provinces, in which the rebels enjoyed the support of England and other Protestant powers as well as, to some extent, of France, had only been halted in 1609 by a truce. And the French Wars of Religion (1562–98) had at least in their later stages been as much an international conflict as a civil war, with Spain supporting the Catholic extremists and England and German Protestants supporting the Huguenots. Were the renewed hostilities after 1618 therefore just a direct continuation of these earlier conflicts?[50]

This view implies that the period between about 1604 and 1609, when the Anglo-Spanish war and the Spanish–Dutch war respectively ended, and 1618–21 was no more than a short in-terval during which the old enemies recovered their breath, resuming the fight again with the old objectives at the earliest possible moment. This, however, is not entirely convincing, not even for the conflict between the Dutch and the Spanish crown which seems to fit this model best. After all, what had been at stake during the later sixteenth century was the very survival of Protestantism in the Netherlands, as well as in France and ultimately also in England. This is not to say that the religious antagonism was the only or even necessarily the principal cause of the conflicts mentioned, but there cannot be much doubt that a Spanish victory would have greatly facili-tated the triumph of Catholicism in the whole of western Europe.

After 1610, however, Spain's objectives were more limited and gave less primacy to religion. Even Spain had to accept that it might be best to let the Protestants in the northern Netherlands go to hell in their own way;[51] influential Spanish councillors continued to argue for a resumption of the war after 1609 but they no longer saw the suppression of Protestantism as a principal war aim.[52] As the course of the Thirty Years War was to show, Spain, however reluctantly, had largely come to terms with the fact that there were countries in Christendom in which Catholicism could not be enforced in the foreseeable future. This is not to deny that many Protestants in England and other countries still saw Spain as the agent of Antichrist, bent on enforcing idolatry every-where. The very real threat to the survival of Protestantism in western Europe which Spanish hegemony had presented in the late sixteenth century continued to haunt the political imagination of Protestants even when the actual danger they faced had somewhat dimished.

If the confessional element in Spanish foreign policy was less pronounced after about 1600 than it had been in earlier decades, it would be equally wrong to see the Thirty Years War as a struggle in which Spain together with the Emperor con-sciously tried to erect a universal monarchy where all other princes and powers would be reduced to the status of mere clients if their countries were not simply conquered and incorporated into the Habsburg dominions. Again there was certainly no lack of contemporary propaganda designed to rally Europe's princes and republics to the anti-Spanish cause by appealing to their fear of a Spanish *monarchia universalis* and of the 'beastly Spanish servitude'. This propaganda may even have been based on genuine perceptions of Spanish policy dominant among Spain's opponents.[53] But Spanish re-sources were limited and, more importantly, even the ambi-tious Conde-Duque Olivares and other Spanish statesmen were well aware that they were not inexhaustible. They there-fore tried to limit their war aims, though probably not enough to assuage the fears of Spain's neighbours, or to avoid a situa-tion in which too many political and military commitments slowly eroded Spain's remaining strength.[54]

In fact Johannes Burkhardt's recent and otherwise ad-mirable account of the Thirty Years War is least convincing where the author tries to argue that a universal monarchy was indeed a realistic option between 1618 and 1648 (or 1618 and 1659). Burkhardt further suggests that Olivares in Spain and later Richelieu in France consciously tried to create just such a universal monarchy, as opposed to achieving a more limited *hegemony* for their own country as the greatest power among other autonomous states.[55] At least the argument about Olivares's and Richelieu's political intentions is clearly at odds with most recent accounts of Spanish and French policy during the war. This is not to deny that Burkhardt is right in insisting on the character of the war as a struggle about the future of the European system of states and about the structure of the states belonging to this system. But the alternatives were less stark than he claims. A Habsburg universal monarchy was hardly ever on the cards, not least because neither Philip IV and Olivares nor Ferdinand II had any clear plans for such a monarchy, as was to become apparent in the later 1620s and the years around 1635 when their power was greatest.[56] The opposite solution, the dissolution of the existing composite monarchies or multiple kingdoms[57] – the realms of the Spanish and Austrian Habsburgs – as well as the total disintegration of the Holy Roman Empire, seemed a more likely outcome of the war during certain periods of the conflict.

Ultimately, foreign policy in western Europe before 1618 was dominated neither by the endeavour to build a universal monarchy nor by religion, but by more secular issues – questions of security, of prestige and reputation, but also, in particular in the Spanish and Dutch case, economic interests. In the Holy Roman Empire, however, religious tensions did not really culminate until after 1600. It is therefore possible to argue that the outbreak of war in Germany, in which the fate of Protestantism was clearly at stake – though even the German war was not really dominated by exclusively religious issues before 1629–30 and even less so after 1635 – brought the religious issues back to the forefront of conflict in western Europe too. This came about at a time when the rulers and leading statesmen in Spain, England, France and the Dutch Republic had already to some extent changed their priorities. The outbreak of war thus threatened the cohesion of the great monarchies of western Europe, or to be more precise, of the French and the Stuart monarchies (the Spanish case was different), at the very moment when their rulers and statesmen had become more confident that they were about to overcome the disruptive forces of confessional confrontation.

For various reasons neither France nor England were interested in a revival of open religious warfare, or even of a

European conflict which could be *interpreted* as a religious war in the years before 1618. The French monarchy would be in a particularly vulnerable position in such a case. In 1598 Henry IV of France had managed to put an end to the religious civil war in his country as well as to the war with Spain. Henry IV had been a Protestant for long periods of his life, but had finally converted to Catholicism in 1593 before he was crowned King of France, while granting toleration to his former co-religionists in 1598. But if the confrontation between Protestantism and Catholicism were again to dominate international relations, the war between Huguenots and Catholics would most likely revive in France too. Each side would seek alliances with the foreign powers which acted as leaders of the Protestant and the Catholic camp respectively; the Huguenots with the Netherlands and perhaps England, and the more militant Catholics, who still suspected Henry IV of being a crypto-Protestant anyhow, with Spain. Henry IV's foreign policy before his premature death probably aimed to avoid a religious war – though not necessarily war as such – in Europe by creating a system of alliances bridging the gulf between Protestant and Catholic states while trying at the same time to counterbalance Spanish influence in Germany and Italy.[58]

Under Henry's rule France seemed to be preparing for a major war with Spain while intervening in the dispute about the succession to the Duchies of Jülich, Cleves and Berg in 1609–10. Henry's intentions in 1610 are not entirely clear. He may have wanted to deal Spain a fatal blow by establishing a French presence on the lower Rhine which would have allowed France to cut supplies to the Spanish Netherlands. Or he may have been trying to prevent the outbreak of a primarily religious war – a clear threat to France's newly won internal stability – by co-operating with the German princes, who in return would have had to subordinate their interests to French priorities.[59]

However, Henry IV was assassinated by a Catholic fanatic in 1610 while preparing for armed intervention in the Jülich-Cleves crisis. Henry's violent death was extremely convenient for Spain, but it also showed that tensions within France were still too great to allow her to pursue an active foreign policy based on co-operation with Protestant states and princes. The regent Marie de Medici and her advisors who governed France after 1610 shunned all major commitments abroad; peace now seemed the best means to ensure domestic stability. It was left to Cardinal Richelieu who in 1624 became first minister to the new King, Louis XIII, to find a way to eliminate the Huguenots as an autonomous political faction without allowing the ultra-Catholic *dévots*, who favoured close co-operation with the Papacy and Spain, to direct French policy.

If the potential repercussions of a major European war fought on primarily religious lines would have been devastating for France, England was also interested in avoiding such a conflict. James I of England (1603–25) tried to defuse political and religious tensions in Europe. Shortly after his accession to the English crown he had brought 15 years of open warfare and an even longer period of armed confrontation to a close by concluding peace with Spain. The son of the Catholic Mary Stuart, Queen of Scots, who had been executed in England in 1587 because of her involvement in a number of conspiracies against Elizabeth I, James I faced problems which were different from those confronting Henry IV of France, but not necessarily less severe, as the attempt to assassinate him in 1605 – an attempt motivated by Catholic religious fervour but also by English anti-Scottish feeling – was to show.[60] James I's 'appeasement' policy towards Spain has often been considered unrealistic and even foolish by historians, but England could ill afford a major war, as was to become apparent between 1625 and 1630 when it was fought. England's administrative structure, especially her taxation system, was not up to the strains which a major international conflict entailed. Moreover, religious dissensions in the kingdoms of the Stuart monarchy, inevitably linked to different concepts of foreign policy, were likely to be exacerbated once war broke out.[61]

James I governed a composite monarchy (England, Scotland and Ireland) where not only Protestantism and Catholicism (still espoused by a majority of the landowning classes in

Ireland and a small but not altogether irrelevant minority in England) confronted each other, but also various mutually exclusive varieties of Protestantism itself: Calvinist Presbyterians in Scotland, the Puritan advocates of a further reformation and of strict anti-Popery in England, and finally those theologians and laymen who favoured a cautious, or perhaps not so cautious, return to some of the traditions of the pre-Reformation Church and who wanted the Church of England to pursue a religious *via media* between Geneva and Rome. After 1603 James I managed to avoid open religious conflict in his three kingdoms surprisingly well, but as events after 1618 were to show, the precondition for a domestic religious *détente* was a certain amount of political and religious *détente* in international relations.[62]

The fact that despite continuing religious tensions, the conditions for such a limited *détente* between the hostile religious communities in western Europe (although not in Germany) seemed to improve after about 1610, must have encouraged James in his peaceful policy. There was a chance, or so it seemed at least, to create a sort of third party between the extremists of both sides, consisting possibly of Gallican French Catholics, moderate and conformist English Protestants and, perhaps, Dutch Arminians.[63] After 1598 a brand of Catholicism flourished again in France, though not unopposed, which aimed to limit the Pope's power and return to the pre-Reformation Gallican, that is specifically national, traditions of the French Church. Thus during the Estates General of 1614 the Third Estate demanded that the assembly officially reject the power of the Pope to depose secular rulers, and that all officeholders and priests should be required to swear an oath in accordance with this resolution.[64] In the Netherlands, on the other hand, influential theologians tried to mitigate the rigidity of strict Calvinism. This movement led by Jacob Arminius was certainly highly controversial in the Netherlands. Its alliance with the political factions which supported a lasting peace with Spain made it hardly less so, and even James I repudiated many of its basic theological tenets. His sympathy, visible at least to some extent after the outbreak of the Thirty Years War, was limited to the Arminians' more moderate stance *vis-à-vis* the Catholic Church.[65] Nevertheless Gallicanism as well as Arminianism could possibly offer points of departure if not for a genuine 'ecumenical' movement – the religious and theological antagonism between the confessions remained too great for that – then at least for a political *détente* between the competing churches, one which would have excluded the extremists on both sides, Jesuits as much as radical Puritans. And it was such a *détente* which James clearly welcomed, before 1618 as much as later.

Though generally pursuing a cautious conciliatory policy towards Spain, James I had come close to committing himself to a more openly anti-Catholic foreign policy by signing an alliance with the Protestant Union in Germany in 1612, and giving his daughter Elizabeth in marriage to the Elector Palatine Friedrich V in the following year. During these years, after the death of Henry IV, a triumph of the pro-Spanish *dévots* in France seemed possible and James apparently thought it necessary to give some encouragement to Spain's opponents on the Continent.[66] But this was merely a passing phase, though few Protestant statesmen in the Empire realised it.

In the 1620s James I's peace policy, which was intended to be based on solidarity between all monarchs against what he saw as the seditious activities of Rome and Geneva alike,[67] came to grief. This was partly a result of the fact that the conflicts in the Holy Roman Empire, which James probably never quite managed to understand, rekindled religious tensions in western Europe which had never entirely disappeared anyhow, and increased their influence on foreign relations. But James's policy also failed because the state that James most needed to win as a partner if lasting peace was to be established in Europe, Spain, had other priorities.

At the beginning of the seventeenth century Spain was clearly still the dominant power in Europe. But in the past Spain's ascendancy had been as much or more the result of the weakness of her rivals as of her own inherent strength. In about 1600 the population of Castile, the real heartland of the

Spanish monarchy, hardly numbered 7 million people and was already in decline.[68] This compared very unfavourably with the French population of at least 17 million. Of course, the Empire of the Spanish Habsburgs comprised a vast number of other kingdoms and provinces, Aragon, Portugal, Sicily, Naples, Milan, and the Burgundian provinces: from the Franche Comté in the south to Flanders in the north not to mention the extensive colonial empire in South America and the mostly Portuguese possessions in Africa and Asia. But the outlying provinces were as much a burden as a factor of strength. They had to be defended against hostile neighbours and were often reluctant to make any major contribution to the defence of other, more distant parts of the Spanish composite monarchy.[69]

The problem for Spain was that her limited economic and financial resources were hardly adequate to maintain the position which she had achieved in the sixteenth century, especially if French power were to revive.[70] But if Spain, or Castile, could ill afford another prolonged war after 1609, she could not really afford peace either, or so it seemed. Although war with the Dutch had repeatedly brought the Spanish crown finances to the brink of total collapse, war had also meant protection for Spain's fragile economy, both in agriculture and industry. Now that the Dutch could again trade freely with Castile, the heartland of the Spanish monarchy was exposed to economic competition that it was ill-equipped to meet. Cheap imported grain and dried fish from northern Europe competed with the more expensive Iberian products. Even more importantly, Dutch cloth imports hastened the decline of textile manufacturing in Castile. Long before the the truce expired in 1621, a general conviction had taken hold among all strata of the Spanish population that peace with the Dutch was not worth making sacrifices for because it would be Spain's ruin, at least in economic terms. This conviction was, if possible, even stronger in Portugal, for while the truce of 1609 brought an end of hostilities in Europe, warfare in the Far East continued. Here the once extensive Portuguese trading Empire crumbled under the impact of Dutch competition and armed naval expeditions. Nor were the Portuguese and Spanish colonies in the New World secure from Dutch attack.

Given the threat to the Portuguese and Spanish colonial empires, it was clear that those Spanish councillors who opposed renewing the truce, which would have extended it beyond 1621, saw the objectives of a renewed war to a very considerable extent as economic ones. A Dutch retreat from the Spanish and Portuguese spheres of influence in Asia and, even more importantly, America was essential. Moreover the river Scheldt, which the Dutch had continued to blockade after 1609, had to be re-opened for trade (with the Scheldt open, they hoped that Spanish-controlled Antwerp, once the most important port in the Netherlands, would regain its position as an outstanding centre of international trade). Dutch concessions to Spanish claims for some sort of suzerainty over the Republic and to their demands that toleration be officially granted to Catholics in the North were ultimately of secondary importance.[71]

Immediately after the truce with the Dutch, Spanish policy, under the guidance of Philip III's favourite and leading minister, the Duke of Lerma, had given priority to the Mediterranean. The battle against the forces of Islam, fought at home with the expulsion in 1609–10 of the Moriscos (the descendants of Muslims who had invaded Spain in the Middle Ages and who had been forced to convert to Christianity in the early sixteenth century) as well as in northern Africa and the Mediterranean as a whole, lay at the heart of Lerma's policy. He preferred to leave the Spanish Netherlands to their own devices under the government of Archduke Albert of Austria (1599–1621), one of Emperor Maximilian II's sons, married to Philip II's daughter Isabella.

But as early as 1617 the balance of factions at the Spanish court had begun to shift.[72] With the return of the former Spanish ambassador in Vienna, Don Baltasar de Zúñiga, to Spain, advocates of a more active policy in northern Europe had an influential spokesman in the Spanish Council of State. In January 1617, while he was still ambassador at the imperial court, Zúñiga had persuaded Archduke Ferdinand of Styria,

Emperor Matthias's successor designate, to sign an agreement in which Ferdinand promised to cede to Spain extensive feudal rights in northern Italy annexed to the imperial crown. Zúñiga's successor as ambassador, the Count Oñate, continued to reinforce the ties between the two principal branches of the Habsburg dynasty, clearly in preparation for a renewed war with the Dutch Republic. In the so-called Oñate treaty of March 1617 Philip III of Spain waived his own pretensions to the Bohemian and the Hungarian crowns, which Ferdinand was to inherit from Matthias, and promised to support Ferdinand's claim. Ferdinand also received military assistance against the Republic of Venice with which he was at war. In return Ferdinand agreed to cede the Habsburg dominions and rights in Alsace – officially they belonged to an independent branch of the Habsburg dynasty with its seat in Innsbruck – to Spain, when an opportunity arose.

Though kept secret at the time, the Oñate treaty had momentous implications. It strengthened Ferdinand's hand in dealing with possible resistance in his hereditary dominions or in the Empire. Spain, on the other hand, was already all but committed to an active policy north of the Alps, a commitment which Lerma had tried to avoid. When in 1618 the Spanish Council of State had to decide whether Spain would support Ferdinand actively against the Bohemian rebels, Lerma, who opposed this move, was easily outmanoeuvred by Zúñiga.[73] In October 1618 Lerma lost all his offices, was dismissed from the court by Philip III and retired in disgrace to his estates.

However, even without the crisis in Bohemia, Spain would in all likelihood have pursued a more militant policy in central Europe than during the years of Lerma's ascendancy. Opposition to a renewal of the truce with the Dutch was in any case strong for the economic reasons which have been mentioned, but also because the truce seemed to compromise Spain's prestige and reputation as a great power. Even without the rebellion in Bohemia, a major military conflict in central Europe was therefore likely and it became even more likely because this reluctance to extend the truce was shared by the Dutch.

Paradoxically Spain's economic loss after 1609 had not necessarily been the Republic's gain, or not to an extent that was seen as satisfactory by the Dutch population at large. Food prices had risen after 1609, partly because of increased exports to Spain and the Mediterranean, and this posed a threat to the living standards of the urban population. Moreover, under the impact of competition from Flemish textile manufacturers in the Spanish-controlled southern provinces, Dutch textile production had not benefited from the increased opportunities for export as much as expected. In some places it was in fact struck by a severe crisis due not only to Flemish and English competition but also to a change in the structure of demand for cloth. Lighter and cheaper fabrics were now favoured. Dutch manufacturing towns such as Leiden, Haarlem, Delft and Gouda had been struck particularly hard by the crisis in textile production and it was here that opposition to the peace policy of the leading statesman of the period, Johan van Oldenbarnevelt, was strongest.[74] Supported by this opposition movement Maurice of Orange, the Stadholder of five of the seven provinces of the Republic and the most important advocate of a more militant foreign policy, had Oldenbarnevelt arrested in August 1618 and executed as a traitor the following year. The Synod of Dordrecht (Dord), an assembly of Dutch divines (November 1618 – May 1619), also attended by the representatives of a number of foreign reformed churches (for example England, Scotland, the Palatinate, some Swiss cantons, and Bremen), sealed the triumph of the war party's theological wing, the strictly Calvinist Counter-Remonstrants, over the more liberal Remonstrants who, inspired by Arminius, had sought Oldenbarnevelt's protection.

Neither Lerma's fall nor Oldenbarnevelt's execution and the defeat of his followers both in the theological disputes of the Dutch Reformed Church and in the debates on the future course of Dutch domestic and foreign policy made war a foregone conclusion.[75] Nevertheless, the Bohemian revolt unleashed a struggle which at least Spain had already all but accepted as inevitable, although it would certainly have been dominated by different issues and would have taken a very different course without the initial focusing of Habsburg–Catholic and Protestant forces on Bohemia. After the expiry of the truce with the Dutch, Spain would in any case have tried to secure her supply route (the 'Spanish road') from Italy via the Valtelline, Tyrol, Upper Swabia and along the Rhine to Flanders. It is, however, unlikely that this in itself would have led to as general a conflagration in the Empire and in Europe as did the Bohemian revolt.

2

1618: BOHEMIA AND THE EMPIRE

The Crisis of the Habsburg Monarchy

On the morning of 23 May 1618 the assembly of the Bohemian Protestants – comprising lords, knights and a number of delegates from the royal boroughs – met near the royal castle, the Hradshin, in Prague. Following a brief discussion, the members of the assembly went to the castle where they insisted on seeing the regents governing Bohemia in the absence of Matthias, the King and Emperor. After a heated exchange of words between the leaders of the assembly (Count Thurn, Colonna von Fels and Wenzel Ruppa) and the regents, Thurn and his friends declared two of the regents, Martinitz and Slawata, traitors because they had undermined the rights and privileges of the Protestant Estates of the kingdom. They asked the noblemen and other people present to punish them for their crimes there and then and let them die a traitor's death. To the applause of the angry crowd Martinitz and Slawata were thrown out of the windows of the council chamber of the Hradshin, and one of the clerks of the council, a certain Frabricius, shared their fate for full measure.

This defenestration was not as spontaneous as it may have seemed. Not only was there a historical precedent which the irate Protestants could follow – a similar defenestration had taken place in 1419 during the Hussite revolt – but Thurn and his close friends had planned this 'execution' carefully. Its real purpose was to close the door to any compromise between the reigning dynasty, the Habsburgs, with their Catholic advisors, and the Protestant opposition. By killing the regents, the Protestants would burn their boats. Even for those who were reluctant to risk an armed confrontation – probably still the majority – there would be no turning back.[1] However, the 'execution' was bungled. Martinitz and Slawata, and Fabricius too, miraculously survived. Later Catholic propaganda credited the Virgin Mary with personal intervention, though the rubbish which filled the castle moat and the large cloaks which the regents and the clerk were wearing probably softened their fall sufficiently to ensure their survival without divine intervention.

The defenestration of May 1618 was the culmination of a history of religious and political conflict going back to the reign of Rudolf II (1576–1612) and beyond. Though the Habsburgs, with the possible temporary exception of Maximilian II, had always been loyal supporters of the Roman Church, they had not been able to enforce Catholicism in their own dominions during the sixteenth century. In Bohemia, religious opposition to Rome had a particulary long tradition. Ever since the Hussite movement in the early fifteenth century, Bohemia, and to a lesser extent Moravia too, had been alienated from Rome. Although the moderate Hussites, the Utraquists, and the Catholic Church had eventually come to some sort of compromise, the position of the Roman Church, which had lost nearly all its estates during the period when Bohemia was under Hussite rule, remained weak. The prelates were excluded from membership of the Estates and until the late sixteenth century the amount of landed property belonging to ecclesiastical institutions and corporations was very limited. As late as 1600 only about 5 per cent of all land in Bohemia was in the hands of the Catholic Church (about 18 per cent in Moravia),[2] although at this stage donations by noblemen and the patronage of the crown had already laid the foundations for a recovery.

During the sixteenth century, the Reformation had made inroads in Bohemia. Although the Utraquist Church was in many ways an independent national church,[3] the theological and liturgical differences between it and the Roman Church had been reduced to a number of fairly minor points before the Reformation. During the sixteenth century, however, many Utraquists virtually became Lutherans or even Calvinists. Calvinism also influenced some of the members of the Bohemian Brethren, a smaller religious community whose roots lay in the theologically more radical wing of the fifteenth-century Hussite movement. In Moravia the variety of religious creeds was even greater. Non-Catholics did not enjoy the same legal privileges here as the Utraquists did in Bohemia, but in practice liberty of conscience was largely assured during the sixteenth century. Thus not only Lutheranism and Calvinism but also various sects, such as those influenced by early sixteenth-century Anabaptism, had adherents there. In fact, a tolerant undogmatic piety which could not easily be identified with any of the existing confessional churches continued to survive in Moravia until the early seventeenth century. It was this very lack of a clear confessional identity, however, which made it easier for Catholic theologians and clergymen to win converts among the members of the various 'Protestant' religious communities, and quite a number of members of the high nobility converted to Catholicism in Moravia before 1618, sometimes after having experienced a genuine spiritual and emotional crisis.[4]

Thus not only in Moravia, but elsewhere in the Habsburg dominions too, the Catholic Church slowly regained some of its strength through the application of the Tridentine Reforms and the missionary activities of religious orders of which the Jesuits were the most active. Nevertheless, Rudolf II was as unsuccessful during his reign (1576–1612) as his predecessors in suppressing Protestantism, and before the turn of the century he probably did not even try to do so. The Habsburgs were not strong enough to risk an all-out religious war against their own subjects, and they had to be all the more cautious as Protestantism enjoyed powerful support in their German-speaking dominions, in the duchies above and below the river Enns (Ober- und Niederösterreich), as well as in Styria, Carinthia and Carniola. Staunchly Catholic Tyrol was the only exception in this respect. In 1568–71 the Emperor Maximilian had made important concessions in Lower Austria, which legalised the status of the Protestant parishes in this principality. Maximilian had even approved the Prayer Book and liturgy which the Protestants were to use. Implicitly these concessions applied to Upper Austria as well, although the Protestants there had rejected any interference by the Emperor in their internal affairs. An officially approved Prayer Book would have constituted an interference in their eyes, and so no final settlement could be reached. In the 1570s the great majority of the lords and knights of Upper and Lower Austria were Protestants. Nevertheless, the status of Protestantism was not secure. The Toleration Edicts signed by Maximilian had been granted to the nobility who were allowed to hold Protestant services in the chapels of their castles and manor houses. The status of Protestant ministers in the towns was much more precarious, and in fact the most important town in Austria, Vienna, remained largely Catholic. Recent estimates suggest that even in the 1570s only about 50 per cent of all parishes in Upper and Lower Austria were really in Protestant hands.[5]

Thus there was always the potential for a Catholic recovery, which could be activated by bishops and priests determined to reform their own church and attack Protestantism. In Inner Austria, which had been governed by a younger branch of the Habsburgs since 1564, such a recovery was already well under way by about 1600, although, at the meeting of the Inner Austrian Diet in 1578, the Protestant Estates had managed to gain even more far-reaching concessions than the Lower Austrian Estates had achieved earlier. Faced with the threat of Turkish invasions, Archduke Charles had granted freedom of worship not only to the nobility but also to the citizens of his capital Graz and of three other major cities.[6] However, if the Turkish threat had initially been an advantage for the Estates, it was later exploited by the Archduke's Catholic councillors. With Turkish troops so close – the distance between Graz and the first Turkish outposts in Hungary was hardly more than about 100 miles – the Estates could not afford to renege on their commitment to pay for the defence of the Inner Austrian principalities. After all, they would have been among the first victims of a Turkish invasion. Thus the usual weapon wielded by assemblies of the Estates, which was to make the granting of supply conditional on a redress of grievances, was ultimately of little use here.

After missionary activities and the foundation of a Jesuit university in Graz in 1585 had prepared the ground, the Catholic bishops, supported by troops, suppressed all Protestant worship in a series of Counter-Reformation campaigns in 1599–1601. Protestant churches were reconverted into Catholic ones or destroyed, non-Catholic religious books burned and clergymen sent into exile. Although noblemen retained their liberty of conscience until 1628 as long as they did not take part in Protestant acts of worship, the victory of Catholicism was almost complete; only in a few remote rural areas did Protestantism survive for a few more decades and in some cases until the eighteenth century.

The political and religious conflicts in Bohemia and the other dominions of the Habsburg monarchy which culminated in the defenestration of 1618, must be seen in the light of these events. The Counter-Reformation in Styria, Carinthia and Carniola, largely completed by about 1601, demonstrated what the future had in store for Protestants in the Habsburgs' other principalities and kingdoms. When Archduke Ferdinand, who had ruled Inner Austria since 1596 (his father Charles had died in 1590 but Ferdinand did not come of age until six years later), turned out to be the most likely successor to his cousin Matthias as ruler of all the Habsburg dominions after 1612, tensions were bound to mount even further.

In fact the Habsburg monarchy had already come to the brink of collapse in the period 1606–12. The Emperor Rudolf II, who had always been susceptible to bouts of deep depression, became ever more mentally unbalanced after a serious illness in 1599–1600. While his policies became increasingly erratic, councillors and personal favourites who supported the cause of militant Catholicism gained significantly more influence than in the preceding years. The Emperor made the mistake of provoking his non-Catholic subjects by gestures revealing his support for the Counter-Reformation, while his real policy lacked all unity of purpose and clear direction. Matters came to a head after 1604. Rudolf's unconciliatory and at the same time rather weak policies had led to a rebellion in those parts of the Kingdom of Hungary which were under Habsburg rule. The rebels were allied with the Prince of Transylvania, a semi-independent principality dominated by its Magyar nobility, which the Habsburgs as well as the Turks (the latter rather more successfully) claimed as part of their sphere of influence.[7] They wanted the ancient privileges and liberties of the kingdom to be confirmed and insisted on religious toleration for non-Catholics. The Emperor's brother Matthias, who had been entrusted with the command of the imperial army in Hungary, reluctantly made a number of concessions to the Hungarian Estates in 1606 including religious toleration even for Calvinists. Moreover, as has already been mentioned, he signed the Peace of Zsitvatorok with the Turks in the same year.

Rudolf II disapproved of the concessions made to the Hungarian Estates and of the treaty with the Turks. Matthias, however, had the backing of his brothers Maximilian and Albert and his cousin Ferdinand, who had asked him to act as head of the German branch of the Habsburg dynasty because in their eyes Rudolf was incapacitated. The conflict between Rudolf and Matthias soon escalated. Each side tried to mobilise the Estates against its opponent and some of Matthias's troops even invaded Bohemia in 1608. Rudolf had to cede the government of Hungary, Moravia and Austria (the Duchies of Upper and Lower Austria) to his brother. In Bohemia, Silesia and Lusatia he maintained his position only by making major concessions to the nobility and the Estates in general. The Letter of Majesty (1609) which Rudolf had to sign to gain support against his brother recognised not only Protestantism – granting full freedom of worship – but also a long list of liberties and rights claimed by the Estates of Bohemia. The representatives of the Estates became virtual co-regents and their right of resistance was to all intents and purposes legally established. What is more, Matthias had to grant similar concessions to the Estates of the principalities in which he had managed to establish his rule against that of his brother. The way seemed free for the Habsburg monarchy to be transformed into a confederation of principalities and kingdoms dominated by the aristocracy, with the monarch as a mere figurehead.

Matters did not stop there. In 1611 Rudolf recruited troops to strengthen his position once more and to fight his brother. The commander of these troops was Archduke Leopold, Bishop of Passau and Strassburg. The devastation caused by Leopold's army in Austria and Bohemia gave Matthias a pretext to invade Bohemia. With the support of the Bohemian Diet, Rudolf was forced to abdicate – in fact he was deposed. Matthias was *accepted* or, as the Estates later claimed, *elected* as King of Bohemia in his stead. Rudolf died about a year later. He had retained the title of Emperor, but in fact ruled a realm which no longer extended beyond the walls of his palace.

The years 1608–11 had marked the high tide of Protestant and aristocratic power in the Habsburg dominions. Legally the Protestant Estates had never enjoyed such extensive rights. However, at an informal level their position was already being undermined. The imperial court, removed to Vienna once again under Matthias, now served as a focus for the forces of the Counter-Reformation. If the Bohemian Estates had some influence on appointments to state offices in the Kingdom of Bohemia, for example, advancement at court was completely in the Emperor's gift and here Catholicism was a precondition for gaining favour. By granting patents of nobility to reliable Catholics or converts, whose number was growing during these years, the Emperor and his councillors were able to undermine Protestant control over the institutions which had always been their major stronghold, the Diets and committees of the Estates. This was certainly true for Upper Austria and even more so for Lower Austria.[8]

If Catholicism was on the advance by informal means, the chances for a suppression of Protestantism were further enhanced in 1617, when Ferdinand of Styria was crowned as King designate of Bohemia. Although Ferdinand was known to be an ardent and intolerant Catholic, Matthias's advisors persuaded the Bohemian Estates to accept the Archduke as Matthias's successor. The Estates did not even assert their right to elect the king, a right which they had claimed when Rudolf was forced to abdicate in 1611 to be replaced by Matthias, and which they had repeatedly though not consistently claimed on earlier occasions, in particular during the fifteenth century. In 1617, however, the official version that Ferdinand had merely been accepted by the Estates as the rightful heir, not elected, went virtually unopposed.

The defenestration of 1618 was in many ways a belated answer to the carefully stage-managed coronation of 1617, when the radical Protestants had been outwitted. The attempt to kill those councillors who were most sharply opposed to the constitutional arrangements based on the Letter of Majesty of 1609, Martinitz and Slawata, was a sort of pre-emptive strike intended to establish the supremacy of the Protestant Estates before Matthias's death and before Ferdinand had a chance to impose his will in Bohemia. There had indeed been infringements of the privileges granted in 1609: for example, Protestant churches built on land which the Catholic Church claimed as its property had been closed and destroyed – illegally as the representatives of the Estates argued. But these measures were more a welcome justification for the revolutionary act than its real cause, which must rather be sought in the fears which all non-Catholics harboured with respect to the future.

The defenestration, though it did not actually result in loss of life, certainly made any future compromise between the Habsburgs and their opponents difficult, as Count Thurn and his supporters had indeed intended. Ferdinand of Styria and Archduke Maximilian of Tyrol, the Grandmaster of the Teutonic Order, reacted to the events in Prague by having the Emperor's favourite and chief councillor, Cardinal Klesl, arrested and deported to Tyrol where he was kept as a prisoner. Klesl was seen as too weak and too likely to make concessions to the rebels. Matthias made some futile protests against

Klesl's arrest, but ultimately had to accept the *coup d'état*. Without his chief minister, Matthias, never a strong or energetic ruler, was paralysed, and political decisions were increasingly taken by Ferdinand, Matthias's successor designate. In March 1619, the elderly Emperor died a bewildered and isolated man. Matthias's death, weak as he may have been as a ruler, made a peaceful solution of the Bohemian crisis even less likely than before. The Bohemians were faced with the alternative of either accepting Ferdinand as their King after all, or taking the ultimate step of deposing him. On 19 August 1619 they did indeed pass a resolution deposing him with the assent of delegates from Moravia, Silesia and Lusatia. Thus unanimity was achieved among the Estates of the dominions of the crown of St Wencislaus.[9]

At this point their chances of transforming Bohemia with its neighbouring principalities into a sort of aristocratic republic with an elected monarch, perhaps more as a symbolic than a real head, seemed *prima facie* better than ever. Poland's constitutional development during the seventeenth century shows that such an aristocratic republic was more than a mere utopia in eastern and east-central Europe. The Bohemians found support not only in Moravia but also in the ancient centre of the Habsburg monarchy, in the Duchies of Lower and Upper Austria, as well as in Hungary, and beyond the borders of the monarchy, in Transylvania. Ferdinand, Matthias's heir, was ill prepared to confront his rebellious subjects. Nevertheless, the Bohemian revolt was crushed within little more than a year. The support which Ferdinand received from his allies, Spain and Bavaria, was certainly of the utmost importance in helping him to achieve a swift victory. But the opposition against Ferdinand was never quite as strong and unified as it seemed. One of its inherent weaknesses was its inability to rally truly popular support, especially outside the towns. In the last resort, the interests of the nobility and the peasantry were difficult to reconcile.

One of the best examples of noble attitudes is provided by the Calvinist leader of the Protestant nobility in Upper Austria, Erasmus von Tschernembl. Well-acquainted with the resistance theories current in Calvinist circles all over Europe, he nevertheless denied the right of resistance to those below his own rank. During the Upper Austrian peasants' rising of 1594–97 he had declared that the rebellious peasants could justly be executed merely because they had been disobedient, even if they had not actually taken anybody's life.[10] Such attitudes would not have mattered so much had the tensions between nobility and peasantry not been so acute.[11] Many noblemen, not just in Upper Austria, but also in the other rebellious provinces, were afraid that a prolonged civil war would destroy the traditional political and social order, and were reluctant to take such a risk in resisting Ferdinand to the last ditch.

The German Princes and Bohemia

It should be stressed that despite the serious religious and political tensions in the Holy Roman Empire there seemed at first to be a chance of containing the Bohemian crisis and preventing a general conflagration. The attitude of the Protestant princes in Germany was initially rather cautious, and in many cases it became even more cautious as the crisis escalated. The fact that the crisis was not contained was ultimately due to two factors: Palatine intervention and, paradoxically enough, Ferdinand's weakness.

The Elector Palatine and in particular his regent in Amberg (in the Upper Palatinate or Oberpfalz, a province bordering on Bohemia and ruled by the Elector Palatine), Prince Christian of Anhalt, had been in touch with the Bohemian opposition right from the start. What Anhalt had been trying to bring about before 1618 was an international coalition with a leading role for the Palatinate and himself, uniting all opponents of the House of Habsburg and of Counter-Reformation Catholicism. Now the hour for bringing these plans to fruition seemed to have struck. Anhalt certainly encouraged the Bohemian Estates' decision to depose Ferdinand in August 1619. Their further decision to proceed to the election of

Friedrich V, the Elector Palatine, as the new King of Bohemia, barely two weeks later on 26/27 August, had also initially been in accord with Anhalt's wishes, although at this stage he had already begun to doubt the wisdom of his own radical policy.[12] However, whatever doubts Anhalt may have harboured, Friedrich accepted the Bohemian crown and was thereby irrevocably committed to open war against Ferdinand of Austria.

This decision finally transformed the Bohemian crisis if not into an all-embracing European conflict, then certainly into a war in which the future of the Holy Roman Empire was at stake. But we must also take Ferdinand's position into account. His attempts to subdue the Bohemians and their allies were far from successful. In June 1619 Bohemian troops took up their positions before the walls of Ferdinand's own capital Vienna and threatened to lay siege to the town while Ferdinand was forced to discuss their grievances with the angry representatives of the Lower Austrian nobility in the Hofburg. Legend has it that one of the Austrian noblemen, Andreas Thonradel, buttonholed Ferdinand and shouted at him: 'Give in, Nandl, or you are done for'. This may indeed be a legend, but the remarkable sang-froid which Ferdinand showed when the Estates confronted him with their 'Sturmpetition' (literally 'storm petition') was real enough.[13]

An unshakeable faith in the justness of his own cause coupled with courage, or perhaps just great insensitivity at moments of danger, was one of the future Emperor's most remarkable personal traits. In situations such as the confrontation with the irate noblemen, Ferdinand's lack of imagination may to some extent have worked in his favour. Unable to understand the convictions of his opponents, he was equally incapable of imagining the disasters which might befall him if he continued to pursue his policy in the face of opposition. The steadfastness and resolution which made him so different from his cousin Rudolf II enabled him to survive even periods of crisis without giving in to his enemies. In the eyes of his opponents, however, he was the archetype of a tyrant and a bigot, and he was indeed extremely intolerant in religious matters.

But so were the majority of his contemporaries, whatever their religious persuasion.[14]

Nevertheless Ferdinand's lack of imagination and his altogether rather mediocre intellect were definitely a disadvantage when he was confronted with unfamiliar challenges, and in a way the task of governing the whole of the Habsburg monarchy was such an unfamiliar challenge. For about 20 years before 1617 he ruled a medium-sized territory, Inner Austria, not really larger than the Palatinate or Saxony. Now he was the ruler of one of the greatest monarchies in Europe. If he was on unfamiliar ground here, this can be asserted with even greater justification of his role as Emperor. In fact, it has been convincingly argued that Ferdinand never really developed a coherent policy for the Empire.[15] In a way he was out of his depth outside his hereditary lands. This explains to some extent why in the later 1620s he took recourse to the same sort of purely confessional policy in the Empire which he had previously pursued, ultimately successfully, in his own dominions. But in the Empire this policy was to lead to disaster.

During the Bohemian crisis, and in fact for most of the early 1620s, Ferdinand lacked not only a clear political concept for the Empire. More than anything else he lacked the means to implement whatever policy he decided to pursue. His attempts to regain control over Bohemia proved futile in 1619. What is more, the Bohemian Estates, though unable for the time being to take Vienna, were about to push Ferdinand back to his Inner Austrian stronghold. Moravia, Silesia, Upper and Lower Austria, as well as large parts of Hungary occupied by troops from Transylvania allied with the Bohemians, were lost to the Habsburgs. In this situation Ferdinand could hope to defeat his enemies only if he received outside help. Spain had already granted Ferdinand considerable financial assistance in 1618, and within a few months of the fall of the Duke of Lerma in autumn 1618, the advocates of an active Spanish policy north of the Alps were able to overcome the last opposition to intervention in Bohemia and the Holy Roman Empire.[16] Spanish financial and military support was certainly highly important for ensuring Ferdinand's political survival in

1619–20. In many ways the Elector Palatine had chosen the worst possible moment for a confrontation with Ferdinand. On the one hand Spain had already decided to give her interests in central Europe a higher priority than in the preceding years and to prepare for a renewal of the war in the Netherlands, but on the other hand this war had not yet started again, so that the Spanish monarchy still had enough resources available to support Ferdinand in Bohemia and in Germany.

Bavaria was as important an ally as Spain. In October 1619 Duke Maximilian and the reconstituted Catholic Liga agreed to send their army to support Ferdinand. Maximilian, however, insisted that after a victory, he should be compensated for the costs he would incur during the war. The Archduchy of Austria or parts of it were to be occupied by Maxmilian's troops as security until Ferdinand reimbursed Bavaria for the costs of the military intervention. Ferdinand also assured Maximilian, though this was not yet part of a formal written agreement, that after the Elector Palatine was defeated, Maximilian would be rewarded with substantial parts of the Palatine dominions and a transfer of the electoral dignity from the Palatine branch of the Wittelsbach dynasty to Maximilian's own Bavarian branch.

In a word, because Ferdinand was not strong enough to crush the Bohemian rebellion himself, he incurred political as well as financial debts. Therefore his political creditors, Bavaria and to a lesser extent Spain, were able to dictate policy to him after 1620. It could be argued that an extension of the conflict would have been far less likely had Ferdinand been able to deal with the Bohemian rebellion himself, relying on his own military and financial resources. For in the last resort Ferdinand seems to have cared less about the Empire than about his own dominions.

The preceding remarks have stressed the inherent weakness of Ferdinand's position. In fact, a number of accounts of the origins of the Thirty Years War have emphasised that his position would have been untenable without outside help and have stressed the importance of Spanish intervention in particular.[17] No doubt Spain's intervention was important. But Ferdinand's fortunes also gradually improved after the summer of 1619 for quite a different reason: his in the end unanimous election as Emperor on 28 August 1619, hardly two weeks after his deposition as King of Bohemia. Palatine policy in spring and summer 1619 had really been based on the assumption that the election of a new Emperor after Matthias's death in March could be postponed until the Bohemian crisis had been resolved and Habsburg power in the Empire destroyed or at least severely curtailed. However, it was not the Elector Palatine who traditionally organised the election of a new sovereign after the death of an Emperor, but the Empire's Archchancellor, the Archbishop of Mainz. Needless to say, he was a staunch Catholic and devoted to the House of Habsburg.

Very few Protestants were prepared to take the ultimate step of preventing a meeting of the prince electors by force, although in Heidelberg, the Palatine capital, such plans were debated. When the electors did meet in Frankfurt in August 1619 – the ecclesiastical princes and Ferdinand in his capacity as King of Bohemia had come in person, the other electors had sent authorised representatives – the Elector Palatine was unable to present a plausible alternative candidate to Ferdinand. His best bet seemed to be to promote the candidature of the Duke of Bavaria; the three archbishops who were members of the electoral college and who, together with Bohemia, held the majority against the Protestant electors, would not in any case have voted for a candidate who was not a Catholic. However, Maximilian was not prepared to compete against Ferdinand. Thus the Archduke and recently deposed King of Bohemia (the electors did not recognise the deposition so that he could cast the Bohemian vote for himself) was elected not only by the spiritual members of the college but also by Saxony and Brandenburg. Even the Palatine representative ultimately had to concur with the majority decision of the Kurkolleg, which traditionally tried to achieve a unanimous election.

From the moment he was elected and crowned Ferdinand had an enormous political capital at his disposal. Even without an army at all, his authority was considerable. However many battles the Bohemians and the troops of the Elector Palatine might win, Ferdinand would still be Emperor, whereas a single lost battle could easily spell doom for his opponents. Without the Emperor's assent, no legitimate political settlement could ever be reached in Germany. This was as true in 1648 as it was in 1619. Ferdinand, on the other hand, could outlaw his enemies for breach of the Empire's peace and *crimen laesae majestatis* (high treason), and by carefully exploiting and manipulating the existing legal framework he could declare whole principalities forfeited and use these titles and dominions to reward his allies. Never clearly defined and often fragile, the Emperor's authority was nevertheless a factor of considerable significance in a political situation as confused as that created by the Bohemian rebellion.

The Elector Palatine now found it increasingly difficult to justify his policy in legal terms. Legal scholars favourable to his cause argued that the two *personae* of the Emperor had to be distinguished. On the one hand he was the ruler of the Holy Roman Empire, on the other a private person, and according to this theory Ferdinand claimed the Bohemian crown only as a private person. Thus a nobleman supporting the Elector Palatine in a war about the Bohemian succession was not guilty of felony or treason against the Emperor. This was an important point, for the less powerful princes in particular and even more the imperial free knights were frightened by the prospect of incurring the Emperor's wrath.[18] But these arguments ultimately failed to reassure them.

From the moment Ferdinand was elected Emperor the system of alliances which the Palatine politicians had built before up 1618 started to disintegrate. Saxony, the most powerful Lutheran principality, had never been sympathetic to the idea of a direct confrontation with the House of Habsburg and Catholicism. Johann Georg of Saxony, who would have had considerable support in Bohemia, had already rejected an offer to be elected King of Bohemia instead of Ferdinand. But he was not going to allow the Elector Palatine, Friedrich, his main Protestant rival among the princes of the Empire and a Calvinist, to gain Bohemia for himself. After all, this would have made Friedrich Johann Georg's liege lord, for Saxony held a number of fiefs of the crown of Bohemia. Johann Georg therefore decided early in 1620 to support Ferdinand against the Bohemian Estates and their allies. Saxony's support was by no means unconditional. In March and April 1620 Ferdinand had made a number of important concessions. The privileges which the Protestants in Bohemia, Moravia, Silesia and Lusatia enjoyed were to remain inviolate. In other words religious toleration was to be granted, in as far as those who claimed these privileges remained obedient to the Emperor – an important qualification which was later used to suppress Protestantism altogether in Bohemia and Moravia. Furthermore, the Elector of Saxony was to take the Margravate of Lusatia in pledge for the repayment of the costs which he would incur during his military intervention in favour of the Emperor.

More important even than these concessions made to Johann Georg personally were the decisions taken at a conference of princes supporting Ferdinand's cause. Most of them were Catholic but they also included Johann Georg of Saxony and Landgrave Ludwig of Hesse-Darmstadt. The conference was held in Mühlhausen in Thüringia in March 1620. Here the members of the Catholic Liga declared that they would not try to regain former ecclesiastical possessions in northern and eastern Germany (in the Lower and Upper Saxon Circle of the Empire) by force. This concession, which was particularly important for the status of the numerous bishoprics in the area, which had been secularised or were about to be secularised, was confirmed by the Emperor. It was a precondition for Ferdinand's success in persuading the Protestant princes of northern and eastern Germany to stay neutral, at least for the time being, although further attempts to gain their active support failed.

Nevertheless, the decisions taken in Mühlhausen ensured that the war which could no longer be avoided would not, for the time being, be an all-out religious conflict, at least outside the imperial dominions. In fact, in July 1620 the members of the Protestant Union and the princes of the Liga signed a treaty of neutrality in Ulm. Under its terms neither side was to attack the other, so that the war would be limited, in theory, to Bohemia and the Habsburg dominions. This was, of course, an arrangement which strongly favoured Ferdinand II, Maximilian of Bavaria and their allies. Maximilian remained free to intervene in Bohemia and the Rhine Palatinate was in no way protected against a Spanish invasion. So why did the members of the Union sign the treaty? To some extent the French diplomats, who acted as mediators between the hostile camps, were responsible for the wording and the contents of the treaty of neutrality. At this stage it was the principal aim of French policy to prevent the outbreak of a major war in the Holy Roman Empire. A Habsburg victory would strengthen Spain, France's old rival and potential enemy, whereas a Protestant victory could not be welcome to the French King and his councillors, nearly all devout Catholics, either, not least because such a victory might well strengthen the Protestant opposition within France. After all, the Elector Palatine's predecessor had been one of the most powerful patrons of the Huguenots during the French Wars of Religion in the sixteenth century.[19]

In any case, France was in no way capable of intervening in a major European conflict herself. Louis XIII, the French King, had gained power in 1617 only by having his mother's favourite, the Italian Concino Concini, assassinated. His mother, Marie de Medici, had become regent after the death of Henry IV in 1610 and had directed French policy in the following years, avoiding all involvements in international conflicts. Relations between mother and son remained tense for a considerable time after Concini's assassination. In summer 1620 troops mobilised by Marie de Medici's supporters were even involved in a minor battle with the royal army,[20] and it was only too likely that the dowager Queen's household would become a dangerous centre for a radically Catholic opposition should Louis XIII pursue a pro-Protestant foreign policy, something which he was not inclined to do at this stage anyhow. He preferred to concentrate on reducing the privileges of his Protestant subjects in southern France, and in particular in Navarra and Béarn. In Béarn, a lordship which until 1617 was united with France only in a loose dynastic union, Protestantism had remained dominant after 1598, the date of the Edict of Nantes, and Catholicism was barely tolerated there. An armed intervention by the royal army in 1620 established Catholicism as the official religion in Béarn as in the rest of France,[21] but now the French Protestants, fearing a revocation of the Edict of Nantes, felt threatened and became restive. With civil war a permanent danger, the French decision to stay neutral while trying to contain and limit the crisis in Germany was probably inevitable. French neutralism, however, was bound to shatter the morale of the Protestant Union which was already rather low.

Not only did France remain neutral, but England and even the Netherlands were equally reluctant to support the Elector Palatine. The Dutch did support the Elector Palatine financially – in 1620 about one-eighth of Friedrich's troops in Bohemia were paid for by the Dutch Republic or were in fact Dutch regiments – but in the last resort they had to concentrate their resources on defending themselves against the Spanish attack which was expected in 1621 when the truce with Spain expired. James I of England, on the other hand, had disapproved of his son-in-law's adventurous policy from the very beginning.[22] What was more, England's resources were hardly adequate to finance a major army on the Continent or even to grant Friedrich generous subsidies. When it dawned on the Elector's allies that the network of international alliances which his diplomats had constructed during the preceding years was falling apart before the first battle had even been fought, their own determination to fight against the Emperor and the forces of the Counter-Reformation began to evaporate. Largely isolated in Europe, the Palatinate began to lose its German allies too. Thus the Treaty of Ulm prepared the ground for the decisive victory which the Catholic armies were to achieve over the following months and, in fact, years.

The decline of the Union which ended in its official dissolution in May 1621 was to some extent due to the fact that this alliance had initially been founded to defend the position of the Protestant princes and towns in southern and western Germany. It was widely assumed before 1618 that the principal theatre of operations in an armed confrontation would be the Rhine valley, either the upper Rhine with its patchwork of Protestant and Catholic territories, or the lower Rhine as in 1610–14. Here, outside intervention by the Union's actual or potential allies, the Dutch, English and French, would have been much easier. Moreover, these powers would have had a much stronger incentive to intervene in this strategically important zone than in Bohemia, a kingdom which was too far removed from the principal centres of political and military conflict in western Europe.[23]

The Catholic Triumph

With the Union neutralised Maximilian was free to send his and the Liga's troops into Bohemia. Friedrich V, the Elector Palatine, had been crowned King of Bohemia only in November 1619. A year later his troops were defeated by the Catholic army in the battle of the White Mountain near Prague on 8 November 1620. Friedrich V's rather inept foreign policy and his failure to win allies had certainly considerably hampered all efforts to defend Bohemia. However, internal dissension among the Bohemian Estates, and the fact that the system of taxation and administration in the kingdom remained as inefficient under the new government as under the Habsburgs, had also undermined the Bohemian army's ability to fight. Moreover, the general collapse of order during the Bohemian campaign in 1620 and the barbarous behaviour of Catholic as well as Protestant soldiers who indulged in looting and other excesses had created a climate of social unrest. In some areas the peasants had already assembled not only to defend themselves but also to plunder the castles of their lords, and a major peasant uprising seemed quite possible.[24] The prospect of a social revolution further dampened the fervour of Ferdinand's Protestant opponents in Bohemia, and made it impossible to mobilise adequately Bohemia's financial and material resources.

After the battle of the White Mountain Maximilian's and the Emperor's regiments soon subdued the whole of Bohemia and Moravia. It was left to Johann Georg of Saxony to accomplish the same in Lusatia and Silesia. The conditions which he imposed in these provinces were much less harsh than those suffered by Bohemia. The Silesian Estates in particular managed to obtain guarantees for their ancient privileges and for the survival of Protestantism.[25] As it turned out these promises made by Johann Georg in the Emperor's name were not entirely worthless; they were partially incorporated in the Westphalian peace in 1648, so that Protestantism survived at least in northern Silesia.

In contrast to the provinces conquered by the Saxon troops, Moravia and especially Bohemia were subjected to a savage campaign of repression which was to last for several years. The leaders of the Bohemian Estates who had not been able to escape were executed. Protestantism was suppressed during the 1620s, contrary to the spirit if not to the letter of the promises Ferdinand had given Johann Georg.[26] Moreover, entire sections of the old established elite were expropriated and their possessions distributed among Ferdinand's supporters or sold off to them at bargain prices. The lower nobility (*Ritterstand*), to some extent already in decline before 1618 for economic reasons, was now largely marginalised politically and socially. For the next two centuries the Austrian duchies as well as Moravia and Bohemia were to be dominated by a Catholic aristocracy of noble magnates with close links to the imperial court which shaped their mentality and culture. Although a number of native families who had always remained loyal to the old church, or had converted to Catholicism in time before 1618, continued to hold their own, many members of this aristocracy were of foreign origin, hailing from other parts of the Habsburg monarchy, from southern Germany, Italy, or even Spain or Ireland.[27]

Such were the long-term consequences of the battle of the White Mountain. The more immediate problem facing Ferdinand and his allies after the victory, however, was how to deal with Friedrich V. The Elector and temporary King had fled Bohemia immediately after the battle of the White Mountain, but he was not yet prepared to abandon his claim to the Bohemian crown entirely, and even less inclined to accept the probably quite harsh punishment which Ferdinand was likely to inflict on him – for example a transfer of the Upper Palatinate and possibly even of the electoral title to Maximilian of Bavaria. Although Spanish troops had already started to advance on the Lower Palatinate in 1620 and had occupied a number of towns west of the river Rhine, Friedrich and his councillors could hope that their military position would improve once the main theatre of operations shifted away from Bohemia towards the Rhine valley.

In spite of the gradual dissolution of the Protestant Union, Friedrich could still count on a number of allies in this area, in particular the Margrave Georg Friedrich of Baden-Durlach and the Landgrave of Hesse-Kassel. England and the Dutch States General, which had failed to send help in any substantial way in 1620, were also more likely to mobilise assistance now that what was at stake was not only the fate of Protestantism in the Habsburg dominions, but the very constitution of the Holy Roman Empire and the balance of power in central Europe. However, Friedrich and his advisers had once again miscalculated their chances of success. It was fatal for his political fortunes that an international political alliance capable of intervening in Germany was not formed until 1624–25.

The Dutch were too busy defending themselves against Spain, which had been putting considerable pressure on their borders since the resumption of hostilities in spring 1621, to intervene in Germany on any considerable scale. In fact the fall in January 1622 of the fortress of Jülich, which had been garrisoned by Dutch soldiers since 1610 and was now besieged by Spanish troops, would have made Dutch intervention in Germany almost impossible anyhow. Only when the war moved to north-western Germany did the States General take a more active part in the struggle in the Empire. But even then their contribution was largely limited to financial support and providing the Elector Palatine's disintegrating forces with a safe haven in the Netherlands where they could regroup and support the Dutch in their fight against Spain, or gather enough strength to renew the war in Germany. The Elector himself took refuge in The Hague, provisionally in 1621 and permanently the next year, and here his court-in-exile was established. It became an important point of contact for militant Protestants, many of them exiled, from all over Europe throughout the 1620s.

But the war in the Netherlands and the war in Germany remained by and large two distinct conflicts. Certainly Spain was engaged in both, but repeated attempts by Spanish diplomats to persuade the Emperor, the Catholic German princes, and even Protestant rulers and towns to join the Spanish monarchy in its fight against the Dutch, were never really successful.

If the Palatinate could expect little help from the Dutch in 1621, appealing to James I of England for help proved equally futile. Although about 2,000 English soldiers were sent to strengthen the defences of the the Palatinate in 1620, James had not yet given up his dream of being Europe's peacemaker. Moreover, he himself, the various factions of his court (including his favourite George Villiers, Marquess and later Duke of Buckingham, and the Prince of Wales) and the Parliament assembled in 1621 were at cross-purposes about the political strategy most suitable for countering the Habsburg advance in Germany.

Thus Friedrich V was once more left to his own devices. In fact, Count Ernst of Mansfeld, a well-known military entrepreneur who had already fought for Friedrich in Bohemia, managed to recruit more than 40,000 soldiers in Alsace to defend the Palatinate in 1621. During the 1620s Mansfeld was to gain a considerable reputation as a commander who could assemble large armies on the cheap in a short time, but who was also liable to lose these troops in an even shorter time through wastage, sickness and desertions, and who was reluctant to risk the regiments he had assembled in battle. In

1621–22 Mansfeld's army was supported by smaller contingents under the command of Georg Friedrich of Baden and Christian of Brunswick – the Protestant administrator of the Bishopric of Halberstadt, who was a great admirer of Elizabeth Stuart, Friedrich V's wife, and a reckless adventurer, like many younger sons in search of glory and a hereditary principality of his own.

None the less, the Protestant troops were no match for the army of the Catholic Liga commanded by Count Jean Tserclaes Tilly. Tilly, a veteran who had served his military apprenticeship in the Spanish army of Flanders and in the Habsburg army in Hungary, had already beaten the Protestant forces in Bohemia in 1620 and had occupied the Upper Palatinate around Amberg in 1621. Now, in his campaign against Mansfeld and his allies, he could count on the support of the Spanish troops operating mainly on the left bank of the Rhine. As the Margrave of Baden, Christian of Halberstadt and Mansfeld proved incapable of co-ordinating their operations, the Margrave of Baden and Christian were defeated separately in the battles of Wimpfen (6 May 1622) and Höchst (20 June 1622). Mansfeld's position became untenable. Officially dismissed by the Elector Palatine, he decided to retreat to the Netherlands together with Christian and the remnant of his troops. The Lower Palatinate was now lost. Heidelberg was taken in September, Mannheim in November. Whereas the western part of the Electorate left of the Rhine was occupied by Spanish troops, the eastern districts came under the control of Maximilan of Bavaria, the head of the Liga. Maximilian had already occupied the Upper Palatinate the year before and he clearly hoped to secure this province and at least parts of the Lower Palatinate for himself and his heirs.

The Elector Palatine had in fact been officially outlawed by the Emperor in early 1621. Normally a proper trial had to be held in the Chamber Court in Speyer or the Aulic Council in Vienna before a prince of the Empire was outlawed. At least the imperial proclamation against the culprit had to be approved by the Estates of the Empire in the Imperial Diet, or if the Diet was not sitting, by the prince electors. However, the lawyers advising Ferdinand II argued that a trial was unnecessary in cases where the crime was 'notorious'. Not even the consent of the prince electors need be obtained, they suggested. A mere memorandum by the Aulic Council assessing the merits of the case was sufficient. The Emperor had at first, for political reasons, hesitated to accept this argument, but after Friedrich's defeat in Bohema he was duly declared an outlaw.[28] This entitled Ferdinand – or so it could be argued at least – to confiscate Friedrich's forfeited fiefs, possessions and dignities. This was an important point. It gave the Emperor a chance to reward his allies, in particular Maxmilian of Bavaria, but also created a precedent for punishing other 'rebels' later. The imperial sentence against the Elector Palatine in January 1621 showed that the war had already begun to change the constitutional balance in the Holy Roman Empire in the Emperor's favour.

For the time being, however, the Duke of Bavaria benefited most from Friedrich V's defeat. Ferdinand had already transferred Friedrich's electoral dignity to him in secret in September 1621. In February 1623 Maximilan was officially invested with the title of Prince Elector in Regensburg, where an assembly of princes (*Deputationstag*) had met. However, Ferdinand did not yet dare to tranfer the dignity of elector to the Bavarian Wittelsbachs in perpetuity. For now only Maximilian was to bear the new title.[29] A return of the title to the Palatinate branch of the Wittelsbach dynasty remained possible. This was a concession the Emperor had to make in the face of opposition among the Protestant princes and even among some moderate Catholics to the transfer of the electoral dignity. Furthermore, the Spanish ambassador had tried to prevent the fatal decision altogether; Philip IV of Spain and his advisors knew that relations with the former Elector Palatine's father-in-law, James I of England, were bound to suffer if Friedrich were permanently reduced to the status of a landless outlaw stripped of his titles.[30]

In 1623, however, there was little Friedrich could do to counter the imperial decision. He did manage to assemble an army once more with Dutch support. While Mansfeld advanced eastwards from the Netherlands and took up a position in Eastern Frisia near the Dutch border, Christian of Halberstadt tried to move southwards with about 21,000 men. He planned to enter Bohemia, where he hoped to join forces with the Prince of Transylvania, Gabriel Bethlen. Bethlen had taken up the fight against the Habsburgs once again and, supported by troops which the Turks had supplied, managed to invade Hungary – where he could count on local support – and Moravia.

However, Tilly had already moved to northern Germany with superior forces before the fresh Protestant offensive got off the ground. Christian of Halberstadt decided to retreat to the Netherlands but he was stopped by Tilly's forces at Stadtlohn, in the territory of the Bishop of Münster near the Dutch border, on 6 August 1623. Christian's army was totally defeated and only a few thousand of his troops managed to escape into the Netherlands. In Eastern Frisia Mansfeld was wise enough to disband his army early in 1624 before worse could befall him, or rather, before lack of supplies and money made his position totally impossible.

After Stadtlohn, the war in Germany was over for the time being. Without outside support none of the German princes was really able to confront the victorious army of the Liga. On the other hand, the calm which returned after 1623 was deceptive. The balance of power in the Holy Roman Empire had changed so drastically since 1618 that this in itself was likely to provoke Friedrich V's former allies outside Germany and other European powers to intervene. Moreover, during the years 1619–22 the theatres of operations had been areas traditionally under imperial control or the Emperor's influence – his hereditary dominions and southern Germany where he had always had a great network of clients at his disposal. However, northern Germany, where Tilly's troops were garrisoned in 1624, and the areas east of the river Elbe were a different matter. Here armies fighting for the Roman Catholic Church and imperial authority were moving on more difficult ground. Northern and eastern Germany were not only areas where Protestantism was very firmly entrenched, they were also regions where in a manner of speaking the imperial writ did not run in the sixteenth century. With the important exception of electoral Saxony, the Emperor had always had few clients and allies there. There were probably even fewer after the reign of Charles V, who had at least had a powerbase in the Low Countries bordering on north-western Germany.

Thus, although Ferdinand and Maximilan had been victorious throughout the early 1620s, no permanent settlement of the issues which had fuelled the conflict so far, or had been raised during the course of the war, was yet in sight in 1624.

3

1629:
COUNTER-REFORMATION
AND HABSBURG SUPREMACY

Germany and Europe in 1629: The Edict of Restitution, Alès and Mantua

The series of victories which the Catholic armies had achieved between 1620 and 1624 was to be continued during the following five years. At the same time more and more countries were drawn into the war. In the early 1620s the war had not yet been a genuinely European conflict. It had focused on two principal issues: the struggle for power in the Empire and the Dutch–Spanish war which was renewed in 1621 after the expiry of the truce. Moreover, these two issues had remained largely distinct, as has already been emphasised. Certainly, Spanish troops fought in the Palatinate as well as against the Dutch, and the States General gave support, mostly financial and logistical, to the Elector Palatine and his allies. But no major Dutch army had come to the rescue of the Palatinate nor could the Spanish count on the active support of the German Catholic Liga against the Dutch. From 1624 onwards, however, the conflict was increasingly internationalised. Powers such as England and Denmark, and ultimately France, too, which so far had stayed on the sidelines, took up arms at last and tried to redress the military and political balance in central Europe. With these new participants the issues dominating the conflict became ever more complex and intricate.

The complicated pattern of alliances and counter-alliances in the later 1620s, one of the most crucial and most eventful phases of the war, may often seem confusing. The political problems of this period are, however, easier to understand if we look first at the essential changes which the military and diplomatic confrontations of these years brought about; that is, if we take a closer look at the political situation in Europe at the end of the 1620s, and then return to the events of the preceding years.

In more than one sense the year 1629 was a watershed in the course of the Thirty Years War. It both marked the apogee of Habsburg power in Europe and saw the first signs of its decline. The association between the Habsburgs and the cause of the Counter-Reformation was re-affirmed and made explicit in the Edict of Restitution in 1629. None the less it now came under increasing strain. These stresses were visible not only in the armed confrontation between Spain and France, two Catholic powers, in northern Italy after 1628, but also in severe tensions between Bavaria and the Emperor at the end of the 1620s. Furthermore, the military commitments undertaken by Spain proved to be too expensive to sustain for a country with ultimately rather limited economic resources. Thus the series of defeats which the Protestant princes in Germany and later the great Protestant powers of northern Europe had suffered in their struggle against the Habsburgs and against their Catholic opponents was about to come to an end in 1629. This was the very moment when the Emperor's effective authority in Germany seemed greater than ever, and when Spain seemed to have a chance to deal a fatal blow to her Dutch enemies with help from the imperial army, and possibly even an imperial navy.

What was at stake in the late 1620s was on the one hand the position of the Habsburg powers, and on the other the fate of Protestantism. Was Europe to be dominated by the Spanish and German branches of the Habsburg dynasty? The victories which armies fighting for the Emperor continued to achieve in Germany after 1624 seemed to be laying a secure foundation for permanent Spanish and imperial hegemony in

Europe. At the same time, the victories won by Spanish or imperial troops during the 1620s were also victories for the cause of the Counter-Reformation, and battles won by other Catholic armies, in particular the troops of the Catholic Liga in Germany, tended to favour Spanish and imperial interests, at least indirectly. As events were to show after 1628, however, this equation of the interests of the House of Habsburg with the cause of Catholicism was too much at odds with the re-quirements of *realpolitik* to work in the long run. Not only major Catholic powers, especially France, but also Catholic rulers of lesser status, such as the Duke (newly created Prince Elector) of Bavaria, were very much aware that their interests were ultimately incompatible with the political objectives pursued in Madrid and Vienna. Moreover, even Ferdinand II, the Emperor, and Philip IV, the Spanish King, found it in-creasingly difficult to co-ordinate their policies, each having clearly distinct political priorities.

Nevertheless, in the years immediately before 1629 these fissures in the structure of the Catholic–Habsburg alliance had not yet become sufficiently visible to change the course of the war. In fact, in 1627–28 co-operation between the various Catholic princes of Germany and Europe appeared to be closer and more effective than ever. During the late 1620s the religious antagonism had, *prima facie* at least, finally become the dominant element in the war, which by now involved most European powers. It was a struggle in which Spain and France, despite the continuing tensions between them, had at least one enemy in common: England.

In the early 1620s England had remained neutral, as had other Protestant powers, in particular the Scandinavian king-doms, Denmark and Sweden. From the mid-1620s on, however, the Protestant camp had gradually become more coherent, at least outside the borders of the Empire. England had entered the war against the Habsburgs in 1624–25, fol-lowed by Denmark. In the second half of the 1620s the great Protestant powers of northern Europe – the Netherlands, England and Denmark, but not Sweden – came together in an alliance which was at once anti-Habsburg and anti-Catholic.

However, their opponents, the Catholic powers, had also achieved a greater degree of unity. Whereas France, neutral in the early 1620s, had moved towards the brink of open war with Spain in 1624–25, the leading French minister, Cardinal Richelieu (appointed in 1624), had decided to take a less hostile stance towards Spain in early 1626; French domestic problems had reasserted their primacy. In fact, in early 1627 relations between England and France deteriorated rapidly while at the same time religious tensions within France escalated once more. The result of these developments had been an alliance between England and the French Huguenots, and open warfare between France and England during the years 1627–28. For a short time a general *rapprochement* seemed possible between France and Spain. It was favoured more than ever for religious reasons by the French *dévots*, who still exerted considerable influence at the Bourbon court at this stage. In March 1627 France and Spain signed an offensive alliance and pledged mutual support in their struggle against England. Olivares, the leading Spanish minister, as well as Richelieu saw this alliance very much as a tactical move, a mere temporary expedient, but Olivares did in fact decide to send a naval squadron to La Rochelle in autumn 1627 to support Louis XIII's troops. However, the squadron arrived too late in the year to be of any real assistance.[1]

Given the dominant position of the religious factor in international politics during the admittedly brief period 1627–28, it was only logical, or so at least it must have seemed at the time, that the conflict between Protestantism and Catholicism in Germany, which had always been an important element in the war, would also be expressed more openly than before. And in fact the Emperor Ferdinand II went a long way towards finally transforming the war in Germany into an all-out religious conflict early in 1629.

On 28 March 1629, after a long and virtually unbroken series of Catholic victories on the battlefields of central Europe, Ferdinand II had a document published all over Germany which was to have a potentially revolutionary impact: the Edict of Restitution. It provided for all ecclesiastical rights and possessions secularised since 1552, the year of the signing of the peace treaty of Passau on which the *Religionsfriede* of 1555 was based, to be returned to the Roman Catholic Church. This applied in particular to the great prince-bishoprics of northern Germany which had come under the control of Protestant 'administrators' before 1618 – normally members of the neighbouring princely dynasties. However, a large number of monasteries and their property were also affected. The background to the Edict of Restitution and its impact will be discussed later (see below, pp. 94–8).

What needs to be emphasised here once more is that the edict was very much in tune with the turn taken by international relations in Europe in the late 1620s. It was the logical climax of a drift towards ever sharper antagonism between Protestantism and Catholicism all over Europe – or so it must have seemed at the time. However, at the very moment when the edict was being promulgated and published in the Empire, the structure of the conflict in western and southern Europe had already begun to change again. The Emperor's lawyers and theologians who had prepared the edict in 1628 had clearly not foreseen these changes. Or at least they had underestimated their impact which was to transform the edict into a political miscalculation of gigantic proportions. If a chance for a concerted religious crusade against Protestantism all over Europe ever existed, it was already gone by spring 1629. The seemingly clear confessional frontlines of the years 1627–28 were blurred once more.

In France, Louis XIII's army had on 29 October 1628 taken the most important Huguenot stronghold, La Rochelle, which had been besieged since 1627. Repeated attempts by the English fleet to lift the siege of the town had all failed. In fact, England decided to withdraw from the conflict with France in April 1629 (Anglo-French Peace of Susa) and abandoned the French Protestants to their fate. The bitter but brief confrontation between France and England was now over. What is more, exactly three months after Ferdinand II's edict called the status of Protestantism in Germany into question, in

France the French King passed the Édit de Grace of Alès (28 June 1629). Like the Edict of Restitution, the edict of Alès dealt with the relationship between Catholics and Protestants. However, whereas Ferdinand's edict threatened the very survival of Protestantism in Germany, the Edict of Alès re-established the peace between Protestants and Catholics in France which Henry IV had achieved at the end of the 1590s, although it also modified the earlier arrangements considerably. The Huguenots had to make great sacrifices after the military confrontations of the 1620s and the fall of La Rochelle. They had to abandon all their fortresses and strongholds and they lost their political autonomy. Nevertheless their status as a religious community remained, for the time being at least, intact.

Admittedly the comparison between the situation in Germany and France is of limited validity. In France the Protestants were a comparatively small minority comprising about 4–5 per cent of the population. To disarm them without fuelling an endless confessional war was much easier than in the Empire, where most of the more powerful secular princes and almost the entire population of eastern and northern Germany were Protestants. Nevertheless, the fact remains that the confessional conflict which had gained a considerable momentum in France in the 1620s was successfully defused in 1629. France was once again free to pursue an active foreign policy, although the extent to which alliances between France and Protestant powers were legitimate remained a subject of heated debate and acrimonious political conflict among French Catholics throughout the 1630s and even later.

The fact that Cardinal Richelieu had managed to extricate France from domestic and international conflicts which had been fought primarily along religious lines meant that at the very moment when Ferdinand II's commissioners began to enforce the Edict of Restitution, this policy could no longer count on the tacit or open support of Catholic Europe as a whole. The assumptions about the nature of European politics on which the edict had rested became invalid at the very moment of its publication. While Ferdinand II gave priority to

the cause of the Catholic Church over other political considerations, France was about to enter a war against the foremost
Catholic power of Europe, Spain, thus pursuing a policy dic-
tated more by reason of state than by religious orthodoxy.

In December 1627 the Duke of Mantua in northern Italy had
died without direct heirs. A French nobleman, Charles de
Gonzague, Duke of Nevers, a distant relation of the late Duke
of Mantua, had the best claims to the Duchy and the
Marquisate of Montferrat, also ruled by the Dukes of Mantua.
Both Montferrat and Mantua, although fairly small principalities, were strategically important as they controlled the access
to the Lombardian plain from east and west. The Spanish, who
governed the Duchy of Milan and had dominated most of Italy
for many decades, considered Nevers, the prospective heir of
these principalities, plausibly enough as a French ally or client.
They were not prepared to abandon their sphere of influence
in northern Italy or even to grant France a foothold in this
area, which they had always jealously guarded against the
influence of all other powers. However, dislodging the Duke of
Nevers and his troops from Mantua and Montferrat proved to
be more difficult than the Spaniards had anticipated, as both
the city of Mantua and the most important town in Montferrat,
Casale, were important fortresses difficult to take by assault.
The position became even more complicated in military terms
when France, which saw Nevers as the rightful heir, refused to
forego this chance to curb Spanish power in northern Italy and
decided to intervene. A French army crossed the Alps in
February 1629 to oppose the Spanish forces. Although the
Mantuan war ended in 1631 with the Peace of Cherasco which
confirmed the Duke of Nevers as ruler of Mantua and
Montferrat, the conflict between Spain and France which had
begun in 1629 was to continue in one form or another –
diplomatic manoeuvres, war by proxy, minor military operations during the years 1631–35 and all-out warfare thereafter –
until 1659, longer than the war in Germany.[2]

Thus Europe in 1629 offers a picture with many contrasting
elements. In Germany an attempt was made to impose a peace

settlement based on the undisputed military superiority of the Catholic armies, which would have been unacceptable even to those Protestant princes and Estates which had so far remained largely loyal to the Emperor, or at least neutral. In France, on the other hand, we see a decisive defeat of the Huguenots and their English allies, but also the return of a more lasting peace between the confessional groups. This was in itself the precondition for a profound change in French foreign policy. Now, for the first time since 1618, France was prepared to confront Spain directly in war, if necessary.

At the same time England made its exit from the scene by concluding peace with France (April 1629) and Spain (November 1630). Charles I of England's attempt to influence the course of events on the continent by military intervention during the period 1625–28 had failed. It was not repeated during the 1630s, despite all the pressure exerted by court factions and sections of the political nation favouring a more active pro-Protestant foreign policy. The objectives which England had pursued in the later 1620s – the defence of the Protestant cause everywhere in Europe; a restoration of Charles I's brother-in-law, the Elector Palatine, to his title and dignity; and a destruction of Spanish hegemony in Europe and, possibly, the New World – had proved too ambitious.

Like Charles I, another Protestant king, Christian IV of Denmark, also had to admit defeat in 1629. In the peace treaty of Lübeck (7 July 1629) he managed to maintain his position outside the Empire and in the Duchy of Holstein but largely lost his influence in northern Germany, in the Circle (*Reichskreis*) of Lower Saxony. The attempt to form an alliance against the Habsburg powers and to dislodge them at least from northern Germany had failed.

The Failure of the Anti-Habsburg Coalition 1625–1629

What were the reasons for this defeat? Clearly, the anti-Habsburg coalition which had slowly emerged in 1624–25 was torn right from the outset between the conflicting aims of a confessional war – promoting such aims promised maximum support at home, at least in England – and a more conventional cross-confessional dynastic alliance which would include Catholic princes. These conflicting aims bedevilled English policy during the years 1624–29 in particular. In many ways the resources which the Stuarts had at their disposal to intervene in the war were inadequate anyway. Indeed, in the 1630s the Stuart monarchy was to be considered a *quantité négligable* at most European courts, with the exception perhaps of Madrid, where considerations of naval strategy loomed larger than in Vienna or Munich. Nevertheless, in the mid-1620s England was uniquely qualified to take the lead in a Protestant alliance against the Habsburgs. At a time when Spain was about to shift the weight of her operations against the Dutch to naval warfare, the invervention of the English fleet could make a real difference to the balance of forces at sea. From a comparatively secure position and with the remaining prestige of the successor to the Queen who had withstood Spain in 1588, the English King, still Europe's potentially most powerful Protestant monarch, could therefore encourage, support and finance the military activities of other powers in central Europe.

If England had hesitated before 1624 to take a firmer line, this was due not only to James I's invincible desire for peace, but also to the hope that a settlement with Spain might still be reached without a war. Spain's interest in the Palatinate, the main bone of contention from the English point of view, was indeed limited. Although the Lower Palatinate – the districts left of the Rhine were occupied by Spanish troops – was of considerable strategic importance for Spanish supply routes along the Rhine, Madrid may have been prepared to abandon the occupied territory provided it received sufficient guarantees for the security of the Spanish position along the Rhine.[3] However, a solution of the Palatinate problem was impossible without Bavarian co-operation, for it was Maximilian of Bavaria who occupied the eastern half of the Lower Palatinate and all of the Upper Palatinate, and who had been officially invested in 1623 with the electoral title of the outlawed Count

Palatine. Spain was not really capable of forcing Maximilian of Bavaria to abandon his conquests. Nor was Madrid willing, or even perhaps able, to exert enough pressure on Ferdinand II to persuade Maximilian to agree to a solution which was acceptable to Friedrich V, the (former) Elector Palatine, and England.

In fact, the heir to the English throne, the Prince of Wales (later to be King Charles I), and King James's favourite, the Duke of Buckingham, found out for themselves that negotiating with Spain was fruitless. In a rather unorthodox move they had travelled to Madrid in spring 1623 to win a Spanish bride for Charles and to secure the restoration of the Elector Palatine, Charles's brother-in-law. But the negotiations proved to be abortive. After their return to England in October 1623, Charles and Buckingham were determined to go to war with Spain in order to take revenge on the Spaniards who had humiliated them in Madrid, to restore the Elector Palatine, but also to resist any further growth in Habsburg power in Europe.[4]

The problem was finding allies for such a policy, both in England and abroad. Charles and Buckingham needed allies at home because the ageing King, James I, continued to oppose any major military engagement. Thus a considerable amount of political pressure had to be exerted to persuade him to break off any further negotiations with Spain. This was only possible by mobilising public opinion (that is, primarily the opinion of the 'political nation', the social and political elite) for war. In fact, Charles and Buckingham went even further. When Parliament met in March 1624 to grant the necessary taxes for the impending struggle with the Habsburgs, they encouraged members of both Houses to criticise the King's peaceful foreign policy. They also supported an attempt to bring down the King's most important councillor opposing war, the Lord Treasurer Cranfield, by means of a parliamentary impeachment. Cranfield was indeed eliminated politically and had to resign.[5]

But in their attempt to mobilise enthusiasm at home for war against Spain – an enthusiasm which was indispensable if Parliament was to be persuaded to grant enough taxes to finance the war – Charles and Buckingham unleashed political forces which they were ill equipped to control. Their appeal to anti-Popery, the widespread fear and hatred of the Roman Catholic Church, created political expectations which they were unable to fulfil.[6] The war which they wanted to wage against Spain was not intended to be a religious crusade. On the contrary, France was to be won as England's ally, and to cement this alliance Charles was to marry Louis XIII's sister, Henrietta Maria. This was classical dynastic policy. But a King who was married to a Catholic and who had signed a marriage contract granting some degree of toleration to his wife's co-religionists in his own kingdom was hardly the ideal champion of the Protestant cause. Nor were the Duke of Buckingham's credentials as a militant Protestant any better. As Charles's principal advisor, as he had been his father's favourite, he was largely held responsible for the voyage to Madrid in 1623 and for the attempt to marry Charles to a Spanish Infanta – a marriage which was anathema to all those raised in the anti-Spanish and anti-Catholic tradition going back to the reign of Elizabeth I. Yet it was this very tradition to which Charles and Buckingham had to appeal in 1624–25 to legitimate their policy in England.

Of course, the problem of combining a foreign policy inspired more by 'reason of state' than religious fervour with the necessity of legitimating it at home in confessional terms was not unique to England. Richelieu was to experience similar problems to some extent in France in the 1630s (see below, pp. 117–25). Nevertheless, it was particularly difficult to find a solution to this question in England. England had only a very small Catholic minority – although the majority of the King's subjects in Ireland were Catholics – but the confessional identity of the Church of England had remained somewhat dubious ever since the late 1550s when Elizabeth I had once again dissolved the links with Rome which her sister Mary had re-established. Was the Church of England part of an international Protestant community whose centre was in continental Calvinism? Or was England rather to follow a *via media* between Rome and Geneva?[7]

James I had managed to shelve these questions about England's true religious identity for most of his reign, but the Catholic offensive in central Europe had caused many militant Protestants in England to ask whether their own church and their own country were armed for the – possibly final – battle with the forces of darkness and, indeed, the Antichrist, which they saw closing in on them. The theological and ecclesiastical compromises which they had been prepared to tolerate in earlier years now seemed far less acceptable.[8] Tensions were exacerbated by the fact that there was also an opposing movement in the English church which wanted to stress the distance between continental Protestantism and the Church of England more strongly than in the past. Members of this movement, often called Arminians, did so partly for theological reasons, but probably also because the dangerous radicalism of continental Calvinists seemed all the more disturbing at a time when this radicalism threatened to involve England in a war which did not affect her true interests – as those in England who still preferred peace with Spain to co-operation with the Dutch believed.[9]

Charles I soon discovered that the confessional and political passions which his decision to go to war with Spain had unleashed at home actually reduced England's ability to win this war. Parliament had already been reluctant to grant adequate supply for a war against Spain during his father's reign in 1624. At this stage James I's visible lack of commitment to a warlike policy and the less than clear aims of a military intervention may have further dampened the never very pronounced enthusiasm for a costly war. But no really satisfactory grants of parliamentary subsidies were made in later years either: domestic tensions, fuelled at least to some extent by the distrust which Charles's and Buckingham's religious stance inspired, were partly responsible for this attitude.

Before his death in April (N. St.) 1625 James I had in any case preferred to avoid an open confrontation with Spain. He decided to spend the little money he had been granted for the war on recruiting an expeditionary force which the ubiquitous Count Mansfeld was to lead against the Catholic forces in

Germany. This strategy proved to be a disaster. France's expected co-operation was withheld when Richelieu discovered that James I was still determined to avoid open war with Spain. Mansfeld's hastily recruited troops, badly trained and equipped and ill supplied, were dumped on the Dutch shore, where they died in their hundreds and thousands in the winter of 1624–25.[10] When Charles I succeeded James I, he decided to attack Spain directly after all and to concencrate on a naval campaign. The lack of supplies was, however, still a problem, as the Parliament of 1625 had granted only two parliamentary subsidies. The English and Dutch fleet's attack on Cadiz in November 1625 resulted in another defeat. Cadiz was now much better defended than in the Elizabethan period, and the English forces had not seen battle for more than 20 years.

In the meantime, attempts to forge an alliance with France foundered. Since May 1625 Charles had been married to Henrietta Maria, Louis XIII's sister, but he was not able to get active French support. Richelieu was initially interested in closing the strategically important Alpine valley of the Valtelline, which connected the Spanish Duchy of Milan with the Tyrol, to Spanish troops. But other issues now took priority. In January 1625 the latent conflict between the French crown and Huguenot noblemen and towns had escalated once more, and a French alliance with Protestant powers such as England or the Dutch was hardly helpful for the attempt to subdue the Huguenots. Instead France decided to seek a settlement with Spain. In the Treaty of Monzón (March–May 1626), the French abandoned the Valtelline which was now open once more to Spanish troops and supplies.

Instead of a wider anti-Habsburg alliance, a narrower coalition had to be formed. The Dutch and the English had already signed an offensive alliance in September 1625. This alliance was extended three months later by the accession of Denmark. The Hague alliance of December 1625 formalised earlier agreements between England and Christian IV of Denmark who had already been promised support for his campaign against the Catholic Liga and the Emperor. Initially, in

1624 and at the beginning of 1625, the English and Dutch diplomats had still hoped to gain the King of Sweden, Gustavus Adolphus, for the war against the Habsburgs as well. But Gustavus had demanded much more extensive English military and financial support than Christian IV as the price for his troops intervening in Germany. Given the parlous state of the English crown's finances, the cheaper Danish offer had been preferred. Gustavus Adolphus was not prepared to co-operate with his Danish rival and inveterate enemy even under the auspices of an international Protestant alliance. Instead he resumed his war against Poland which was to keep his troops busy until September 1629. As it turned out, however, England proved incapable of fulfilling even her limited treaty obligations towards Denmark. Having been denied supply by Parliament in 1626, Charles I decided to levy a forced loan, in other words to impose disguised taxation without parliamentary consent. Enough money could be scraped together in this way to finance the navy, but not enough to pay the promised subsidies to Denmark.[11]

In the meantime, relations with France had deteriorated further and in spring 1627 Charles and Buckingham decided to go to war with France. Initially in 1624–25, when England had decided to abandon her neutrality, the war had had three objectives: to reinstate the Elector Palatine, to contain Habsburg power in Europe, and to defend the Protestant religion. The last objective, though it loomed large in domestic justifications for the war, was probably the least important for its architects. Now in 1627, with England fighting principally against France (the war against Spain dragged on at the same time without major battles), to all appearances only the religious objective remained. In reality, naval competition between England and France also played its part in the crisis which led to the Anglo-French war. Another factor was Buckingham's personal chagrin caused by France's apparent refusal to honour her obligations as England's ally.

Although the House of Commons had accused Buckingham in 1626 of having abandoned the French Protestants, and, indeed, of having helped the French King in his war against them, his military support for the Huguenot stronghold La Rochelle did not really make him any more popular. Many were now inclined to see the war against France as the Duke of Buckingham's private affair, and described the army as 'the Duke's faction' under arms.[12] The constitutional conflicts which England's intervention in the European war had provoked could be patched up for the moment when Parliament met once more in spring 1628, but military success remained elusive. The Duke of Buckingham was assassinated in August 1628 by an officer influenced by the widespread hatred for the favourite. The English fleet nevertheless tried once more to relieve La Rochelle but to no avail. In October 1628 the Protestant fortress fell to the French army commanded by Richelieu in person.

As there was no longer any point in continuing the war against France, Charles I might have returned to the original fight against Spain, but with the imperial and Catholic forces victorious all over Germany prospects for a restitution of the Elector Palatine were now even worse than they had been four years before. Moreover, the mutual distrust between the King and large sections of the political nation represented in Parliament which had built up during the preceding years did not augur well for England's ability to wage war. Charles therefore decided to dissolve Parliament in March 1629 and to seek peace not only with France but also with Spain.

England's intervention in the war had failed. Moreover, the war had re-opened the debate on the true identity of the English church, which James had managed to mute at least until the early 1620s. It was this debate which proved to be more destructive than anything else for domestic peace in England, and which was to make a considerable contribution to the outbreak of civil war in England thirteen years later in 1642. In some ways this war can be seen as a delayed result of England's brief participation in the European power struggle, in which many people in England continued to take a keen interest after 1629.[13]

With England paralysed, or at least weakened, by domestic strife since early 1626 and war with France since 1627, the

Stuarts' principal ally in northern Europe, Christian IV of Denmark, found himself in a very uncomfortable position. The Treaty of the Hague with England and the States General had stipulated that England was to make monthly payments of £30,000 (120,000 Taler) to maintain Christian IV's army, England's own troops in northern Germany and Count Mansfeld's army which, having been reformed after the terrible losses suffered in the winter of 1624–25, had taken up positions in Eastern Frisia. Further subsidies were to be paid by the Dutch (20,000 Taler per month) and by the French who made a promise later separately in a different, more informal agreement. As it turned out, Christian himself received only about 547,000 Taler from the English crown during the years 1625–28, and very little of this after 1626. Admittedly more English payments were made to Mansfeld and to an English regiment fighting in northern Germany, but English expenditure for the war in northern Germany still probably fell about two-thirds or maybe even three-quarters short of the expected sum.[14]

Dutch and especially French payments (534,000 and 716,000 Taler respectively in the period 1625–28) were made more promptly and came closer to the sum, smaller than the English share, initially promised. However, this could not disguise the fact that Christian IV's position was comparatively weak. This was all the more true as the Danish Estates, which had little sympathy for the ambitious policy pursued by Christian in his capacity as Duke of Holstein, refused to finance the King's military adventures. He therefore had to rely largely on the income from his demesnes and the custom tolls levied at the Sound in Elsinore. Admittedly, he had managed to get himself elected military commander of the Circle of Lower Saxony in April 1625. This *Reichskreis* was indeed his stronghold. Not only was he Duke of Holstein, he also controlled either personally or through members of his family, the territories of the Bishoprics of Verden and Halberstadt. Moreover, his son possessed an expectancy, as co-adjutor to the present prince-bishop, for the important see of Bremen, which like other ecclesiastical benefices was being transformed into a secular principality. Nevertheless, support from the other members of the Lower Saxon Circle, in particular the several branches of the ducal families of Brunswick and Mecklenburg, was lukewarm.

The first military encounters between the troops of the Liga under Tilly's command and Christian IV's army in summer 1625 remained inconclusive. Both sides felt that they were too weak for a major battle. When hostilities recommenced in 1626, however, Tilly's position had improved considerably while Christian's had deteriorated. Nervous about the outcome of the war in northern Germany, Maximilian of Bavaria had asked the Emperor to take part in the war with an army of his own. So far Ferdinand had limited his military activities mostly to his own hereditary lands and their eastern border in Hungary, where the Prince of Transylvania posed a permanent threat. He now entrusted the Czech nobleman, Albrecht von Wallenstein (or Waldstein), with the command of a new imperial army to be recruited by Wallenstein himself. Born in 1583, Wallenstein had belonged to the minority of Bohemian and Moravian noblemen who had supported the Habsburgs in their fight against the Protestant Estates in 1618–20. Having converted to Catholicism in his youth, he had benefited enormously from the destruction of the Protestant elite after the battle of the White Mountain, when he had acquired vast estates, the former property of Protestant noblemen now outlawed and expropriated. Thanks to his enormous fortune he was able to pay for the initial recruitment of the new army himself without any major payments from the Imperial Treasury, at least for the time being (see below, pp. 157–9).

Wallenstein's new army, growing within a short time to a strength of about 50,000 men (though not all were stationed in northern Germany) changed the balance of military forces. Although Wallenstein's men were ill-trained, they were sufficiently effective to beat those of Count Mansfeld – so far the unrivalled master in the art of recruiting vast armies cheaply and quickly. In April 1626 Mansfeld attempted to prevent Wallenstein's troops from crossing the river Elbe by taking the imperialists' bridgehead at Dessau, but failed. Wallenstein turned the battle into a disastrous and bloody defeat for Mansfeld. However the old *condottiere*, having lost three-quarters of his army of 20,000 men, was able to assemble new regiments within a couple of weeks, partly by uniting his forces with those of other Protestant commanders. He now turned south-eastwards and attacked Silesia. In a series of forced marches his troops, or what was left of them after this *tour de force*, reached Moravia in August 1626. Mansfeld was closely followed by Wallenstein, but he hoped to unite his army in Moravia or Hungary with the Transylvanian troops commanded by Gabriel Bethlen.

The Transylvanian prince had once again attacked Habsburg Hungary, but as before he lacked the stamina for a protracted campaign, all the more so as the Turks, on whose protection and support he relied, had suffered a severe defeat in the eastern part of their empire in Baghdad in 1626. The Persian army had beaten back the Sultan's troops which had tried to reconquer southern Mesopotamia. Unable to risk another major conflict on the western border of their empire, the Turks refused to support Gabriel Bethlen. Bethlen signed a treaty with the Emperor in December 1626 in Bratislava (Preßburg) which ended the hostilities once more. This left Mansfeld's remaining regiments, numbering hardly more than 4,000 or 5,000 men, stranded. The *condottiere* himself tried to leave the scene of his defeat via Ragusa but died en route near Sarajevo. The regiments which he had left in Upper Silesia maintained their position for a while, but they were too isolated and too few in number to pose a real threat, and they were forced to surrender by the imperial army the next year.

Meanwhile, Christian of Denmark had been beaten decisively by Tilly at Lutter am Barenberge on 26 August 1626. A number of strong fortresses in Holstein and in the Archbishopric of Bremen garrisoned by Christian's troops delayed the final Danish defeat, but in 1627 when Wallenstein's forces, growing all the time, advanced into Holstein, Christian's fate was sealed. His infantry had to surrender in September in Eutin; his cavalry followed a month later, after having retreated north to Jutland. Christian was defeated once and for all. The Danish Islands, however, not to mention Norway and Scania (both under Danish rule), were beyond Wallenstein's reach because he had no fleet. This fact, as well as the fear of a direct Swedish intervention in Germany and the outbreak of war in northern Italy in 1628, which required imperial intervention, explains why Christian ultimately managed to gain comparatively favourable terms in his negotiations with the Emperor. The prince-bishoprics which he had tried to claim for members of his family in northern Germany were lost, but the Peace of Lübeck, signed in July 1629, left Christian's possessions north of the Elbe – Holstein, Schleswig and Jutland – intact.

The Dukes of Mecklenburg who, in contrast to other Protestant princes in northern Germany, had supported Christian to the end, partly because parts of their duchy were occupied by Danish troops, lost their entire principality which the Emperor declared forfeited through felony and treason. In vain did the nobility of Mecklenburg protest that their dynasty had governed their country for nearly a thousand years (which was somewhat exaggerated).[15] The Dukes were sent into exile. Their duchy, however, was not, like the Palatinate earlier in the war, given to another princely dynasty which had been more loyal, but to the imperial general Wallenstein, who was created Duke of Mecklenburg in 1628. This was not only a convenient way of rewarding the victorious commander and of repaying, at least partly, the enormous debts which the Emperor owed him, but it was also a revolutionary act.[16] If the Emperor could advance his servant, a mere Bohemian nobleman, to the status of a prince of the Empire and entrust him with the government of an ancient duchy (the Princes of Mecklenburg had been created Dukes in 1348), he could just as well reduce the princes of the Empire to the status of mere subjects and servants. With the investiture of Wallenstein as Duke of Mecklenburg, Ferdinand II had already begun to overreach himself. But the inherent weakness of the Habsburg position in Germany and Europe was not to become fully apparent until 1629–30.

The Fragility of Habsburg Supremacy

The defeat of Denmark had removed the last obstacle to Catholic and Habsburg ascendancy in northern Germany. Nevertheless, the victories won against the Protestant alliance proved to be far less decisive in the long run than they seemed at the time. The continuing fragility of the Habsburg position was due to a combination of factors. Particularly important were the failure of the Habsburgs to match the power of their opponents at sea, crucial to the progress of the Spanish–Dutch war; the growing tensions between the Emperor and his Catholic allies in Germany; and the final alienation of Protestant loyalty and neutrality in the Holy Roman Empire as a result of the Edict of Restitution.

Olivares and the Spanish Council of State planned to shift the main thrust of the war against the Dutch away from land to naval warfare, and to introduce measures designed to strangle the Dutch economy as early as 1625. This strategy promised to be less costly than an offensive on land, which Spain could no longer finance. After the fall of the Dutch fortress of Breda to Spanish troops in June 1625, a victory of high symbolic but little real military significance, celebrated by Velazquez in his famous painting, the Spanish army in Flanders and Brabant had been reduced in size. It gradually lost its capability to mount a major offensive on its own.[17]

Instead the Dutch economy was to be destroyed by breaking the trade links between the Netherlands and the rest of the world on land as well as at sea. This was a rather ambitious plan, but the victory of the imperial and Catholic armies in northern Germany in 1626–27 seemed to offer some chance of success in this respect. Olivares tried to gain the co-operation of Wallenstein's and Tilly's armies for a major offensive to attack the rear of the Dutch lines. Moreover, Wallenstein was to occupy a number of harbours in northern Germany which were to serve as naval bases for a Spanish–imperial fleet to be supported by Polish ships if possible. The intention was to cut the Dutch off from the Baltic, one of their most important areas of trade. The co-operation of the

German Hanseatic towns, in particular Hamburg and Lübeck, was essential for this plan to succeed, and Spain was prepared to offer the Hanseatic towns special trading privileges within the Spanish Empire in Europe and overseas to win their support.[18] But it was clear that any sort of Spanish presence in the Baltic would provoke Sweden which had so far remained neutral. Moreover, towns like Hamburg and Lübeck, strongly fortified and therefore capable of defending themselves against the imperial forces, were reluctant to antagonise the Protestant powers of northern Europe, who were not only important trading partners, but also their only possible allies in case the Emperor and the armies of the Catholic Liga should try to re-establish Catholicism in northern Germany.

Wallenstein himself, though appointed 'General of the Oceanic and Baltic Seas' by the Emperor in February 1628, pursued the project of a naval offensive, so dear to the Spanish, only half-heartedly. He did try to occupy Stralsund, an important harbour on the Baltic coast opposite the island of Rügen, but the siege of the city in 1628 (May–July) was abortive. Stralsund, supported by Danish and Swedish troops, held out against the imperial army. The failed siege of Stralsund further strengthened the resolve of those Hanseatic towns which had not yet been occupied to resist co-operating with Spain and the Emperor.

The failure of the far-reaching Spanish plans for a concerted effort to destroy Dutch naval power in the Baltic was, however, only one of many setbacks Spanish policy suffered during these years. The reduction in the number of Spanish troops in the Netherlands gave the Dutch a chance to go on the offensive themselves and with the outbreak of war in northern Italy at the end of 1627 the Spanish position was further weakened, as supplies and reinforcements, needed more urgently in the South, failed to materialise. Despite help from imperial troops under the command of Count Montecucculi in summer 1629, the Spanish army proved unable to defend the important fortress of s'Hertogenbosch, which fell to the Dutch in September 1629. Overseas in the Indies the war was taking an even more disastrous turn for the forces of the Spanish Empire. In September 1628 Piet Hein, the Admiral of the Dutch West Indies Company, had captured the Spanish treasure fleet off the coast of Cuba in Matanzas Bay. This surprise coup improved the Company's finances considerably and thus created the basis for further and more ambitious campaigns in Central and South America. These were to result in the occupation of Portuguese north-eastern Brazil by Dutch forces in February 1630. The immediate impact of these Dutch victories in the New World on events in the Old may have been limited, but the need to mount an extensive counter-attack in the Caribbean and in South America made it even more difficult for Spain to finance the war in Europe, which was clearly overstretching her resources.[19]

This, however, was not yet fully apparent in early 1629, and at least in central Europe the Habsburg position still seemed secure. This explains to some extent why Ferdinand II now decided to commit himself to a more radical Counter-Reformation policy in the Reich than before by signing the Edict of Restitution mentioned above (see pp. 76–7) in 1629. It was ratified on 6 March and published on 28 March. Officially the edict was only an interpretation of existing law, in particular the Religious Peace of Augsburg of 1555. In fact, however, it assumed the character of a new law superseding the Peace of Augsburg, at least in some respects, without officially denying its validity.[20] As a legislative act the edict was revolutionary in itself, regardless of its contents, for in the Empire new laws could be passed only by the Emperor in conjunction with the Imperial Diet, not by a mere imperial *fiat*.

If Ferdinand's attempt to claim powers which no other Emperor before had enjoyed in the last hundred years was disquieting enough for the German princes, the regulations of the edict were even more disturbing for those among them who were Protestants. Not only was ecclesiastical property secularised after 1552 to be returned to the Church, but it was feared that the status of former monasteries which had been dissolved or transformed into hospitals or similar institutions by Protestant princes before 1552, but which had claimed to be independent of territorial jurisdiction and subject to no ruler but the Emperor at some stage in the late Middle Ages, would now also be disputed. Many Protestant territories would thus have been forced to come to terms with the existence of rich and powerful Catholic ecclesiastical corporations within their borders, and some would have been virtually dismembered. Protestant worship remained legal in the Empire after 28 March 1629 – as long as it was Lutheran and not Calvinist, for the edict had expressly outlawed Calvinism – but it was clear that in the long term Protestants were to be reduced to the status of a politically powerless minority.

In retrospect, the decision to pass and enforce the edict was a fatal error of judgement. The success of the Habsburg armies in the Empire during the first decade of the war would have been much more difficult, if not indeed impossible, to achieve had the Protestant camp been united. The neutrality and at times even support of Protestant princes such as the Landgrave of Hesse-Darmstadt, the Elector of Brandenburg, and more important than any body else, the Elector of Saxony, had been indispensable for achieving Ferdinand II's objectives in the Empire. Although Brandenburg and Saxony were by and large not directly affected by the edict, it was only too likely that they would be alienated by such a radical measure. So why did the Emperor provoke these princes by endorsing potentially unlimited Catholic claims to secularised former church property all over Germany?[21]

Some of Ferdinand's councillors had indeed warned him against such measures, which would turn the constitutional and political conflict in Germany into a straightforward religious war. He had been advised to concentrate on strengthening his position in the hereditary lands; to exploit the relative weakness of the Sultan in Hungary; and to avoid all measures which would increase his dependance on Maximilian of Bavaria, whom many councillors in Vienna saw as an inveterate though secret enemy of the Habsburgs.[22] But paradoxically, fear of an open conflict with Bavaria probably contributed to Ferdinand's endorsement of a strict Counter-Reformation policy in the Empire. This policy was now the lowest common denominator for further co-operation with Bavaria and the Catholic ecclesiastical princes. Furthermore, constitutional traditions prevented the Emperor from incorporating the confiscated territories of outlawed princes into his hereditary dominions. If, however, former Catholic bishoprics were restored to their status as ecclesiastical principalities, there was nothing to stop the Emperor from having members of his family elected as prince-bishops, thereby extending Habsburg power into northern Germany. Thus Ferdinand's son Leopold Wilhelm could expect to take over the important Archbishoprics of Magdeburg and Bremen, for example.

A final point must be mentioned. As Wolfgang Seibrich has recently emphasised, in those areas of the Empire occupied by Catholic troops a piecemeal restoration of ecclesiastical property had already been under way before 1629. But it was the prince-bishops who benefited from this restitution or (as in the Upper and Lower Palatinate, for example) institutions and congregations favoured by secular Catholic rulers and under their direct or indirect control, not necessarily the older monastic orders which had been the original owners of the secularised property. These orders with their manifold ancient privileges were considered too independent-minded and, as they were often of a more contemplative character, not aggressive enough in the fight against heresy. Ferdinand could not really have an interest in strengthening the power of the bishops as territorial rulers, or of the secular Catholic princes. By endorsing a process already under way, however, he could hope to gain control over its future progress in order to prevent the autonomy of the territorial princes in the Empire from being consolidated further. Furthermore, by stressing his role as supreme judge in all questions relating to the status of religious communities and their institutions in the Empire, he enhanced his own authority.[23] Finally, we should not forget that at the time, the Counter-Reformation policy endorsed by the Edict of Restitution seemed to be in line with the overall pattern of events in Europe in 1627–28, a period which had seen a hardening of confessional frontlines in international conflicts (see above, pp. 75–8).

None the less, the price Ferdinand paid for this move was high. Protestant princes who so far had been prepared to co-operate with him, in particular Saxony, became increasingly restive. Their later support for Sweden was at least partly motivated by fear that Ferdinand, reneging on the promises he had given in Mühlhausen in 1620 about the Protestant possessions in the Upper and Lower Saxon Circles,[24] would suppress Protestantism in the Empire altogether, or at least reduce the Protestants to the status of a barely tolerated minority.[25] The example of the Counter-Reformation in Bohemia, Moravia and the Austrian Duchies, where Protestant worship had been largely eliminated in the years before 1629 and many Protestants sent into exile, could not be very reassuring.

If the Edict of Restition had been designed to appease Bavaria, it clearly failed to achieve this objective. Maximilian with his ecclesiastical allies had indeed consistently promoted the cause of a Catholic restoration and a restitution of ecclesiastical property in the years before 1629. He had all the more reason to do so because he feared that negotiations for an eventual peace settlement would jeopardise his position in the Upper and Lower Palatinate and his claim to the formerly Palatine electoral dignity. He had indeed been confirmed in these possessions and as hereditary Prince Elector by the Emperor in February 1628 in exchange for the return of Upper Austria (occupied by Bavaria since 1620) to direct Habsburg government. Nevertheless the prospect of peace between England and Spain, which was becoming more likely since the outbreak of hostilities between France and England in 1627, was worrying because Spain would have been only too glad to sacrifice Bavarian interests to such a settlement. If, however, the Emperor could be persuaded to endorse the restitution of all ecclesiastical property secularised after 1552, a genuine compromise settlement in the Empire leading to the restoration of the Elector Palatine would be rendered much more difficult, not to mention the fact that Calvinism, which the Elector Friedrich V professed, was outlawed by the edict so that the Palatinate was excluded from any future peace anyhow.[26]

Thus the Edict of Restitution certainly met some of Maxmilian's demands, but he nevertheless remained dissatisfied with the course of imperial policy. With most other Catholic and Protestant princes of the Empire he remained irritated by the enormous power wielded by Wallenstein as imperial general. Wallenstein now had an army of more than 100,000 and perhaps, if we take official figures at their face value, up to 150,000 men; this was a much larger force than the 30,000 to 40,000 men which the Liga kept under arms.[27] Wallenstein's army was to a large extent paid for by contributions which the general's soldiers 'collected' or rather extorted from the population of provinces in which they happened to be garrisoned. Thus most German principalities, regardless of whether their rulers had fought for or against the Emperor, had to pay for the imperial army.[28] This in itself ensured that the imperial general became the most hated man in Germany, but opposition to him was further increased by widespread fears that Ferdinand II might use his army to stamp out any resistance to his authority.[29] Wallenstein's promotion to the status of Duke of Mecklenburg was widely seen as an ominous sign in this context and as a breach of traditional constitutional practice.

Opposition to Wallenstein which had been articulated on more than one occasion during the period 1627–29 culminated in June/July 1630, when the prince electors or their delegates met in Regensburg. The feeling against the general was particularly strong at this time because of the policy Ferdinand II had pursued during the past year. He had decided to send about 50,000 of Wallenstein's soldiers to Italy to support the Spanish troops trying to take Mantua in spring 1629. Among the Catholic princes, let alone the Protestants, an alliance with Spain which involved the Empire in war in northern Italy and – predictably – the Netherlands as well, and would prolong hostilities indefinitely, was extremely unpopular. Then as later, the princes were very reluctant to foot the bill for a Habsburg policy which they saw as purely dynastic and detrimental to the interests of the Empire, not to mention the fact that even Catholics feared that Spain was determined to undermine the German princes' 'liberties'.[30] Radical measures seemed to be called for. The electors therefore now demanded Wallenstein's dismissal as general and the reduction of the imperial army to less than a third of its actual size, that is from about 120,000–150,000 to some 40,000 men.[31] Without his most important commander and virtually irreplaceable military entrepreneur, Ferdinand II would be unable to undertake any further military adventures, or so they hoped.

Surprisingly enough, Ferdinand II agreed to comply with the prince electors' demands and dismissed Wallenstein in August 1630. Bavaria was already involved in negotiations with France about an alliance, officially defensive in character but clearly directed against Spain and at least implicitly the Emperor as well, and Maximilian was thus able to exert a certain amount of pressure on Ferdinand. Moreover Ferdinand wanted his eldest son, the future Ferdinand III, to be elected King of the Romans (Emperor designate) which was impossible without the prince electors' goodwill. But all this is insufficient to explain the Emperor's decision to surrender the tool which was indispensable if he wanted to impose his will on the princes of the Empire.

Part of the explanation is probably that under the influence of some of his advisors Ferdinand had already begun to distrust Wallenstein, who would have been difficult to control should he decide to demand ever greater rewards for his services. In addition, having committed himself to a strictly Catholic policy through the Edict of Restitution, Ferdinand had to consider Wallenstein's army, among whose soldiers and even commanding officers there were many Protestants, as less than reliable even if Wallenstein himself should remain loyal.[32] But in the last resort Ferdinand's compliance with the wishes of the electors showed that he had no plans to transform the Empire into an absolute monarchy. He was not prepared to commit himself irrevocably to a policy which would have led to open military conflict with most princes of the Empire including the Catholic ones. Such a commitment would have been inevitable if he had maintained Wallenstein's army, if only for the simple reason that this army was just too large and costly to be maintained for merely defensive purposes.

Having avoided open conflict with Bavaria and the other princes by dismissing Wallenstein, who accepted his fate with surprising equanimity, Ferdinand had to appoint Tilly, the old general of the Catholic Liga, joint commander of his own and the Liga's forces. The Emperor may have thought that he had thus saved the chance to reach some sort of lasting peace in the Empire at last. A peace treaty with France concluded in Regensburg shortly afterwards, in October 1630, against the wishes and to the great chagrin of Ferdinand's Spanish allies but in compliance with the demands of the German prince electors, seemed to remove a major obstacle to such a settlement. In spite of the sack of Mantua, which had recently been taken by the imperial army, the Emperor was to recall his troops from Italy and promised to invest Charles de Gonzague, the Duke of Nevers, with the Duchy of Mantua. France also agreed to recall her troops and further promised not to assist the Emperor's enemies in any way, either militarily or financially. Had the French promise been kept this would have been an important point, for in July 1630 Gustavus Adolphus with his troops had set foot on Usedom, an island off the coast of Pomerania. However, Richelieu repudiated the Treaty of Regensburg, which had indeed been signed without his prior consent. The war in Italy continued until 1631 (engaging imperial troops), and France gave Sweden the financial support she needed, contrary to the terms of the Regensburg agreement. Ferdinand's policy thus turned out to be based on a number of serious miscalculations. He had antagonised even the most cautious and moderate Protestants by the Edict of Restitution, had dismissed the general and his army who might have been able to oppose the Swedes successfully, and in the final resort had abandoned Mantua, freshly conquered by imperial troops, to the French without gaining anything substantial in return.

4

1635: AN ABORTIVE PEACE

The Swedish Intervention 1630–1635

The years after 1629 saw a rapid and dramatic collapse of the Habsburg and Catholic position in Germany, for the reasons outlined in the previous chapter. Not only the war for Mantua but also Sweden's intervention in 1630 totally changed the course of events. The dominant role which Sweden was to play during the later phase of the war in Germany was in many ways quite astonishing. Sweden was a comparatively small country with fewer than 1.5 million inhabitants (including Finland and the Baltic provinces of Estonia, Ingria and Livonia). The degree of urbanisation was very limited: essentially Sweden was a country of farmers and peasants, though in the years before 1630s the Swedish gun foundaries had achieved an outstanding position in the European arms markets, supplementing Sweden's extensive exports of iron and copper ore. The Swedish mines were rich in these minerals, and foreign immigrants had provided the skills which the native population lacked, necessary for producing guns. Moreover Sweden largely controlled trade in the eastern Baltic, which provided the Swedish crown with substantial revenues from customs duties levied in the harbours of Estonia (conquered between 1561 and 1582), Ingria (conquered 1617) and Livonia (conquered in the 1620s).

During the 1620s Sweden had remained neutral (apart from military support for Stralsund) and had concentrated her military efforts on the war against Poland going back to the turn

101

of the century. Although England and the Netherlands had tried to establish an alliance with Sweden in the mid-1620s, these plans had foundered on the rivalry between Sweden and Denmark and on Sweden's excessive – as Charles I of England thought – demands for subsidies. Nevertheless, as early as 1627–28 the King of Sweden, Gustavus Adolphus, and his Chancellor, Axel Oxenstierna, had come to the conclusion that in the long term Sweden could not stay out of the conflict in Germany.[1] Concern for the fate of the Protestants in Germany and the liberties of the Germany princes did not at this stage loom large among the motives for intervening in the war. Rather, it was the presence of a large imperial army on the coast of the Baltic in Mecklenburg and Pomerania and, for a time, Schleswig-Holstein and Jutland as well, which Gustavus Adolphus and his advisors found disconcerting. Moreover, though imperial and Spanish plans to create an imperial fleet in the Baltic came to nothing in the years 1627–29, there was no guarantee that the Emperor would not one day be able to gain the support of the Hanseatic towns for his maritime policy after all, and thus threaten the political and economic ascendancy for which Gustavus had laid the foundations since his accession (1611).

However, at the heart of the King's concern about the imperial presence in northern Germany was probably the impact this presence might have on Sweden's relations with Poland. Since the turn of the century Sweden had been in conflict with Poland. This conflict was sometimes interrupted by temporary truces but never entirely resolved. It was at once political, dynastic, economic and confessional. In 1587 Sigismund Vasa had been elected and crowned King of Poland; after the death of his father John III of Sweden (in 1592) Sigismund legally became King of Sweden too. However, as a Catholic he was unpopular in his country of origin and was ousted by his uncle Duke Charles of Södermanland. All attempts by Sigismund to regain power in Sweden failed and in 1604 Charles was crowned King of Sweden. However, Sigismund, who was to rule Poland until his death in 1632, never entirely abandoned his claim to the Swedish crown, which his son and successor, Wladislaw, continued to uphold. The ensuing tensions between the two countries were further exacerbated by the claim both kingdoms laid to the Baltic provinces of Estonia and Livonia. These provinces with their great harbours (in particular Riga and Reval/Talinn) were important for Sweden because they gave her control over a large share of the exchange of goods between Russia and the rest of Europe and also provided her merchants with much-needed access to international trade.[2] On the other hand Sigismund of Poland, having already abandoned Sweden, was not at all willing to abandon rich Livonia as well.

Open hostilities between Poland and Sweden commenced in 1600. Though they died down after 1605 and were settled temporarily by intermittent truces, they resumed in earnest in 1617, and, after another truce, once more in 1620–22. In 1626 Sweden had largely conquered Livonia and the Swedish army now attacked the Poles in Prussia at the mouth of the Vistula. However, the advance of Wallenstein's troops into northern Germany in 1626–27 offered the frightening prospect of a Polish–Habsburg alliance which Sweden would be unlikely to be able to withstand. In fact Wallenstein sent 12,000 of his men to Prussia in 1629 and these troops to some extent improved the Polish position. When Gustavus Adolphus signed a truce with Poland (mediated by France) in 1629 at Altmark to free his hands for the war in the Empire, his principal objective was to counter directly the threat which the presence of imperial troops in northern Germany posed. The Danish–Swedish war of 1611–13, at the beginning of Gustavus Adolphus's reign, which had ended in a crushing defeat for Sweden, had shown how vulnerable Sweden was. It was clear that the country could not afford a wait-and-see policy with respect to the worsening situation in Germany. Moreover, an offensive policy seemed to recommend itself on grounds of military finance too. The Swedish army, oversized in relation to Sweden's limited economic and demographic resources, could only be maintained as long at it fought outside the kingdom and as long as contributions, taxes and customs duties from conquered provinces supplemented the income from purely Swedish sources.[3]

Though considerations of security were undoubtedly dominant in motivating Sweden's intervention in Germany at least
initially, the confessional element in Gustavus Adolphus's
policy, often dismissed as mere propaganda in recent Swedish
historiography,[4] should not be underestimated. Religious principles and more secular political interests had become inseparable in the Swedish case. Having gained the crown through
the deposition of a legitimate ruler – Sigismund Vasa – the legitimacy of the Swedish branch of the Vasas as a ruling dynasty
was questionable. In the last resort the claims of the elder,
Polish line could only by rejected by reference to religious and
confessional principles. For Gustavus Adolphus the defence of
the Protestant faith was therefore not just a convenient
justification for intervention in Germany, it was also closely
linked to the principles on which the legitimacy of his own
and his dynasty's rule rested. In this respect Sweden's position
in the early seventeenth century is perhaps comparable to that
of England after 1688 and under the early Hanoverians:
foreign policy served to defend a potentially controversial political and religious domestic settlement as well as the status
and interests of the state in its competition with other powers.[5]
Some historians, in particular Günter Barudio, have also depicted the Swedish King as the idealistic champion of constitutional principles, of the rule of law and a free constitution,
fighting for these ideals abroad as well as at home.[6] But it is
highly unlikely that Gustavus would have taken any great interest in the constitutional problems of the Holy Roman Empire
if these problems had not had serious implications for
Sweden's own security. In addition the King was not entirely
free from autocratic ambitions himself, in spite of the comparatively strong position of the nobility and Estates in Sweden.[7]
And in later years the Swedish troops which Gustavus
Adolphus brought to Germany took as little account of traditional privileges when exacting contributions from German
princes and their subjects as did the imperial armies.

Having landed his troops on the island of Usedom in July
1630, Gustavus Adolphus's first problem was to find allies. On

his own he could hardly hope to defeat the seasoned imperial troops, though the Emperor's decision to dismiss Wallenstein in the summer of 1630 certainly weakened the position of Sweden's opponents. France, which had already helped to bring about the truce between Poland and Sweden in 1629, signed a treaty with Gustavus in January 1631 (Treaty of Bärwalde) promising Sweden 400,000 Taler per annum to help finance the Swedish expeditionary corps. However, the Protestant princes of the Empire remained reluctant to support Sweden openly. The Elector of Saxony had called a meeting of all Protestant Estates of the Empire in February 1631; officially the purpose of this meeting, which took place in Leipzig, was only to co-ordinate the policy of the Protestant Estates for the imminent negotiations with the Emperor about the Edict of Restitution and other grievances. However, in the end, the assembly issued a manifesto (in April 1631) which protested in strong terms against the edict and the intolerable contributions imposed on the Estates of the Empire by the imperial and Catholic armies. Furthermore, a defensive alliance of all Protestants was to be created, the Leipziger Bund, with an army of 40,000 men.[8]

Officially the policy of this confederation was to be no more than an armed neutrality between the Emperor and Sweden. However, events forced the hand of Johann Georg and the other Protestants princes. While the Swedish troops advanced into Brandenburg, Tilly, the Catholic commander-in-chief, besieged Magdeburg, one of the few cities officially allied to Sweden. On 20 May 1631 Magdeburg was taken by assault. Not unusually in such cases, the garrison was massacred. In addition, however, the entire town was burnt down, probably inadvertently rather than deliberately. Up to 20,000 men and women lost their lives, either slaughtered by the soldiers or, the majority, dying in the flames. The impact of this event on Protestants all over Germany can hardly be overestimated. In the sixteenth century, during the Schmalcaldic war (1546–47) and the subsequent years when Protestantism was virtually outlawed, Magdeburg had been one of the very few Protestant towns to defend itself successfully against Charles V and his armies. Ever since, it had been a symbol of heroic Protestant resistance against 'Popery'; now it was laid waste and its inhabitants murdered in their thousands.

The outcry this provoked could not be ignored by the Protestant princes as their own territorial Estates and court preachers joined in the call for revenge. Until May 1631, Ferdinand II could still count on a residual loyalty among many Protestants, or at least Lutherans, despite the Edict of Restitution. Now Germany was swamped by innummerable pamphlets and popular songs accusing the Emperor of having been seduced by Jesuits who wanted to transform the Empire into an absolute monarchy along Spanish lines. One song exlaimed 'Shame on you, Emperor, that you allowed Germany, that innocent flower, to be defiled and laid waste',[9] and another in Low German dialect called on the Germans to arise: 'Wake up, Germany, keep out the Jesuits … defend your liberty, … lest one hear shortly that the German Empire is no more.'[10] Gustavus Adolphus, the 'Lion from Midnight [i.e. from the north]', though perhaps not entirely innocent with respect to the catastrophe of Magdeburg which his troops had failed to relieve in time, became the hero of German Protestants. He was the only ruler credited with the capacity to defend the true faith and at the same time to restore the pristine splendour and ancient constitution of the Empire.[11]

After Magdeburg, Brandenburg, admittedly already hard pressed by Swedish troops, signed an alliance with Sweden, and gradually other Protestant princes followed. Saxony still hesitated but joined Brandenburg in September, when Tilly threatened to occupy the Electorate with his troops. Considerably strengthened by the troops of his new German allies, Gustavus Adolphus defeated Tilly decisively at Breitenfeld on 17 September. This was one of the greatest battles of the entire war, where 41,000 Protestant troops fought the 31,000 men under Tilly's command. Breitenfeld was a major turning point of the war. Tilly lost two-thirds of his men who fell in battle, were taken prisoner or simply deserted; the Catholic position collapsed not only in northern Germany but also along the Rhine and in the south-west. In spring 1632 the Swedish troops invaded Bavaria and occupied Munich (May); Johann Georg's troops had marched into Bohemia and taken Prague even earlier.

The Swedish invasion of Bavaria had at least one advantage from Ferdinand II's point of view: Maximilian of Bavaria was now more than ever committed to his alliance with the Emperor. His attempts to withdraw from the struggle in the Empire and to pursue an independent policy which had culminated in a treaty of neutrality and non-aggression signed by France and Bavaria in Fontainebleau in May 1631 had failed. Co-operation between Bavaria and Catholic France may have been possible, but not between Bavaria and Protestant Sweden, not least because Bavaria could not afford to abandon the German ecclesiastical princes, her most important allies and clients, to the fury of the Swedish army.

Ferdinand II now decided to recall the only commander who seemed capable of reorganising his army and resisting the Swedish advance, Wallenstein. In December 1631, in a decision confirmed in April 1632, Wallenstein was once again appointed commander-in-chief of the imperial armies, with almost unlimited authority not only in military matters but also with regard to diplomacy. Wallenstein did indeed manage to recruit new troops and to stop the Swedish advance. In summer 1632 he took up a strongly fortified position near the important city of Nuremberg, threatening Gustavus Adolphus's lines of supply. The King tried in vain to provoke Wallenstein to a pitched battle. His attacks on Wallenstein's fortified camp were similarly unsuccessful. Exhausted, the Swedish troops retreated to Saxony closely followed by the imperial general. On 17 November 1632 the Swedes and the imperialists did at last meet in open battle at Lützen near Leipzig. Though the Swedes were able to hold the battlefield, the contest was indecisive. Far more importantly, the Swedish King was killed during the fight.

His most senior councillor, the Chancellor Oxenstierna, now took over the direction of affairs in Germany, while a Council of Regency was installed in Stockholm as Gustavus's daughter Christina was still under age. But Oxenstierna could hardly hope to achieve the popularity in Germany which the late King had enjoyed. Even among the officers of the Swedish army Oxenstierna commanded far less respect than his royal master had done. Confronted with the danger of a widespread mutiny among badly paid officers and soldiers Oxenstierna had to make far-reaching promises. Whole counties and bishoprics were abandoned to the leading commanders as 'donations' or just as objects of plunder to compensate them for their arrears of pay. The problem of satisfying the financial demands of the officers and military entrepreneurs who had kept the Swedish army going since its intervention in Germany was not to go away for the rest of the war. In fact, Swedish policy in Germany was to a large extent determined by the need to find a lasting solution to this question, a solution which would prevent unpaid troops under the command of the enraged officers descending on Sweden herself, or on those provinces which Sweden intended to keep after a peace had been signed.

Oxenstierna hoped to defuse Sweden's financial problems in Germany by forming an alliance which was intended to unite Sweden's allies in western and southern Germany. The Heilbronn League founded in April 1633 never quite fulfilled the purposes for which it had been established. But at least it stabilised the situation for the moment, for by 1633 there were already clear signs that Sweden's allies were seeking a settlement with the Emperor, if necessary, at Sweden's expense.[12] However, for the time being, the Swedish troops benefited from the fact that the imperial commander-in-chief did not press home the political and military advantages which he undoubtedly enjoyed after Gustavus Adolphus's death. But in the winter of 1633–34 Wallenstein's dilatory tactics plus his inscrutable diplomatic manoeuvres and secret negotiations with the Swedes and the Elector of Saxony made him highly suspect at the imperial court. For reasons which will probably never be entirely clear, Ferdinand II decided to have his supreme commander taken prisoner by force or, if that proved too difficult, to have him assassinated. The fact that Spain was preparing to send a major army to Germany in

1634 probably hastened this decision, as the Spanish were not prepared to submit to Wallenstein's decisions while he insisted on his right to command all Catholic troops in the Empire, including Spanish contingents. On 25 February 1634 Wallenstein was murdered by some of his officers in Eger whence, already fearing for his life, he had hoped to escape to the nearby Protestant troops. Ferdinand II now entrusted his own son, Ferdinand (III), with the supreme command of his troops.

In September 1634 the new commander-in-chief succeeded in having his forces near Nördlingen join the army of his Spanish namesake, the Cardinal Infante, who had led 15,000 men from Italy across the Alps to southern Germany. On 6 September 1635 the 33,000 imperial and Spanish troops defeated the 25,000 strong Swedish–Protestant army opposing them. Nördlingen was the sign for Sweden's allies to desert their erstwhile protector, an opportunity which many of them had undoubtedly been awaiting for a considerable time. Sweden's position in Germany collapsed almost completely within a matter of months. In August 1635 Oxenstierna himself was taken prisoner in Magdeburg by mutinous Swedish troops and officers once again demanding arrears on their pay. Oxenstierna had to promise them that they would receive cash and donations in Sweden if no solution to the financial problems could be found in Germany.[13] This was enough, for the time being, to calm the colonels and their men and persuade them to release the Chancellor. But even so, the Swedish regiments, or what was left of them, had to retreat to Mecklenburg and Pomerania, provinces already thoroughly plundered and devasted between 1627 and 1634. Sweden's position seemed desperate, or almost desperate. In fact the Council of Regency in Stockholm repeatedly considered unconditionally abandoning all remaining strongholds in Germany, with the exception, perhaps, of Stralsund.[14]

In the end France's open intervention in the war in spring 1635, diverting Habsburg resources and troops from the war in northern Germany, allowed Sweden to make a recovery after 1635. But this was a slow and laborious process.

The Peace of Prague

In 1632, for a brief moment, it seemed possible that the Empire would be dissolved or transformed into a Protestant confederation led by Sweden and comprising most of the principalities and cities east of the Rhine and north of the Danube. However, even before the battle of Nördlingen many of the Protestant princes allied with the Swedish crown had resented Swedish leadership. This was true in particular of Johann Georg of Saxony who saw himself as the natural leader of the German Protestants; reluctant to leave this role to a foreign monarch like Gustavus Adolphus, he was certainly not prepared to concede it to a 'mere penpusher' (a 'Plackscheißer') such as the Chancellor Oxenstierna, who directed Swedish policy in Germany after Gustavus Adolphus's death.[15] It was therefore hardly surprising that the Prince Elector sought an understanding with the Emperor after Nördlingen and cancelled his alliance with Sweden.

Ferdinand II was equally interested in ending the war in Germany. The problem of having his son Ferdinand (III), the victor of Nördlingen, elected as King of the Romans was still unresolved and even if the five Catholic prince electors held a clear majority in the College of Electors, the assent of Brandenburg and Saxony was important if the other Protestant princes were to accept the new Emperor after Ferdinand's death. Moreover, in late 1634 tensions between France and Spain were already growing (see below, p. 122). Madrid was eager to win the Emperor's support for the all-out war against France which seemed to be inevitable. However, Ferdinand II could only support his Spanish cousins effectively if he managed to put an end to the conflict in the Empire. In fact, Spanish diplomats actively tried to promote the cause of peace in the Empire during the years 1634–35. They commissioned pamphlets which appealed to national sentiment in Germany and tried to mobilise this sentiment against France. The notion of a 'German nation' which had to defend its honour and greatness against its enemies – hardly ever mentioned before 1630 by Spanish authors –

assumed a prominent place in Spanish official documents and political tracts in the early 1630s,[16] whereas Richelieu and his pamphleteers appealed more to the idea of German 'liberty' threatened by Habsburg absolutism.

Though few German princes and statesmen were convinced that an alliance with Spain was the best way to promote Germany's greatness, the 'beloved German fatherland' was indeed referred to frequently enough in German pamphlets and tracts in the mid-1630s. The disasters of the preceding years and the presence of foreign armies on German soil had certainly sharpened the sense of national identity in Germany. Nevertheless, the gap between patriotic rhetoric and practical politics remained enormous,[17] as most princes were extremely reluctant to sacrifice their own interests to the common good, however defined, of the 'geliebte teutsche Vaterland' which they and their pamphleteers so often invoked.

The compromise achieved in 1635 between the Protestants and the Emperor was therefore fragile right from the start. Initially the Prince Elector of Saxony, the principal spokesman for the Protestants and Sweden's erstwhile allies, had tried to uphold as many of the old demands of the Protestant princes as possible. Thus the *reservatum ecclesiaticum*, which forced ecclesiastical rulers to abdicate if they converted to Protestantism, was to be abolished and a key date or 'normative year' (*Normaljahr*) was to be introduced for all disputes about Church lands and the rights and privileges of religious minorities living in a principality governed by a ruler of a different religion. In Johann Georg's view this date should be 1612. Thus a bishopric or monastery secularised or administered by Protestants in that year would remain so permanently and the Protestant subjects of a Catholic ruler openly practising their religion at this time could also continue to do so. The idea of a *Normaljahr* was a promising one and was indeed to become one of the keys to the peace settlement of 1648. However, even by November 1634, when Johann Georg had signed a preliminary treaty with the Emperor's emmissaries in Pirna, he had had to abandon a number of his demands.

The final treaty was signed on 30 May 1635 in Prague. It was to be valid not only for the Emperor and Saxony, but for all princes and Estates of the Empire prepared to accept its terms and not explicitly excluded from the imperial amnesty to be proclaimed immediately. By this time Ferdinand II had managed to modify the terms even further in his own and the Catholic princes' favour. Even so there was opposition to the concessions at the imperial court. In particular, a number of theologians and imperial confessors, among them the influential Jesuit Wilhelm Lamormaini, were opposed to the Peace of Prague. In general, those clergymen associated with the pro-Spanish party at court were inclined to make concessions whereas those closely linked to the Roman Curia were against a compromise. Pope Urban VIII continued to advocate a strict Counter-Reformation policy, not just for religious reasons but also because he was opposed to Spain. Spanish possessions in Italy overshadowed the Pope's own position as a territorial ruler and he rightly saw the Peace of Prague as a decisive step towards closer co-operation between the Emperor and Philip IV.[18]

Although Johann Georg of Saxony had tried to get the Edict of Restitution totally revoked, the Peace of Prague remained somewhat vague on this point. The key date for all confessional disputes was now to be 12 November 1627, not 1612 as Saxony had wished. This date was prior to the publication of the Edict of Restitution, and the edict was indeed to be suspended for the next 40 years. Once these 40 years had passed, however, the Emperor could theoretically enforce the edict again, though not without prior consultation with the princes of the Empire. Even if a full-scale return to the Counter-Reformation policies of the late 1620s was unlikely after a further four decades of confessional *détente*, the year of 1627 was in itself problematic for the Protestants. In 1627, after the battle of Lutter am Barenberge, north-western Germany with its numerous bishoprics was already occupied by Catholic troops, not to mention the Palatinate and southern Germany, or the Counter-Reformation in the Habsburg hereditary lands which was well under way by 1627. In fact, only Protestants in the Circle of Upper Saxony and perhaps in the Lower Saxon Circle as well could feel reasonably safe after 1635. Moreover the 'fine print' of the Prague agreement favoured the Emperor and the Catholics to such an extent that Ferdinand and his successors retained considerable discretionary power which they could use to strengthen their own position and that of the Catholic Church.

An important clause of the Treaty of Prague stipulated that only those princes who had taken up arms *after* the Swedish intervention in Germany in 1630 were to be automatically pardoned for their 'revolt' against the Emperor. Others had to enter into complicated negotiations with the imperial court to receive a pardon. A number of princes and counts of the Empire were in fact excluded from the peace altogether. This applied to nearly all the Calvinists, the Elector of Brandenburg being one of the very few exceptions. The Count Palatine, the heir of the former Elector, fared particularly badly, as the peace confirmed the transfer of his title and dominions, at least those on the right bank of the river Rhine, to Maximilian of Bavaria. Given that the Palatine branch of the Wittelsbach dynasty was closely related to the Stuarts, this decision was bound to have an adverse effect on relations between the Empire and Charles I of England. But then it was widely assumed that England was incapable of influencing the course of events on the Continent anyway. As Maximilian of Bavaria put it in 1636: Charles I had to choose whether he wanted to reinstate the Count Palatine as Elector or whether he wanted to be a truly absolute king ('rechter absolutus rex') himself, for if he went to war once more he would have to obey his own Parliament's orders unconditionally.[19]

However, the Count Palatine was not the only prince to have reason to be dissatisfied with the Peace of Prague. The Calvinist Landgrave of Hesse-Kassel, Wilhelm, was also dispossessed. He had long been in dispute with the younger, Lutheran line of the Hessian dynasty, which had its seat in Darmstadt, over the possession of the central districts of the Landgraviate around Marburg, which had belonged to yet another branch of the dynasty until 1604 when it became extinct. The Emperor had always supported the Lutheran line which had already won an important court case against its Calvinist cousins in the Imperial Aulic Council in the 1620s. Negotiations between Wilhelm of Hesse-Kassel and the court in Vienna, which was reluctant to offer Wilhelm acceptable terms, finally broke down in 1636 and the Emperor thereupon transferred the administration of Wilhelm's principality to Landgrave Georg of Hesse-Darmstadt. The Landgrave of Kassel, who had never abandoned his alliance with Sweden, reacted by signing an alliance with France as well in October 1636.[20]

The Duke of Württemberg, though a Lutheran, was also excluded from the amnesty. Though his hopes of regaining at least some of his dominions were better than those of the Landgrave of Hesse-Kassel or the Count Palatine, his position was precarious enough. For although the Edict of Restitution was not to be enforced for 40 years, judgements pronounced by the imperial law courts in favour of Catholic plaintiffs, at least those judgements made before 1628, were to remain valid. In fact, most of the great monasteries incorporated into the Duchy during the sixteenth century had been reconstituted as independent ecclesiastical corporations by Ferdinand II, and other parts of Württemberg had been transferred to servants and supporters of the Emperor as imperial donations, often to satisfy financial claims. Thus if the Duke of Württemberg had any hope of restoration, he would in all likelihood rule over only fragments of his former possessions.[21]

With the Palatinate destroyed as a Protestant principality and Württemberg much reduced in size, south-western Germany was clearly dominated by Catholic princes, and in particular the Habsburgs after the Peace of Prague. This Catholic–Habsburg ascendancy was further reinforced by an important article of the Treaty of Prague which denied the knights and free cities of the Empire (with the exception of Nuremberg, Strassburg, Ulm and Frankfurt) the benefit of the clause which had established November 1627 as a key date for the religious status of all dominions in the Empire. Because there were so many *Reichsritter* and *Reichsstädte* in Swabia and

Franconia, the cause of Catholicism was greatly strengthened by enforcing the Edict of Restitution in the cities and among the knights, and this remained legally possible even after 1635.

Some historians have in fact seen the advantages which Ferdinand gained in Prague as so significant – after all, the monopoly of Catholicism as the only legal creed in the Habsburg hereditary dominions including Bohemia and Moravia was also confirmed by the peace – that they consider the treaty a decisive step towards the transformation of the Empire into an absolute monarchy.[22] The peace had, indeed, declared all alliances among the princes of the Empire or between foreign powers and German rulers illegal; the Liga had finally been dissolved and all armed forces in the Empire now had to swear allegiance to the Emperor.[23] Nevertheless, Johann Georg of Saxony was to command the Protestant troops in northern Germany independently, only loosely subjected to the imperial high command. Maximilian of Bavaria was able to insist on similar concessions. Officially, as the Emperor's general, he was entrusted with the command of about a quarter of the entire army of the Empire; this Bavarian corps was to a large extent identical with the old Bavarian-led army of the Catholic Liga. Thus even if Ferdinand II had wished to rule the Empire as an 'absolute monarch', he would have lacked the military power to do so. This is not to deny that, compared to the years before the outbreak of the Thirty Years War, the balance of forces in the Empire had been considerably modified by the Peace of Prague. As long as Ferdinand could reach agreement with the prince electors, and in particular with the three secular electors, he could now largely disregard the wishes of the other princes and Estates; the Imperial Diet, which had last met in 1613, seemed likely to disappear once and for all from the Empire's political scene. At the very least it would be reduced to a largely ornamental role.

Whatever the shortcomings of the Peace of Prague, it had at least pointed the way towards a lasting settlement, even if it was not to have such a permanent impact itself. A considerable number of problems were left unresolved and the future status of many ecclesiastical principalities and possessions, in particular, remained as uncertain as ever because the clauses relating to the Edict of Restitution had been left deliberately vague. The tensions between the confessions had been successfully defused in Prague, but they had certainly not dissappeared.

The real problem, however, was that among the Protestants the princes of northern and eastern Germany (for example Saxony, which had acted as a self-appointed advocate for Protestant interests during the peace negotiations, Brandenburg and the various Dukes of Brunswick), had the best reason to accept the compromise with the Catholics and the Emperor. For Protestants in western and southern Germany the settlement was much less satisfactory. Unfortunately, however, though the survival and safety of Protestantism in northern Germany was ensured by the peace, security against attacks by the Swedish army still holding out in Mecklenburg and Pomerania was not. Thus among the Protestants the very princes who were most likely to be the strongest supporters of the new settlement soon discovered that the peace committed them either to a fruitless and ultimately unwinnable war of attrition against the Swedes or to buying them off by making major financial and territorial concessions. This problem was particularly acute for the Elector of Brandenburg who claimed the Duchy of Pomerania by right of inheritance, a principality which the Swedes saw as an indispensable bridgehead in the Empire and as the natural compensation for the sacrifices they had made to free Germany from imperial and Catholic 'despotism'.

In fact, Johann Georg of Saxony and Ferdinand II had largely ignored the international dimension of the war during the negotiations which led to the Peace of Prague. As opposed to the Peace of Westphalia signed 13 years later, the Peace of Prague was a German peace and nothing else. For Ferdinand, who wanted to free his hands for the imminent war against France, the presence of the remnants of the Swedish army on the Baltic coast was a minor problem anyhow. And even

Johann Georg, who had more reason to feel concerned about these troops, apparently believed that Sweden's power was broken and that others, in particular the Brandenburg Hohenzollern, would foot the bill should it be necessary after all to make major concessions to the Swedes to get them out of the Empire. This, however, proved to be a miscalculation, for deperate as the Swedish position might seem in 1635, the monarchy of the Vasas was to make a startling recovery at the end of the 1630s and in the 1640s. Combined with the open intervention of French armies in the war after 1635, in itself a precondition for the revival of Sweden's military fortune, this recovery doomed to failure all attempts to uphold the Peace of Prague.

The French Declaration of War

On 19 May 1635 Louis XIII of France officially declared war on Spain. In traditional fashion a herald was sent to Brussels and ceremonially read out the French declaration of war in the market-place. Like almost all his decisions in foreign affairs Louis took this momentous step on the advice of his leading councillor and minister, Armand du Plessis Cardinal de Richelieu. Of the leading statesmen of the Thirty Years War Richelieu, who directed French policy from 1624 to 1642, is probably one of the most controversial figures. Many of his contemporaries, not just in Madrid and Vienna, but also in France, saw him as an evil genius, who, driven by a relentless thirst for power, was prepared to sacrifice everything, religion as much as the well-being of the French people, to his ambition.[24]

This negative assessment of Richelieu's achievement has recently been echoed, for example, in the work of J. Russell Major who maintains that Louis XIII's reign was 'an almost unmitigated disaster for the mass of the French people and ultimately for the monarchy itself'. According to Russell Major, by pursuing an excessively aggressive foreign policy Richelieu brought misery to the French peasants burdened by ever higher taxes, and created insurmountable obstacles to any but the most superficial institutional reforms of the French state.[25] On the other hand, many of his biographers have depicted the Cardinal as a man devoted to France's greatness, a man who was surrounded by enemies abroad and at home but who nevertheless, fighting against heavy odds, laid the foundations for France's hegemony in Europe in the later seventeenth century, and for the system of government, absolutism, which was to reach its apogee under Louis XIV.[26]

In German historiography of the late nineteenth and early twentieth centuries Richelieu more often than not figured as a *bête noire*. But after 1945 German historians, especially Fritz Dickmann and Hermann Weber, greatly contributed to a major revision of the Cardinal's image.[27] They no longer saw Richelieu as a politician bent on territorial expansion, in particular on establishing some sort of 'natural frontier' for the French kingdom along the Rhine, and inspired by the cold rules of reason of state which denied any confessional, let alone moral, standards in foreign policy. Instead they have tried to demonstrate that Richelieu's policy was informed by a high sense of moral and religious responsibility. Hermann Weber has even spoken of Richelieu's 'noble vision of peace', for in his eyes Richelieu's foreign policy had no objective other than to establish a just and lasting peace for Europe.[28] Thus in Weber's opinion the military campaigns and, in particular, the war against Spain officially declared in 1635 were only means, reluctantly employed by Richelieu to achieve such a lasting peace.

Weber is undoubtely right to question the dated clichés of nineteenth-century German historiography. Nevertheless, British historians working on French history have recently raised the question of whether Richelieu's policy, foreign as much as domestic, should not be seen in an entirely different perspective. Joseph Bergin and David Parrott, in particular, have demonstrated that whatever the Cardinal's personal convictions, Richelieu's policies must be interpreted at least as much in terms of the quest for place and profit as of ideological conflict and high political principles.[29] In the final resort, though opposed and hated by many of the noble magnates of France, the Cardinal wanted to establish himself and his family among these *grands*. Far from sacrificing all personal interests to some abstract principle, be it the greatness and glory of France and her King or the peace of Europe, he in many respects acted very much like other great French noblemen who sought to build up networks of clients and increase their personal fortune and power, at almost any cost. Such an interpretation of Richelieu's personality and political role is far from irrelevant for the assessment of French foreign policy in the 1630s, as David Parrott has emphasised, for this policy was largely based on Richelieu's personal decisions, and for the Cardinal domestic and foreign issues were nearly always closely linked.[30]

There is certainly a consensus that after the Peace of Cherasco, Richelieu was extremely reluctant to confront Spain again in an all-out war. This reluctance had a number of motives. Firstly, though its outcome had ultimately been favourable to France, the war for Mantua (1628–31) had demonstrated that the French armies were no real match for the superior Spanish forces in a pitched battle unless they enjoyed a decisive numerical superiority. In fact, this was to remain so until the early 1640s – the battle of Rocroi (1643) was the first truly major battle which the French won against the Spanish troops. Secondly, open warfare against Spain north of the Alps would have been impossible without an official alliance with the Protestant enemies of the House of Habsburg, the Dutch, the Protestant princes of Germany and the Swedes. France did indeed financially subsidise these opponents of the Habsburgs in the early 1630s, but direct military co-operation would have been a different matter. It would have provoked further resistance to Richelieu's rule in France among the Catholic *dévots*, the 'ultras' of the Catholic Reform and Counter-Reformation who, ever since his intervention in northern Italy in 1629, were inclined to see the Cardinal as a traitor to the cause of the Roman Church anyhow. Finally, the advance of the Swedish armies in 1631–32 seemed to make direct French intervention in Germany at once superfluous and particularly difficult. Why send armies against the Emperor when Ferdinand's fate already appeared to be sealed, and when these armies were bound to get involved in disputes with the Swedes who would hardly see eye to eye with the French in matters relating to religion or the status of ecclesiastical possessions in Germany?

Instead of intervening directly Richelieu put the French armies on a war footing – which led to a spectacular rise in taxation in France (see below, pp. 172–5) – and had them occupy gradually the principalities between the French border and the Rhine. Lorraine was the first territory forced to accept French garrisons in 1632–33; subsequently it was virtually transformed into a French province.[31] The Duke of Lorraine had made the mistake of co-operating with Spain and supporting the domestic opposition to Richelieu in France. In fact, his dynasty had a long history of involvement in French domestic affairs and a younger branch of the ducal house, the Dukes of Guise, had come very close to claiming the French crown themselves after the last of the Valois Kings, Henry III, had been murdered in 1589 (by a supporter of the French Ligue, the radical Catholic movement led by the Guises). For Richelieu, therefore, gaining control over Lorraine was not just strategically important to weaken the Spanish position along the French border and to interrupt the Spanish supply lines from Italy to the Netherlands; it was also motivated by the wish to eliminate a stronghold of his own opponents beyond the French border. After all, Gaston d'Orleans, the French King's brother who, as heir presumptive to the French crown (until 1638), was the natural, and often also actual, leader of the anti-Richelieu opposition in France, had married Marguerite of Lorraine, the Duke's sister, in January 1632.

But Lorraine was only the first principality to be occupied by French troops. Other territories were to follow. In fact, the Prince-Archbishop of Trier had asked the French for protection as early as April 1632. The Archbishop felt threatened by Swedish troops advancing into southern Germany and rightly thought that the presence of French garrisons – France paid subsidies to the Swedish crown – would allow him to stay neutral, whereas the intervention of Spanish troops would only provoke Swedish attacks. Other princes and cities followed suit. The Catholic ones were trying to escape a Swedish occupation, like the Archbishop of Trier, and the Protestant ones were hoping for support against the Spanish troops operating in southern Alsace. In 1633–34 the French King gradually became the protector of a large number of cities and small principalities in Alsace, and his troops had occupied almost the entire area, south of Luxemburg and the Spanish Netherlands, between the French border and the Rhine.[32]

Furthermore, they established footholds on the right bank of the Rhine: the important fortresses of Ehrenbreitstein (opposite Koblenz) and Philippsburg, two of the *portes* (gates of entry) for the French armies which Richelieu had wanted to establish in Germany, Switzerland and Italy since 1629.[33] They eventually advanced into the eastern Palatinate, to the right of the Rhine, and established themselves in Heidelberg (December 1634). Richelieu may have considered the French garrisons bargaining counters for a future political arrangement or indeed a lasting peace with Spain, and at the same time as a useful protection against a possible Spanish attack. But of course the French advance made clashes with Spanish and imperial troops inevitable, and in the eyes of the Conde-Duque Olivares, French policy was provocative and threatening. R. A. Stradling has argued that ever since the war for Mantua, Olivares had developed plans for a large-scale pre-emptive strike against France. Like Richelieu, he was convinced that an all-out war was virtually unavoidable in the long run, and he wanted to fight this war under conditions favourable to Spain, that is, not as a long and costly war of attrition but as a short *blitzkrieg* resulting in the fall of the French Cardinal-minister. Olivares thought that Richelieu would not survive the crushing defeats which he hoped to inflict on the French armies.[34]

For Olivares the French advance towards the Rhine and the Habsburg victory at Nördlingen in September 1634 seemed to make the pre-emptive strike which he had been trying to organise since 1632 at once both more urgent and feasible, if we accept Stradling's arguments. Nevertheless, Hildegard Ernst's study of relations between Madrid and Vienna has shown that the aggressive measures Olivares took against France in 1634–35 were probably motivated less by the wish to destroy French military power once and for all than by the conviction that Richelieu was himself planning a major offensive against Spain for the near future. Another motive seems to have been the desire to embroil the Emperor in the apparently inevitable direct military confrontation between Spain and France.[35] The conflict over Mantua in 1628–31 had created an insurmountable mutual distrust between Paris and Madrid – after Mantua, both sides based their assessment of their opponent's intentions on a sort of 'worst case scenario'. But for Olivares it had also demonstrated that the Austrian branch of the Habsburg dynasty could not really be trusted as an ally. After all the Peace of Regensburg (so disastrous for Spain) between Ferdinand II and Louis XIII (1630) had fatally undermined Spain's position in the struggle for Mantua. Thus the only way to get Ferdinand's support against France would be to provoke an incident which made war between France and the Empire certain.

The Spanish decision to attack the French garrison in Trier in March 1635 was part of this policy of turning the French–Spanish conflict into a confrontation between the Empire and Spain. The French were successfully ejected with the support of the local population, and the pro-French Archbishop Philipp Christoph von Sötern was taken prisoner in the name of the Emperor as a traitor (he was to remain the Emperor's prisoner until 1645). This strategy was not immediately successful as Richelieu decided to declare war only on Spain and not on the Empire or Ferdinand II, but eventually imperial troops were engaged in the fight against France. In March 1636 the official imperial proclamation declaring war on Louis XIII followed.

Admittedly, Spain and France had already come to the brink of open war in spring 1634, long before the battle of Nördlingen and before the ejection of the French garrison from Trier. In May 1634 the Marquis d'Aytona had signed a treaty on behalf of the Spanish crown with Gaston d'Orleans, brother of the French King and Richelieu's inveterate opponent. The Duke d'Orleans had been promised financial and logistical support for an expeditionary force which was to invade France to topple Richelieu. This treaty, though perhaps only a preventive measure against a French attack,[36] seemed to demonstrate to Richelieu that the large-scale Spanish attack on France which he feared was imminent. Moreover, it revealed once more that his own domestic position could not be secure as long as Spain was capable of fomenting opposition against him in France. Richelieu therefore took steps to conclude an offensive alliance with the Dutch Republic against Spain. All the same, he was reluctant to commit himself irrevocably to an open war against what was still the most powerful European monarchy.[37] The battle of Nördlingen, however, greatly contributed to making the drift towards open war irreversible. With Sweden defeated or almost defeated, Richelieu could no longer hope that foreign armies would win his war for him. In addition, the danger of a Spanish attack was now much greater than before.

Nevertheless, in the end it was the defeat the French troops suffered in Trier which acted as a trigger for full-scale war; it threatened to cancel out all the advantages which Richelieu had won over the preceding years, not only in foreign relations but also in the domestic sphere. If a prince of the Empire protected by France could so easily be taken prisoner by Spanish troops, alliances with France were clearly of little value. However, it was not only the reputation of the French crown, but also Richelieu's personal reputation that had to be restored by drastic measures if the Cardinal wanted to survive politically. Richelieu had staked his entire political fortune on a belligerent anti-Spanish foreign policy since autumn 1628, and had made many enemies in France in the process: devout advocates of a confessional foreign policy, protagonists of financial and administrative reform, and all those who opposed high taxation in the name of the 'soulagement du peuple' (relief for the hard-pressed populace). If his policy now turned out to be a failure, Richelieu's opponents would win the day against him at court, as the Cardinal could never be entirely sure of Louis XIII's wholehearted support.

In fact, Richelieu's decision, taken after 1631, to extend France's sphere of influence ever further to the east and to put France and her armies on a war footing had gained a momentum of its own. In the final resort it made the declaration of war of May 1635 inevitable. Even before Nördlingen and the Spanish attack on (or liberation of) Trier, any return to a policy of compromise with Spain had become well-nigh impossible for Richelieu, however much he dreaded the risk of an all-out open war against the Spanish Habsburgs. As David Parrott puts it: 'As long as the confrontation with Spain was the dominant issue in France Richelieu could consolidate his own power in government, together with that of his *créatures* and eliminate his rivals, justifying his government monopoly and harsh measures on the grounds of "absolute necessity" created by the foreign situation.' Any return to the rather passive foreign policy of the years before 1629 was therefore impossible for 'the choice for peace and retrenchment would mean the destruction of Richelieu's own authority, just as the pursuit of the war in Italy since 1629 had whittled away the power of his opponents'.[38]

If we accept Parrott's highly plausible arguments, does this make Richelieu's calls for a just and lasting peace disingenuous, mere manifestations of political hypocrisy? Richelieu repeated these calls frequently enough even after 1635, as Hermann Weber has pointed out. Given that influential circles in France remained opposed to war, Richelieu certainly had reasons enough to proclaim his own support for peace as loudly as possible. But Weber is probably right in claiming that Richelieu, though committed to an anti-Spanish policy for reasons which were based as much on self-interest as on sincere political convictions and principles, did try to lay the foundations for a comprehensive European order. This new political system would guarantee a lasting peace and at the same time confirm France's position as the most powerful, if not the dominant of the European powers.

Spain could base her policy at least in central Europe, if not in Europe as a whole, on a political system which was already in existence: the Holy Roman Empire. For Spain it was sufficient to mobilise the resources and forces of the Empire for her own purposes; this had been the aim of Spanish policy since at least the mid-1620s, and in 1635, with the conflict in the Empire apparently settled, Madrid's chances of achieving it seemed better than ever, at least as far as the struggle against France was concerned. The conflict with the Dutch, in which even Catholic German princes were very reluctant to participate, was a different matter. Richelieu, on the other hand, could at best hope to neutralise the Empire, but a system of inter-state relations in Europe favourable to France could hardly be based on the existing imperial institutions as long as the Emperor was a Habsburg.[39] Richelieu, therefore, had to devise a system which would, if not replace, at least to some extent supersede the Empire as a framework for relations between dynasties and states in central Europe. His memoranda about a lasting peace as the principal objective of French policy must be seen as part of this attempt to construct a new framework for European politics. Olivares did not devise an equally systematic plan for a new European order, or at least not one as consistent and abstract as Richelieu's. In this sense his vision of peace was, if not less 'noble', then perhaps less comprehensive.[40] But this was ultimately due to the fact that he had no need to develop such a vision because there were enough elements in the present system, in particular the constitutional and political institutions of the Empire, which he could work with. Moreover, Spain's vision of peace could never be an exclusively European one as her interests in America were too important to be neglected. These circumstances deeply affected the role of France and Spain respectively during the peace negotiations in Münster in the late 1640s.

5

1648: A NEW ORDER FOR EUROPE?

From Prague to Münster and Osnabrück

In 1635 a peaceful settlement of the conflict within the Holy Roman Empire had almost been achieved, despite the manifest shortcomings of the Peace of Prague. Nevertheless, it was another 13 years before the war ended, and even then it was to continue outside Germany. Undoubtedly the nature of early seventeenth-century warfare, which made it difficult to defeat an opponent so decisively in battle that any further resistance was impossible, contributed to this long continuation of the war (cf. below, pp. 150–3). But other factors must also be taken into account. Not only was the sort of peace Spain and the Austrian Habsburgs initially envisaged entirely incompatible with the objectives pursued by Richelieu, Oxenstierna and the Dutch Republic, but the anti-Habsburg allies could not even agree among themselves about the conditions which they expected a future peace to meet. For France the fight against Spain took priority, something the Swedes, understandably enough, took no great interest in. Sweden agreed with France that the liberties of the German princes had to be secured against the Emperor, but Sweden naturally favoured the Protestants whereas France sympathised with the Catholics. Thus the allies were unable to impose a settlement on Madrid and Vienna not only because they lacked the military superiority necessary to do so, but also because they could not agree among themselves on which settlement to impose.

The Habsburgs hoped for a long time that despite the ever more serious setbacks which they suffered from about 1638–39 on, they would be able to divide their opponents. This hope was not entirely unfounded. Ultimately the Dutch did sign a separate peace with Spain in January 1648 in Münster, but the Franco-Swedish alliance proved unshakeable. In fact, in 1641 when their initial treaty of alliance signed in 1638 was renewed, the two crowns had accepted a proviso stipulating that they would go on fighting until a comprehensive peace had been achieved and that they would not seek a separate settlement with the other side. And as it turned out, the need which the two allies had of each other's support was great enough to prevent a breach of this undertaking.

In the years immediately following the Peace of Prague and the French declaration of war against Spain, a Habsburg victory against the combined forces of their opponents did not seem impossible. While Olivares managed to mobilise hitherto untapped resources in the peripheral provinces of the Spanish monarchy – although the price he had to pay for this unremitting fiscal drive was unrest and ultimately rebellion, as the future was to show (cf. below, pp. 129–30) – Spain achieved a striking military recovery in the Low Countries. In the early 1630s her position in Flanders and Brabant had seemed on the point of collapse. The Dutch had taken the important fortress of Maastricht in 1632, and the nobility and Estates of the Spanish provinces became increasingly restive. The Estates General of the Spanish Low Countries had to be assembled in Brussels to assuage discontent, but even so, many noblemen favouring a peace with the Dutch fled to independent Liège, to France, or even to the Northern Netherlands, and fomented unrest in the Spanish provinces from the security of exile. The Infanta Isabella, the Regent of the Southern Netherlands, had to enter into negotiations with the North about a peace favourable to the Republic. Delegates from the Brussels Estates General participated in the negotiations.

However, in December 1633 Isabella died. Spain resumed direct control of the Southern Netherlands. At this stage support for a lasting peace with Spain and the southern provinces had already diminished in the North because the concessions which Spain and the government in Brussels were prepared to make seemed inadequate.[1]

After Isabella's death Spain renewed the war effort with full vigour, appointing Philip IV's brother Ferdinand, a cardinal, as governor of the Southern Netherlands. Once Madrid managed to send reinforcements to Brabant and Flanders in 1634, and, in particular, after the battle of Nördlingen, the military situation greatly improved. In fact, Jonathan Israel has pointed out that 'the effort by Spain' during the years 1635–40 'was by far the most massive in terms of outlay and manpower of the entire Dutch–Spanish war.' In spite of the war against France, Spain's main efforts continued to be directed against the Dutch. Olivares hoped to be able to force the Dutch to sign a truce favourable to Spain, and only after this had been achieved did he intend to destroy the French armies.[2]

The Dutch troops suffered a number of setbacks during the late 1630s, and the situation was rendered particularly difficult by the occasional intervention of imperial troops stationed along the lower Rhine. None the less, the Spanish army failed to achieve a decisive victory. As the 1620s and 1630s had already shown, obtaining such a victory on land was almost impossible. The laborious sieges which were the normal form of warfare in the Low Countries often proved futile, and hardly ever managed to destroy the enemy's fighting capacity, whatever the ensuing territorial losses once an important fortress was taken. Olivares therefore decided to concentrate on naval warfare again. In 1639 a huge Spanish armada comprising about 100 ships – 86 of them warships – sailed up the Channel. The armada was to take troop reinforcements to the Netherlands as the fall of the fortress of Breisach near Freiburg to the French commander Bernhard von Weimar in 1638 had largely blocked the Spanish road from Italy to the Low Countries. However, its commander, Admiral Antonio de Oquendo, also had express orders to seek battle with his Dutch opposite number, Tromp, and to destroy his fleet.

Although the Spanish naval forces, in particular the Dunkirk squadron, had shown themselves equal to their Dutch opponents in the preceeding years, this was a gamble – and it was to fail. Tromp managed to block the further advance of the Spanish ships between Calais and Dover, and to surround them off the English coast, in the Downs, for several weeks. He finally succeeded in driving them ashore and destroying them on 21 October 1639. Though most of the troops on the ships escaped and were subsequently shipped to Flemish harbours by the English, this was a devastating blow for Spain. All hopes of imposing a settlement on the Dutch were finally gone.

In fact, the next year a rebellion broke out in Catalonia (May 1640) to be followed by a second rebellion in Portugal in December which shattered the Spanish position in the very heartland of the monarchy, the Iberian peninsula. The Catalans resented the infringement of their liberties by Olivares, who had imposed unusally high taxes on a province which traditionally had contributed almost nothing to the costs of imperial defence. They equally resented the presence of undisciplined foreign, that is Castilian and Italian, troops in Catalonia since 1635.[3] The revolt in Portugal was at least as serious as the Catalan one. The Portuguese under the leadership of the the Duke of Braganca proclaimed their independence. Their country had been united with Castile in a dynastic union since 1580, something which for several decades many Portuguese had found acceptable enough. But the Portuguese were almost as unwilling as the Catalans to make substantial contributions to the joint military efforts of the Spanish dominions, in particular if this involved not only supplying Spanish fleets with ships, but also sending troops abroad, as Olivares demanded, to Italy or Catalonia. Moreover, important sections of the native political and social elite had come to see further union with Castile as inimical to Portugal's interests, while the regular clergy and most of the ordinary secular priests had always been opposed to Spanish rule.

In the late 1630s the Dutch had finally managed to establish themselves permanently in northern Brazil, thereby threatening Portugal's income from the flourishing sugar export trade. Spain (or Castile) was clearly unable to defend Portugal's colonial empire as long as her priorities lay elsewhere – with the war in the Low Countries and the contest against France. This was resented all the more strongly because the Portuguese were made to pay higher taxes from the 1620s onwards to contribute to the costs of imperial defence. In the 1630s popular discontent had led to a series of anti-fiscal revolts. Although they were quickly put down by Spanish troops they prepared the ground for the *coup d'état* of 1640 in which many noblemen as well as a number of rich Lisbon merchants dissatisfied with Spanish rule took part, and which was secretly supported by France. Within a very short time Spanish rule collapsed, so that the Duke of Braganca could be crowned King on 15 December 1640. He was related to the last Portuguese King, Sebastian, who had died in 1578. Spain tried to reconquer the country but after a war which lasted for nearly 30 years finally had to recognise Portugal's independence in 1668.[4]

After the defeat of the Downs and the Iberian revolts, Spain clearly lost the initiative in the war against her enemies. Although peace with the Dutch in 1648 and the descent of France into chaos and civil war in 1648–53, during the Fronde, allowed Spain to make a temporary recovery in the early 1650s (Catalonia was reconquered in 1652), in the 1640s she was no longer able to assist her principal allies, the Austrian Habsburgs, in any substantial way, be it militarily or financially: the victory of Nördlingen could not be repeated. This was to have a considerable impact on military developments in Germany. Initially, after 1635, the situation here was favourable for the imperial forces. The French armies were not yet able to intervene on any large scale, though they had managed to secure the allegiance of the most talented German commander in Swedish service, Bernhard von Weimar, and his troops, who were now campaigning in Alsace and southern Germany. But in 1636 a Spanish—imperial offensive inflicted heavy casualties on the French in northern France, and French troops could not make any substantial progress in Germany until 1638. At the end of that year the important fortress of Breisach, controlling the roads on the right bank of the upper Rhine, fell to Bernhard von Weimar. Weimar's death in July 1639 gave Louis XIII complete control not only of Breisach, but also of Weimar's army.

Before the French advance in southern Germany the Swedes, the other principal opponents of the imperial forces, largely had to fend for themselves. The mood among the Swedish soldiers, mostly Germans by birth, but also in the Council of Regency in Stockholm, was one of utmost despondency in 1635–36. It seems likely that Sweden would have been prepared to withdraw from Germany in exchange for some minimum concessions by the Emperor and his allies at this time. However, Sweden still hoped to gain a foothold in Pomerania. The ducal dynasty was expected to die out soon (the last Duke did, in fact, die in 1637). Though claimed by the Brandenburg-Hohenzollern on the basis of a legally indisputable right of inheritance, the duchy seemed an ideal compensation for Sweden's military efforts and, at the same time, a convenient bulwark against any further attempt by the imperial armies to establish themselves on the Baltic coast. More essential even than territorial gains, however, was to find a settlement for the financial demands of the officers and soldiers serving in the Swedish army. An amnesty for Sweden's few remaining allies – the Landgrave of Hesse-Kassel in particular – was at this stage no more than an optional condition.[5]

However, no substantial concessions of any sort were offered to Sweden. It was not only, and not even primarily, the Emperor who was opposed to a more flexible policy, but the princes of northern Germany. Brandenburg feared for her claims to Pomerania, and the Elector of Saxony relished the opportunity to treat his former Swedish ally and protector with contempt. Moreover, any Swedish presence in the Empire seemed to endanger Saxony's claim for the leadership of Protestantism in the Empire, which had been so successfully reasserted in 1634–35.

An extension of the truce with Poland in 1635 (Treaty of Stuhmsdorf), although on unfavourable conditions, freed at least enough Swedish regiments to withstand an attack by imperial and Saxon troops in northern Germany. The battle of Wittstock, which the Swedes won in October 1636, improved their situation and delivered large parts of Brandenburg into their hands, but not until the end of the 1630s did the Swedish troops regain the initiative. By then, the reluctant Oxenstierna had finally ratified an alliance with France (Treaty of Hamburg, 15 March 1638) which supplied Sweden with French subsidies for the next three years. It was, in fact, extended in 1641. In exchange for the subsidies, Sweden had to sacrifice her freedom of decision; she now had to support French policy in Germany, and lost the right to sign a separate peace with the Emperor, a concession to France which was not necessarily in accordance with Sweden's own immediate interests. However, strengthened by the new alliance, Swedish troops beat the Saxon army at Chemnitz in 1639, and managed temporarily to occupy parts of Bohemia.

The situation in Germany had now deteriorated so much for the imperial army that the new Emperor, Ferdinand III (having succeeded his father in February 1637 after his earlier election as King of the Romans in December 1636), decided to convene a full meeting of the Imperial Diet (the first since 1613) in Regensburg. The Estates of the Empire were not only asked to grant new taxes to finance the imperial armies, their meeting was also intended to strengthen the Emperor's hand in peace negotiations with the foreign powers which could no longer be avoided, at least in the case of Sweden. During the Regensburg Diet, which lasted for about a year, from September 1640 to October 1641, the Emperor had to make an important concession to the princes of the Empire. Not only the prince electors should be entitled to send envoys to a future peace conference with Sweden and France, but also all present and former allies of these two powers. Although for the time being the status of these envoys was unspecified – not until August 1645 were all Estates of the Empire finally accepted as participants with full and equal rights in the Westphalian peace conference – this decision was to have momentous consequences.[6] The Estates of the Empire were about to reassert the right to negotiate on their own and to co-operate with foreign powers, which they had relinquished in the Peace of Prague.

However, the meeting of the Diet in Regensburg could not stop the slow erosion of the imperial position in Germany. In July 1641 the new Elector of Brandenburg, Friedrich Wilhelm (the Great Elector), signed a ceasefire with Sweden, as he was neither able to defend himself nor confident of ever receiving any effective imperial protection. In 1642 the Swedes invaded Silesia and Moravia. Though forced to retreat to Saxony, their general Torstensson routed an imperial army commanded by Archduke Leopold Wilhelm in the second battle of Breitenfeld in November. After this defeat Ferdinand's hopes of upholding the Peace of Prague in Germany with only minor concessions to Sweden and, if possible, none at all to France, became increasingly unrealistic.

The way seemed open for serious negotiations on a comprehensive international peace. In fact, in 1643 the first diplomatic envoys arrived in Münster and Osnabrück which had been chosen as the venues for the peace conference. However, negotiations were delayed once again by the oubreak of war between Denmark and Sweden in 1643. This war seemed to offer the Emperor a last chance to defeat the Swedes, but a pre-emptive strike by the Swedish army against Denmark destroyed these hopes within the year. Denmark had to sign a humiliating peace in 1645. She lost the islands of Gotland and Ösel (the latter off the Estonian coast) and the Bishoprics of Verden and Bremen also remained under Swedish control, though this was not confirmed until 1648. Ferdinand III's attempt to support Denmark by sending 20,000 men under the command of General Gallas was a total failure; Gallas returned from Holstein in 1644 with only one-third of his troops. The remainder had been killed, or taken prisoner, or simply deserted, as it had proved impossible to provide them with sufficient supplies.

The next year the Swedes attacked imperial positions in Bohemia, helped by a simultaneous offensive by the Prince of

Transylvania, their ally, in Hungary. At Jankov (Jankau), south-east of Prague, Torstensson beat the imperial army decisively. It did not really recover from this blow until the end of the war, and the Emperor's problems were exacerbated by the French advance in southern Germany. The French troops had already won a great victory against the Spanish at Rocroi in northern France in 1643. In August 1645 a combined French, Hessian and Swedish corps routed an army made up of imperial and Bavarian soldiers at Allerheim, north of Ulm. In September 1645 the Elector of Saxony signed a ceasefire and subsequently a separate peace with Sweden, and Bavaria's further support for the imperial cause also seemed doubtful.[7] Substantial concessions to the French and Swedes could no longer be avoided.

The Peace of Westphalia

On 11 June 1645 the French and Swedish envoys submitted their crowns' propositions for the future peace in Münster and Osnabrück (Münster was the venue for the negotiations between France and the Emperor and the other Catholic princes and Estates, Osnabrück for those between the Emperor and Sweden and her Protestant allies). On 25 September the Emperor's plenipotentiaries submitted their reply. In the meantime, all Estates and princes of the Holy Roman Empire had been invited to take part in the peace conference, including those still loyal to the Emperor. Thus the negotiations were to be at one and the same time an international conference, and a meeting of the Estates of the Empire according to the traditional procedure of the sessions of the Imperial Diet, except that during the negotiations Protestants and Catholics were largely organised separately, in the *Corpus Evangelicorum* and the *Corpus Catholicorum* respectively, in particular in all matters relating to religious questions.[8] The full participation of the Estates of the Empire meant that German 'internal' affairs – religious as well as constitutional disputes – which Ferdinand III would have preferred to keep outside the scope of the conference, would be among the principal issues in Münster and Osnabrück.

Serious negotiations did not really get under way until the autumn of 1645, in particular after November 1645 when the imperial *Obersthofmeister* (Lord Steward) and President of the Imperial Privy Council, Count Trauttmannsdorff, arrived in Münster. Trauttmannsdorff had been instructed by the Emperor to make far-reaching concessions, if necessary, especially to Sweden. In religious matters, that is for all problems related to the status of ecclesiastical possessions and property as well as for the confessional allegiance of the population, the year 1618 was to provide the standard for a settlement if required (instead of November 1627, the key date according to the Peace of Prague). The Duchy of Pomerania was to be ceded in its entirety to Sweden in addition to Rostock and Wismar and parts of the Bishopric of Bremen. The Habsburg possessions in Alsace were, if necessary, to be ceded to France, though France was not to be granted membership as an Estate in the Imperial Diet. These conditions were only to be conceded when everything else failed, but they show that Ferdinand was prepared to make serious sacrifices to attain peace. The most explosive issue of the conference from the imperial point of view – the war between France and Spain – was rather slurred over in Trauttmannsdorff's instructions. Spain was to be persuaded to cede some towns and districts in the Low Countries and along the Pyrenees to France, but otherwise it was officially assumed that the alliance between the Emperor and Spain would be maintained, and that France for her part would be prepared to abandon her Portuguese and Catalan allies. This assumption proved, predictably, to be less than realistic.[9] The Spanish plenipotentiary in Münster, Count Peñaranda, who preferred a settlement with the Dutch to a settlement with France, soon fell out with Trauttmannsdorff, who, in his opinion, was about to become a traitor to the common Habsburg cause.

In fact, driving the two branches of the Habsburg dynasty apart became one of France's principal objectives in the negotiations in Münster. This was despite the fact that

135

Richelieu – and later Mazarin and the French diplomats in Münster as well – would have preferred a universal peace providing for Spain to cede substantial territory along the eastern border of France and possibly in Italy and Catalonia too.[10] But this solution turned out be unachievable. In 1646 it looked briefly as if Spain could indeed be forced to make far-reaching concessions; according to Mazarin's plans the Spanish Infanta, María Teresa, was to marry the infant Louis XIV. The French King was to receive the Spanish Netherlands, or at least some of the most valuable provinces in the Spanish Low Countries and perhaps the Franche Comté as well, as a dowry. But with the death of the Spanish Crown Prince, Baltasar Carlos, in the same year the stakes involved in a marriage between María Teresa, now heiress to the Spanish empire, and Louis XIV became too high. Such a marriage would have made Louis the heir presumptive to the entire Spanish monarchy. The marriage project had to be abandoned and was not revived until 1659.

Moreover, in 1647 the Spanish position improved to some extent: Spanish troops managed to lift the siege of Lerida, a key fortress in Catalonia, by French forces in June; and even earlier, in January 1647, the Dutch Republic signed a truce with Spain which was transformed into a permanent peace one year later. Mazarin's plans for extensive territorial expansion in Flanders, which could not be kept entirely secret, had considerably strengthened the influence of the peace party on Dutch politics and thus facilitated a compromise. This was a great success for Spanish diplomacy and a personal triumph for Count Peñaranda, the Spanish representative in Münster.

Despite the ever more desperate state of Spanish crown finances, a serious revolt in Naples in July 1647, and the crushing defeat that French troops inflicted on the Spanish army of Flanders at Lens in August 1648, Spain was now no longer prepared to make major concessions to France, especially as Mazarin's hold on power in France seemed to be becoming ever more tenuous. From January 1648 unrest grew visibly in Paris and the French provinces. It gained momentum in May with protest declarations by the *parlement* of Paris and the other *cours souverains* (the highest law courts) and took the form of open riots and street fights in Paris in late August. Under these circumstances Spain finally lost interest in a peace with France involving any major, and, as it now seemed, unnecessary concessions.[11]

The best Mazarin could hope for, therefore, was a separate peace with the Emperor. The ultimate objective, however, remained the same: to destroy once and for all the foundations of what was perceived as the dangerous and tyrannical Spanish hegemony in Europe. Ultimately this Spanish hegemony was to be replaced, at least indirectly, by a French one,[12] though Richelieu, who had developed detailed plans for a future peace, saw this French supremacy as no more than a natural precondition for the stability of the new European order. France was to act as the indispensable protector of the many small German and Italian princes against Habsburg oppression, being the only power capable of safeguarding their autonomy.

The principal instruction for the French envoys to Münster, dated 30 September 1643 (the main clauses had been drafted by Richelieu before his death), show clearly that France wanted to destroy Habsburg influence in central Europe by strengthening the autonomy of individual princes in Germany. Two federations or collective alliances were to be created under French protection, one in Italy and one in Germany, and any future settlement was to be defended by all members of these federations who were to act as guardians and guarantors of the peace.[13] In the German case such a solution would have meant that the present system of security, which was provided by the institutions and laws of the Empire, would be replaced or at least superseded by a new one centred very much on France. This was to ensure that the Habsburgs could no longer mobilise the resources of the Empire. This was particularly important as Richelieu and his successor were convinced that it would not be possible permanently to divide the two branches of the House of Habsburg, even if the Emperor were to sign a separate peace and give assurances that he would no longer support Spain.

For Richelieu this system of collective security had assumed priority over any territorial conquests, though this was probably not true to the same extent for his successor, Mazarin. Nevertheless, French control over Alsace, or at least over the Habsburg possessions in Alsace, including the important fortress of Breisach on the other side of the Rhine in the Breisgau, was seen as an indispensable precondition for peace. The French instruction of 1643 also mentioned the Franche Comté, Luxemburg and the county of Artois as territories which Spain was to cede to France, in addition to Navarra and Roussillon. Later, in 1645, it was further envisaged that Lorraine should be retained by France, and that all principalities and dominions between Lorraine and the Rhine should be permanently controlled by the French King as their protector.[14] However, the principal purpose of these conquests was probably strategic. This is clearly apparent in the demand for control over key fortresses such as Breisach and Philippsburg or Ehrenbreitstein. France wanted to drive a wedge between the Habsburg dominions in southern Germany and the Spanish Netherlands in order to cut Spanish supply lines along the Rhine, and also with the intention of preventing the Austrian Habsburgs from supporting their Spanish cousins. Moreover, France was to achieve the capacity to intervene militarily in Germany whenever this seemed desirable.

The French soon found, to their chagrin, that these far-reaching plans were generally unpopular among the German princes. Neither did their demand, supported by Sweden, that the Emperor's rights should be so drastically reduced that he would have become a mere figurehead, find much favour. In their joint proposal of June 1645, the two crowns demanded that in future no successor to an Emperor should be elected during the latter's lifetime – this would have made it impossible for the Habsburgs to use the imperial authority to influence elections. Furthermore, they proposed that in future, decisions of the Imperial Diet should be valid only if they were unanimous. This would have paralysed the Diet and, given the further demand of the allies that all imperial decisions were to be approved by the Diet, transformed the Empire into a mere shadow without any political significance.

Confronted with German resistance to such proposals, the French delegates complained that the princes and Estates of the Empire did not know what was good for them, even when it was presented to them on a silver tray. They loved their country far too much (compared with the Italian states 'ceux-ci sont beaucoup plus touchez de l'amour de leur patrie', as one of the French envoys remarked); and put the territorial integrity of the Empire and the preservation of its constitution above their own interests.[15] In fact, the German princes, or at least the less powerful among them, recognised well enough that it was not in their interests for the political system of the Empire to be totally paralysed. This would only have replaced one master, the Emperor, whose power they now hoped to be able to limit and control, by two new masters, France and Sweden, who could not so easily be contained.

Trauttmannsdorff was therefore able to reject French and Swedish demands for a radical revision of the imperial constitution relatively easily at the conference.[16] Sweden insisted on these points more strongly and consistently than France, partly because it was not quite as difficult to win the support of the Protestant princes who were allied with Sweden for an anti-imperial position than that of most of the Catholic ones. These, with the exception of the Archbishop of Trier (until 1645 the Emperor's prisoner) and a few others, still saw the Emperor as their natural protector. Sweden wanted watertight assurances that no Emperor would ever be able to threaten the Swedish position and interests in the Baltic again, and the best guarantee of this seemed to be a settlement which strengthened the liberties of the German princes and Estates. But during the course of the negotiations Sweden modified her more extreme proposals because it turned out to be difficult enough to gain the territorial concessions and financial compensation for the Swedish army upon which the Swedish chancellor Oxenstierna insisted.[17] Sweden's demand for religious toleration to be granted to Protestants in Austria and Bohemia, which would have allowed the exiled noblemen serving in the Swedish army to return home, had also to be abandoned. Trauttmannsdorff was adamant in rejecting these demands. He declared that his master, Ferdinand III, would rather lose his crown and see his sons slaughtered by Swedish soldiers in front of his own eyes than revise the religious and political settlement imposed on the Habsburg hereditary dominions in the 1620s.[18] As Sweden could expect little serious support from France in her fight for the partial re-establishment of Protestantism in the Habsburg territories, her emissaries had, in the end, to acknowledge defeat in this matter. The Protestant exiles from Bohemia and Austria who had hoped that Sweden would manage to insert a clause in the treaties providing for religious toleration and for the restitution of their confiscated goods, or at least for compensation, came away empty-handed, despite the fact that when the peace was signed in October 1648, Swedish troops were occupying large parts of Bohemia, including the New Town of Prague and the Hradshin, the imperial residence in the Bohemian capital.

On the other hand, Sweden did not greatly care about the Franco-Spanish conflict; a settlement in Germany was quite sufficient to satisfy Swedish interests. But with the conflict with Spain unresolved, it was impossible for France to establish the system of collective security envisaged by Richelieu. Nevertheless, Mazarin as well as Oxenstierna continued to press for an arrangement which would have obliged not only the principal participants in the conference, but each and every prince and Estate of the Empire to uphold all clauses of the peace, if necessary by force of arms. This would in all likelihood have rendered the jurisdiction of the imperial law courts obsolete as a means of settling conflicts in the Empire, and would greatly have facilitated outside intervention in the affairs of the Empire. The imperial envoys tried to counter this proposition by demanding that the Estates of France and Sweden take a solemn pledge to uphold the peace in exactly the same way as the Estates and princes of the Empire.[19] But this attempt to assign to the Swedish Riksdag and the French *parlements* and *États generaux* and *provinciaux* a role similar to that of the Imperial Diet in Germany was bound to fail. The constitutional and political situation was too different in the two kingdoms from that which had developed in Germany. And the instruction for the French envoys (1643) had already firmly rejected any claim that the French opposition at home be granted the same rights that France claimed for the rebellious Portuguese and Catalans, or for the princes of the Empire.[20]

In the end, however, the German princes failed to support the idea of a collective security system safeguarding the provisions of the peace, which would have obliged each one of them to stand security for these provisions in case of a violation. The treaties as signed in 1648 did contain a clause which called upon the signatories to restore the rights of injured parties – in so far as these were based upon the peace – if necessary by force of arms (IPO XVII, 6 and IPM § 116). However, this could be interpreted as giving at most France and Sweden, as principal signatories of the treaties, the right to intervene in German affairs, without granting every prince of the Empire the right to start a new war, allegedly in defence of the peace settlement. For ultimately the treaties were signed by the imperial plenipotentiaries and only a select number of delegates from the Estates of the Empire. The others were free to add their signatures too, but whether they did so or not, the peace automatically applied to them. Thus the signatories to the treaties were the foreign powers and the Empire.[21] The Estates were therefore not truly independent and sovereign participants in the diplomatic transactions but rather, next to the Emperor, representatives of the body of the whole Empire.

In fact, although the treaties explicitly confirmed the right of the princes to conclude alliances among themselves and with powers outside the Empire, thus implicitly also asserting their right to pursue their own foreign policy and even to maintain armed forces (all these rights had been severely curtailed by the Peace of Prague), such alliances had to remain compatible with the loyalty all princes owed to the Emperor and the Empire and were not to disturb the peace among the

Estates of Germany. In theory at least, the autonomy of the princes therefore remained limited; in legal terms they were not fully sovereign. Moreover, long before 1618, the princes had sought other rulers as allies within and without the confines of the Empire. Admittedly this had been in an age when even towns subject to a territorial lord had been members of federations and alliances such as the Hanseatic League; the right to conclude alliances with other political powers had not yet become a hallmark of sovereignty to the same extent as it did later.[22] On the other hand, the right which the treaties granted the princes and Estates to participate in formulating the official foreign policy of the Empire, as they had done in Münster and Osnabrück, proved difficult to enforce after 1648. At later international conferences, as opposed to the Westphalian peace conference, the Empire as a body politic was *de facto* represented by the Emperor's delegates alone in most cases, although some of the more powerful princes sent their own envoys to represent their principalities. But these had little influence on imperial policy.[23]

The peace which, after considerable delays, was finally signed simultaneously in Münster and Osnabrück on 24 October 1648 was in many ways a remarkably conservative document. After attempts by Sweden and France to introduce drastic changes in the constitution of the Empire had failed, a return to the *status quo ante* and to old established customs and prescriptive rights became the principle guiding the settlement of most conflicts, and certainly as far as the purely German side of the provisions was concerned. In fact, both Heinz Duchhardt and Andreas Osiander have recently pointed out that the arrangements agreed on in Münster and Osnabrück differed from the results of the great international peace conferences of the late seventeenth and in particular the eighteenth centuries, in that they were not based on a 'programmatic' consensus (Osiander), but rather on established law, custom and precedent – all subject to interpretation, of course. A programmatic consensus would have implied pragmatic solutions, if necessary disregarding established legal rights, and guided solely by the wish to create an evenly balanced political equilibrium, a 'balance of power' allowing the principal participants to feel militarily and politically secure for the future. Certainly the idea of some sort of equilibrium, and even more of security, was not absent from the minds of the diplomats in Münster and Osnabrück, but essentially it was the rule of law itself which was to ensure that these principles were realised.[24]

The rule of law, the ideal proclaimed by the (often Protestant) legal scholars and lawyers of the period before the outbreak of war, became the fundamental principle governing political life in the Empire more than ever after 1648. This is not to say that innovations which disregarded established customs and rights were avoided altogether. The eighth electoral dignity created for the Count Palatine, who was restored to his dominions in the Lower Palatinate, in compensation for his original title which the Duke of Bavaria now held, was such an innovation. Furthermore, Western Pomerania (Vorpommern), as well as Bremen and Verden and the town of Wismar (in Mecklenburg), were ceded to Sweden (as imperial fiefs), which also received an indemnity of five million Taler, to be paid in several instalments by the Holy Roman Empire and its Estates; the money was to enable the Swedish crown to pay off the officers and soldiers in Swedish service at the end of the war. The Habsburg possessions in southern Alsace and their rather ill-defined rights of suzerainty in northern Alsace went to France (with full sovereignty for France in order to prevent the French King from becoming a member of the Imperial Diet); there were certainly no established legal titles for these territorial changes. Slightly different was the case of the three Bishoprics of Metz, Toul and Verdun which to all intents and purposes had been under French control since the 1550s, but which now became an integral part of the kingdom of France.

Other clauses of the peace provided for the cession of the Bishoprics of Minden and Halberstadt to Brandenburg (as compensation for western Pomerania – only eastern

Pomerania passed by normal right of inheritance to the Hohenzollern), with an expectancy for the Bishopric of Magdeburg (the secularisation of these ecclesiastical principalities was accepted by the signatories). Bavaria was confirmed in the possession of the Upper Palatinate, and Saxony in the possession of Upper and Lower Lusatia in accordance with the provisions of the Peace of Prague. The sovereignty of the Dutch Republic and the Helvetian Confederation was asserted, but both states had already been *de facto* independent of the Empire in 1618, and in the Dutch case all impediments to full Dutch sovereignty had in fact just been removed by the Dutch–Spanish treaty of Münster signed in January 1648.

Otherwise, the provisions of the peace were cautious enough. Admittedly, all existing rights of the princes and Estates were declared inviolate and their territorial superiority (*ius territorii et superioritatis*, 'Landeshoheit' or, as the French translations called this right, 'droit de souverainité', perhaps a deliberate overstatement) was affirmed in strong terms (e.g. IPO VIII, 1; V, 30). Moreover, in future the Emperor was to take no major political decision without the consent of the Estates obtained in the sessions of the Imperial Diet. Thus the Westphalian peace did undoubtedly change the political balance in the Empire in favour of the princes; nevertheless, those of the Emperor's rights which had not been expressly limited or declared void, remained unspecified (in particular his prerogatives as supreme judge in all legal disputes and as highest liege lord, *Lehensherr*, in the Empire); they were not individually enumerated.[25] The Emperor was thus given some leeway for a wider interpretation of these prerogatives once the political situation was more favourable for him than it was in 1648.

Of course, any return to the dominant position he had achieved in 1635 in the Peace of Prague was out of the question after 1648 but, as many principalities, not to mention the counts, knights and *Reichsstädte*, were really too small and weak to exploit the rights which the treaties had granted them (they were, for example, hardly able to develop their own foreign policy on a European scale), they had to seek the protection and patronage of a greater power. And for many of them the Emperor remained the most natural patron – certainly for the Catholics, but also for an increasing number of Protestants. As opposed to the power of foreign monarchs, his authority was now strictly circumscribed by custom and law. The very limitations which the peace of 1648 had imposed on him in the long run made him more attractive as a protector of the weaker Estates of the Empire than, for example, the King of France. Thus the Peace of Münster and Osnabrück did not entirely rule out a re-strengthening of imperial influence and authority at some later stage, as the final decades of the seventeenth and the early eighteenth centuries were to show.[26]

Among the most important clauses of the peace were those which were intended to settle the religious conflict once and for all. Following the precedent set by the Peace of Prague, a key date was introduced as a standard for the resolution of all confessional disputes over property as well as over the confessional allegiance of the population. However, this was to be 1624, not 1627 as stipulated in 1635. The Edict of Restitution was consigned to the dust heap of history for good. In fact, in future all confessional disputes were to be solved in the Imperial Diet not by a majority decision, but in an 'amicable' way by negotiations between the bodies of the Catholic and of the Protestant Estates, the *Corpus Catholicum* and the *Corpus Evangelicorum*, as had already been the practice in Münster and Osnabrück. Although this procedure was rarely resorted to after 1648, the mere existence of the legal option of proceeding in such a way obliged Catholics and Protestants to seek compromise solutions acceptable to both sides. Furthermore, the Reformed Protestants, the Calvinists, now enjoyed the same rights as the Lutherans. Finally, religious minorities, for example Lutherans living in a Catholic principality, were now entitled to practise their religion freely if they had done so in 1624: an important provision which severely curtailed the *ius reformandi*, the ecclesiastical government of the territorial rulers, at least in theory. In the Habsburg dominions, however, where the Counter-Reformation had already been well under way in 1624, Protestantism remained outlawed, as has already been mentioned. The only exception was Silesia where Protestants obtained a limited toleration.

A final assessment of the Peace of Westphalia is not easy. By and large, the treaties defused those problems which had contributed so much to the outbreak of the war that had engulfed most of Europe after 1618. The age of religious wars was definitely over in Germany, though confessional loyalties remained politically important. Nor was there to be another war provoked by fundamental conflicts about the interpretation of the imperial constitution. Admittedly it would have required a certain degree of optimism to foresee in 1648 that a lasting and final solution of the major problems had really been achieved. The presence of foreign troops on German soil, for example, remained a cause of major concern. It took about two years before the Swedish garrisons in Germany were finally dissolved after the Estates of the Empire had managed to pay the indemnity which Sweden had been promised. The Spanish garrison in Frankenthal, in the Palatinate, was withdrawn even later and the same was true for some French regiments and those units commanded by the pro-Spanish Duke of Lorraine stationed along the Rhine.[27]

In the second half of the 1650s the Northern War (1654/55–60) in which Sweden fought against Poland and later, at various stages, against Denmark, Brandenburg and imperial troops as well, posed a threat to the peace settlement of 1648. At the same time a possible intervention of the Emperor in the continuing war between Spain and France threatened to involve Germany once more in the political conflicts of western Europe. The fact that all attempts to end the war between France and Spain had failed in 1645–48 undoubtedly contained the seeds of future conflicts. In 1648, the imperial delegates had signed the peace very reluctantly without Spain, under pressure from the princes of the Empire and in particular Bavaria, abandoning the Spanish Habsburgs to their fate. But it was far from clear that the Emperor was prepared to honour those clauses of the Westphalian treaties which were to prevent him from assisting Spain in her war effort. Concern over the links between Madrid and Vienna increased in the late 1650s and in 1658 the Federation of the Rhine (Rheinbund) was founded under the leadership of the Prince Elector of Mainz, Johann Philipp von Schönborn, and under French protection to keep the Empire neutral even against the Emperor's wishes in the last stages of the Franco-Spanish war. In the Federation Protestant and Catholic princes co-operated; this in itself demonstrated that many of the controversies dominating the Thirty Years War had receded into the background, but it also showed that there was still a widespread fear in the later 1650s that the peace settlement of 1648 would collapse.

This was not to be; the treaties of Münster and Osnabrück proved to be a lasting achievement as far as Germany was concerned. However, matters were different outside the Empire, where peace had not been established in 1648 and continued to be elusive in later decades, as the almost permanent armed conflicts of the period 1672–1714 were to show. But these later wars were not, as a rule, mainly caused by disputes in the Empire, as had largely been the case in 1618. Not until 1740, when the male line of the House of Habsburg became extinct, or in fact 1756 (the outbreak of the Seven Years War) did disputes in Germany become a major cause of a large-scale European war again. Thus, while the treaties of Münster and Osnabrück provided a considerable degree of political stability and domestic peace for Germany, this was true for Europe only in as far as internal German disputes were a potential cause of European wars.

Once France had managed to defeat Spain (1659), containing the Bourbon monarchy soon became a major issue of European politics, and ultimately the central problem. The treaties of 1648 provided no solution for this question. On the contrary, the vagueness of those clauses of the Treaty of Münster which were to settle the future status of the Burgundian Circle (the Spanish dominions in the Low Countries and the Franche Comté, all officially still part of the Empire) pointed to crucial shortcomings of the arrangements agreed on in 1648. Moreover, the equally vague provisions relating to northern Alsace and the fiefs dependent on the three

Bishoprics of Metz, Toul and Verdun, which were officially ceded to France in 1648, as well as the clauses dealing with Lorraine, were all to provide rich material for future disputes. The very vagueness of these clauses was guaranteed to provoke a less than scrupulous ruler, as Louis XIV turned out to be, to exploit the legal loopholes of the peace to enlarge his own dominions at the expense of his neighbours.

The pronounced legalism of the treaties of 1648 and the limitations imposed on the authority of the Emperor certainly did not destroy the Empire, or even bring it close to destruction as many German historians claimed in the nineteenth and early twentieth centuries.[28] But the Peace of Westphalia certainly made the political machinery of the Empire even more cumbersome than in the past. In competition with more centralised political systems, such as the French absolute monarchy, the Empire was at a clear disadvantage. And the fact that most European wars of the later seventeenth and the eighteenth centuries were fought on German soil, often with disastrous consequences for the regions immediately affected, shows some of the shortcomings of the arrangements of 1648, at least from a German perspective.

The Thirty Years War had begun as a German war – though it was to become much more than that. It was to end with a peace settlement which was genuinely European in origin, but ultimately German in scope; a peace treaty drafted by Sweden and France as much as by the Emperor and the German princes. It was to be a fundamental law of the Empire, the most important one after 1555. In spite of the manifest shortcomings of the treaties of Münster and Osnabrück, as years went by, virtually all European powers came to see them as a central element of the European system of states. Only the Pope expressly rejected the peace in 1648, because it made far too many concessions to the Protestants. He published a declaration of protest against it, but his objections had already been anticipated by the signatories of the treaties, who declared them to be of no consequence whatsoever (IPO XVII, § 3).[29] The other European powers did not question the legal validity of the peace during the century and a half following the conference at Münster and Osnabrück, even when they tried covertly or overtly to modify the territorial or other arrangements of the treaties, as France did, for example, in the late seventeenth century. The constitution of the Empire as established in 1648 was seen as a fundamental precondition for the security of all European states, or at least, of all of Germany's neighbours. Only this constitution seemed to ensure that no German Emperor, or in fact any foreign monarch capable of imposing his will on Germany from outside, would be able to dominate the rest of Europe as the House of Habsburg had threatened to do in the late 1620s and again, though to a lesser extent, in the years following the battle of Nördlingen.

6

STATE FINANCE AND THE STRUCTURE OF WARFARE

The Financial and Logistical Limits of Warfare

The Thirty Years War was one of the longest and, in its later stages, most indecisive military contests in the history of early modern Europe. When peace finally came in 1648, the principal belligerents signed the treaties of Münster and Osnabrück not so much because they had achieved their real objectives or because they were forced to acknowledge total defeat, but because they were too exhausted to continue fighting, at least on the same scale as during the past decades. This was certainly true for the Emperor, but France, though in a somewhat more advantageous position from a purely military point of view, was also threatened by domestic turmoil and faced bankrupty in 1648. Peace with at least one of her principal enemies was therefore imperative. The Spanish did go on fighting against France until 1659, and against Portugal, which had seceded from the Spanish monarchy in 1640, until 1668. But they could not have done so had they not ended the war with the Dutch in 1648 by recognising Dutch sovereignty. Perhaps the Swedish army in Germany came closest to achieving all-out victory during the last years of the war. However, even the Swedes found that their forces were overstretched and their resources too limited to avoid making major concessions at the peace conference.

In fact, it remains remarkable that very few battles of the Thirty Years War can really be called decisive. The battle of the

White Mountain (1620), which brought about the total victory of the Counter-Reformation in Bohemia and Moravia, and to a lesser extent the battle of Nördlingen (1634), which ensured the survival of Catholicism in large parts of Germany as well as the survival of the Empire as a monarchy headed by a Habsburg ruler, can perhaps be so described. The same could perhaps be said about the Swedish victories of Breitenfeld (1631) and Jankov (1645). Breitenfeld put paid to the Counter-Reformation policy enshrined in the Edict of Restitution – no serious attempts were made to revive this policy in later years at least in northern Germany – and Jankov forced the Emperor to accept Swedish and French demands for a comprehensive settlement superseding the Peace of Prague signed ten years earlier. Nevertheless, neither Breitenfeld nor Jankov were followed up by swift campaigns which destroyed once and for all the enemy's capability to rebuild his army and strike back.

In fact, during the last phase of the war, after 1635, the capacity of nearly all armies to mount major offensive operations with enough troops to besiege and take important fortified places, and to conquer large stretches of enemy territory permanently, diminished considerably.[1] The number of troops deployed in any battle tended to become markedly smaller. At Breitenfeld, for example, admittedly the largest battle on German soil during the entire war,[2] about 41,000 Swedish and Saxon soldiers had fought 31,000 imperial soldiers. After 1635, however, the Swedes as well as the Emperor were rarely able to send more than 15,000 men and were hardly ever capable of sending more than 20,000 men into battle at any given time. Outside Germany the number of troops participating in individual battles remained greater. At Rocroi (1643), for example, 27,000 Spanish troops fought 23,000 French soldiers, but there the devastation caused by warfare was generally not as extensive as in many regions of Germany, so that supplies could more easily be organised.[3]

Of course, the overall size of armies remained much greater. The different imperial armies, for example, numbered about 70,000 men in 1644, including the troops under Bavarian command and the other allies of the Emperor (but excluding the Elector of Saxony's troops and imperial garrisons in Hungary) – a strength which they were to maintain approximately until the end of the war.[4] The various French armies, including those fighting in Italy and along the Pyrenees, were theoretically much stronger still – about 170,000 infantry and 42,000 cavalry according to official figures of June 1639, for example. But this strength existed only on paper. The actual size of the army was always much smaller than official figures suggest, probably by as much as 45 per cent and for some units by as much as 70 per cent. Certainly a quota of at least 30 per cent must be discounted from official figures for the royal army as a whole, even during those phases of a campaign, in spring, when no serious losses had yet occured due to fighting or a lack of supplies.[5]

The real problem, however, was not even the difference between the official and the actual size of regiments and other units, as demonstrated here in the French example, but one of logistics and finance. In most cases the financial resources of the early seventeenth-century states proved to be as inadequate for achieving the far-reaching political and strategic objectives pursued in the war as did the inchoate structure of military logistics. These two factors – the lack of money and of supplies, or at least of the right amount of supplies in the right place – were largely responsible for the indecisive nature of warfare as well as for the enormous regional destruction caused by the war and the prominent part played by 'private' military entrepreneurs during the war.[6]

Warfare was continually hampered by the shortage of funds. Ever larger areas had to be occupied by garrison troops with a combined strength of several tens of thousands of men to provide money and supplies for a comparatively small mobile fighting army, often not more than about 15,000 soldiers. Many principalities and provinces were so devastated that it was impossible to requisition larger quantities of food or collect the same amount of taxes and contributions as during the earlier years of the war.[7] Even if the necessary cash could be raised and provisions bought, it proved very difficult to get them to the place where they were needed. Problems of transport were almost insurmountable, unless grain and other stores were deposited beforehand along the roads along which the troops marched.

The Spanish had, indeed, developed such a system for getting their troop reinforcements from northern Italy to Flanders in the later sixteenth century. Without relying on actual magazines controlled by the army itself, they managed to make the villages and towns along the 'Spanish Road' set aside provisions in advance. This meant that food did not have to be requisitioned or collected laboriously when the troops arrived, but could be distributed straight away at the predetermined resting places of the troops, the so called *étapes*. As an alternative, frequently used in later years, the Spanish crown employed private contractors to provide the necessary goods at the *étapes*.[8] The system worked reasonably well, but then, at least before 1618, the Spanish troops marched along a predetermined route through areas normally not devasted by war, where supplies could be bought at reasonable prices by the contractors, or collected by the local authorities. When the French tried to organise a similar system of supply for their own troops fighting in Germany and along the border with the Spanish Netherlands in the 1630s and 1640s, they were much less successful. Sabotage by provincial and local authorities, inadequate co-ordination of the efforts of the military and the civilian administrations, the rather haphazard communication between the government departments in Paris and the military commanders in the field, and the general lack of funds all greatly diminished the efficiency of the system. These problems were not really overcome until the reign of Louis XIV, after 1660. Even then, most of the provisions for troops continued to be requisitioned in the areas they occupied, especially when they were in enemy territory. Before 1648 most armies did not even try to establish anything like the French *étapes*.[9]

Financial and logistical problems constantly prevented military commanders from achieving their strategic objectives. Whatever military innovations the 1620s and early 1630s may have brought, the later years of the war, the years after

Nördlingen, saw a stagnation in techniques of warfare. In the long-drawn-out war of attrition which the military and political contest had now become, the main concern was simply to find enough provisions for one's own troops and to deny the enemy access to areas where he could feed his men and levy contributions. The cavalry became the dominant arm of service outside the garrisons. Mounted units, though needing more supplies, in particular fodder for the animals, were able to requisition food over a wider area and could move more quickly to regions which were not yet totally devastated. In Germany many armies now had as many, or more, horsemen than foot-soldiers, whereas in earlier years of the war the cavalry had normally made up between 15 and 25 per cent, or at most 35 per cent, of the fighting forces.[10]

The paralysing impact of logistical problems rather qualifies the significance of tactical improvements made during the war as indicators of a long-term 'military revolution' going back, in its origins, to the wars of the later sixteenth century and allegedly culminating in the reforms undertaken by Gustavus Adolphus.[11] Gustavus Adolphus's biographer, Michael Roberts, has argued that the King of Sweden managed to perfect the improvements accomplished in the Dutch army during the war against Spain before 1609. His infantry was better trained and better disciplined than usual, achieved a higher firing power and was deployed on the battlefield in comparatively small units only about six lines deep. The best infantry of the day, the Spanish, had traditionally fought in massive *tercios*, square formations of up to 30 lines deep. The smaller Swedish infantry squadrons (about 400 men), grouped into larger units (brigades) of about 1,600–2,000 men each, ensured a much higher degree of mobility and flexibility on the battlefield. Moreover, the firing power of the infantry brigades was reinforced by light, mobile artillery pieces; similar artillery units were attached to the cavalry. In fact, the effectiveness of the cavalry was also enhanced by supplementing its firing power with detachments of musketeers following the horse regiments into battle. Moreover, and Michael Roberts has strongly emphasised this point, Gustavus Adolphus revived the offensive role of the cavalry on the battlefield. Whereas it had become customary for horsemen to attack infantry units by trotting up to them, discharging their pistols, and, more often than not, retreating, the King of Sweden had them attack at full gallop with drawn sabre or sword, perhaps after an initial volley of shots.[12] In ordering this change of tactics he was apparently inspired by the Polish horse regiments which he had encountered on the battlefields of eastern Europe.

More recent research, however, has shown that the Swedish horse never entirely abandoned the *caracole*, the attack with firearms at a comparatively slow trot; in fact, attack at full gallop with the *arm blanche* as the principal or only weapon did not become customary in the Swedish cavalry until the 1680s.[13] Moreover even Tilly, Gustavus Adolphus's opponent at Breitenfeld, though trained in the Spanish army, was not as outdated in his tactical approach as has sometimes been maintained. He relied far less on massive, unwieldy infantry squares than the cliché of the determined and courageous but old-fashioned and unimaginative Catholic general would suggest.[14] What did give the Swedish army an undeniable advantage was the combined operation of infantry with artillery, and of cavalry with both musketeers and mobile artillery, but of course even this innovation was soon imitated by others such as Wallenstein's imperial army at Lützen. In any case, the tactical improvements achieved by Gustavus Adolphus could not change the nature of warfare as such. They might be decisive in winning a battle like Breitenfeld, but to win a war more was required. In the first place what a commander needed to achieve victory at a strategic level was money.

Finance and the Role of the Military Entrepreneur in Germany

The financial resources of the various states had been a crucial influence on the war right from the start. When the rising in Bohemia challenged Ferdinand II's power in his own dominions, he found it extremely difficult to raise enough money for an effective campaign against the new rulers of Bohemia. However, the financial problems of the Bohemian Estates were soon just as great as Ferdinand's, and in this contest between the financially insolvent those powers with access to enough cash and credit facilities for an energetic intervention dominated. After ten years of peace in the Netherlands, Spain's resources were still comparatively ample and Ferdinand also managed to gain as his ally the richest German territorial prince, the Duke of Bavaria, who had organised the financial administration of his territory more effectively than most other rulers in the Empire. Because both Spain and Bavaria were able to cover a relatively high percentage of the cost of their armed forces out of their state revenues at this stage, they were able to maintain civilian control over these forces.[15]

The Emperor's position was less advantageous in this respect. Although he received Spanish and Papal subsidies,[16] and could rely on troops paid for by other princes, he resorted to a desperate measure to finance the reconquest of Bohemia and liquidate his debts afterwards: the coins issued by the public mints were drastically debased. In Bohemia the debasement of the coinage culminated in the creation of a syndicate of financiers and noble magnates in February 1622 – Wallenstein and the Protestant banker Hans de Witte were both leading members – which controlled the royal mint and directed the coinage manipulations. If they did not benefit directly from fraudulent practices, and this point is controversial, Wallenstein and the other noblemen who were his partners were at least able to buy confiscated estates in Bohemia at discount prices and pay for them with debased coins. These manipulations, which were also undertaken by other rulers during the early years of the war, compounded the inflationary trend which had already existed before 1618. The result was hyperinflation, the so-called Kipper- und Wipperzeit (starting in about 1618, gaining momentum in 1620–22, and not overcome until 1623), which severely disrupted trade and commerce, and was particularly damaging to foreign merchants from countries with harder currencies trying to sell their goods in Germany.[17]

The monetary manipulations of the early 1620s could not easily be repeated. Ferdinand, still lacking the necessary revenues or credit facilities to wage war on any large scale, later had to employ a military entrepreneur to provide him with both. When Ferdinand decided to recruit a major army of his own in 1625 he entrusted this task to the man who had already been a member of the Bohemian coinage syndicate and who was to become the most famous of the military contractors of the Thirty Years War, Wallenstein. Because of his vast fortune, mostly accumulated since 1620, and his ability to raise credit, Wallenstein seemed predestined for this task. His connection with the Calvinist banker de Witte, who hailed from Antwerp and was able to mobilise the resources of international finance for Wallenstein's army, was certainly one of the essential foundations of Wallenstein's success.[18]

It was a general practice of the time to leave the recruiting of individual regiments and companies to officers who were military entrepreneurs, treating war as a commercial transaction in a manner of speaking, as well as commanders. They advanced the sums which were necessary to recruit, arm and equip soldiers or at least a considerable part of these sums, in the hope that they would later not only recoup their losses but also make a considerable profit. They could achieve this either by pocketing part of the funds which were meant to pay and feed their men, many of whom only existed on paper, which greatly facilitated such fraudulent but widespread practices, or by looting or holding to ransom towns and villages occupied during the war, not necessarily only places which belonged to the enemy. Rewards in the form of confiscated estates which the rulers of the time used to compensate their officers for unpaid debts owed to them were also a possible source of financial profit.

All this was well – or rather badly – established practice in 1625 when Wallenstein recruited his troops. Even the fact that Wallenstein did not recruit only one or two regiments, but acted as a general contractor to recruit a whole army, was not all that unusual. Count Mansfeld, for example, had been similarly active on a large scale as a military entrepreneur during the early years of the war.[19] What was new about Wallenstein's methods was that he extended to an unprecedented degree the system of extorting contributions from occupied provinces and territories. Places where troops were billeted had always been made to provide lodgings, and supply food for the soldiers and fodder for the horses, often without adequate payment. Mansfeld in Bohemia and Spínola in the Palatinate had also demanded cash contributions from the areas where the troops were stationed in the early 1620s, but Wallenstein based his entire system of military finance on these contributions. Essentially, occupied provinces had to pay his soldiers' wages, or at least a very high percentage of them.[20] The enormous contributions extorted in this way by Wallenstein and later by other commanders permanently changed the structure of taxation in the areas under occupation. After 1648 the territoral rulers were to benefit from the fact that the level of taxation had been raised so dramatically during the war; their Estates and subjects had become accustomed to a burden of taxation unheard of before 1618 (cf. below, p. 191).

Wallenstein's system never worked well enough to make recourse to other sources of revenue entirely superfluous. During the first year of his career as imperial commander-in-chief Wallenstein may indeed have been able to finance his army exclusively from contributions raised in occupied territories, as he had apparently promised the Imperial Treasury in Vienna.[21] But this did not work for very long. Not only were towns and villages in principalities officially allied with the Emperor also forced to pay contributions, but massive amounts of imperial revenues from Bohemia and Silesia and later other imperial provinces, such as Moravia as well, were also assigned to the upkeep of the army, as de Witte's biographer Ernstberger has emphasised. In 1629 when Wallenstein's military power had reached its height, the general reckoned that he would receive about a million Taler from occupied territories, a further million from the imperial provinces of Bohemia, Silesia and Moravia, and a third million from the expected proceeds of the sale of confiscated estates and principalities belonging to the Emperor's enemies.[22] This may have been only a rough estimate, but it shows that the sums which the Emperor's *Erblande* (hereditary dominions) contributed to the upkeep of the army were far from negligible.

Even so, in the long run Wallenstein's methods of raising revenues in the Empire created considerable friction, not least because his army was much larger than forces had been at the beginning of the war. Tilly had fought his campaigns with an army numbering no more than 30,000 men in the early 1620s; Wallenstein, however, probably had about 100,000, if not more, men under his command in the late 1620s. Nevertheless, even Wallenstein never thought of deploying all his 100,000 soldiers on the battlefield.[23] Many of his regiments were widely dispersed and their main task was, in fact, to raise contributions. This was not a very efficient system because the surplus which was left for the mobile fighting army on top of the wages and provisions for the numerous garrisons was limited. None the less, it was later imitated by the Swedes and other armies. To occupy whole provinces in this way at least had the advantage of preventing the enemy from raising contributions there.

However, Wallenstein's dismissal in 1630 was at least to some extent due to the fact that Ferdinand II's councillors deemed that the political costs of this sort of warfare were too high. In purely economic terms Wallenstein's system of war finance would probably have remained viable as long as the troops were kept on the move so that the regions where they were quartered did not suffer for too long, or spread out thinly, thus limiting the damage done by billeting. Moreover, although the occupied territories had to pay enormous sums in military contributions, a very high percentage of this money was spent locally to buy food, provisions, horses and weapons. The important imperial city Nuremberg, for example, paid about 440,000 florins in contributions to Wallenstein between 1625 and 1630, but Nuremberg was also an important centre for the manufacture of weapons and for the international trade in arms and military equipment. The amount of money spent by the agent of Wallenstein's banker, Hans de Witte, in Nuremberg therefore far exceeded the contributions which the city paid.[24]

Wallenstein was the most important of the military entrepreneurs of the Thirty Years War, but in many ways his position was exceptional. Though not a prince of the Empire or a
sovereign ruler, he had acquired the newly created Duchy of
Friedland in Bohemia after 1620. He was therefore a prince in
his own right. His vast estates in Bohemia gave him the opportunity to supplement his role as general and military entrepreneur with that of a munitioner and victualler, selling grain and
other provisions to his own army. When he was dismissed as
commander-in-chief, his refusal to supply the troops of his successor Tilly was, in fact, one of the reasons for Tilly's inability
to stop the Swedish advance.[25]

Thus Wallenstein's position was exceptional in more ways
than one. After his premature death in 1634, there was only
one other military commander who acted as a military entrepreneur and general contractor on a similar scale during the
later years of the war. Bernhard von Weimar (cf. above,
pp. 130–1) was indeed the son of a prince of the Empire, but
only a younger one. In fact, he was the eleventh son of Duke
Johann of Sachsen-Weimar, and as he inherited only a tiny
principality he was largely left to shift for himself. Serving the
Elector Palatine during the early years of the war, he later
became an officer in Christian of Denmark's army. After
Christian's defeat he took up service as a general in Gustavus
Adolphus's expeditionary corps in 1631, and as one of the
most important Swedish commanders, he was rewarded for his
services by the Swedish crown with the territory of the
Bishoprics of Würzburg and Bamberg – transformed into a
new Duchy of Franconia in 1633.

Defeated at Nördlingen in 1634, he offered the services of
the remaining troops under his command to Louis XIII of
France. In October 1635 the representatives of the French
crown and Bernhard von Weimar signed a contract which
assigned Bernhard an annual income of 400,000 livres. In
return, the general was to put an army of 12,000 foot-soldiers
and 6,000 horse in the field, much smaller, of course, than
Wallenstein's vast armada. However, there was a clear parallel
with Wallenstein's career – Wallenstein had been created

Duke of Mecklenburg at the height of his career – in that Bernhard managed to elicit a promise from the French that they would confer the Habsburg Landgraviate of Upper Alsace on him as a principality.[26] After Bernhard's death in June 1639, the heyday of the large-scale military contractor and entrepreneur who recruited and commanded whole armies was over, but generals and officers continued to treat war as a business in a more limited way. Even in the French army, which even before 1660 was already under stricter civilian control than other forces, colonels (or *mestres de camp* as they were normally called in the French army before 1661) and captains, who had frequently bought their commissions, remained in many ways owners of their regiments and companies respectively. Charges as colonel could even be sold to women, who of course did not serve themselves but entrusted the position in question to a deputy. As late as 1650 the French secretary of war, Le Tellier, could say that the King's army was a virtual republic in which the lieutenant generals considered their brigades as 'so many cantons'.[27]

Nevertheless, the later years of the Thirty Years War did see a certain tendency to tighten government control over the armed forces. One symptom of the changes which took place during the 1630s and 1640s was the different treatment received by prisoners-of-war, in particular officers. Whereas simple soldiers who had been taken prisoner were often incorporated into the victorious army, officers were released provided they could pay a high enough ranson. During the early years of the war it was normally the commander of the regiment or other military unit which had captured the prisoners who received the ransom, but on the other hand, an officer who had been taken prisoner had to pay the ransom out of his own pocket. The risk of warfare – high enough anyhow – thus became even more unpredictable. As early as 1635 Bernhard von Weimar had stipulated in his contract with the French crown that Louis XIII would pay his ransom should he be taken prisoner, as the King did for the *maréshals de France*. During the last years of the war it became normal practice for the rulers and princes for whom the various armies fought to pay their soldiers' and officers' ransoms when they were taken prisoner, or to exchange them for prisoners which their own forces had taken. Formal agreements were now signed which fixed the amount of money to be paid for each officer according to his rank.[28]

The risks of warfare for high-ranking officers were thus reduced, but they lost the opportunity to make extra profit by taking important enemy commanders prisoner, for not only was the ransom money now fixed, but it also normally went into the prince's coffers, not into those of his commanders. The position even of a military commander-in-chief was now increasingly less that of an independent entrepreneur fighting for a lump sum at his own financial risk and for his own profit, and gradually more like that of a genuine officeholder. Commanders did, however, retain a great deal of autonomy in financial matters until 1648 and beyond.

The later phases of the Thirty Years War also saw a modification of the system of contributions on which the finances of the various armies so largely rested. After the Peace of Prague (1635) the imperial army for one was no longer financed by contributions extorted at will by troops from the occupied territories but at least in theory by regular taxes. The Estates of the Empire which had signed the Treaty of Prague had agreed to pay the costs necessary to finance the army which was to eject the foreign invaders – in particular the Swedes – from Germany. Later the Council of Electors and the Regensburg Diet of 1640–41 granted further taxes, and the assemblies of the various Circles of the Empire, or at least of those Circles which still maintained some coherence and which were willing to co-operate with the Emperor, did the same. Even if the amount of money which a given territory or principality actually paid to the troops under the immediate or indirect command of the Emperor often bore little relation to the amount of taxes granted, some sort of legal system for supplying the imperial army and for paying the soldiers' wages was now established or re-established.[29] When this system worked, which was probably never more than intermittently, it worked best for garrison troops which concentrated on defending those principalities which also paid the contributions to maintain them. It was, however, inadequate for more ambitious military operations. Major campaigns which extended beyond a given geographical and political region could not be fully financed in this way. Such campaigns required central funds, which in the case of the imperial army had to come from the revenues of the hereditary lands (Austria, Bohemia etc.) or, before 1640, from Spanish subsidies.[30]

If such funds were not available, whole armies could be wiped out by famine, disease and desertion during a major offensive, sometimes without a single battle, as the imperial advance into northern Germany and Holstein in 1644, for example, was to show.[31] However, the revenues raised in the imperial hereditary lands were never really enough to create a sufficiently large central fund to supplement the contributions raised in the Empire, and they became even less adequate in the late 1640s, when the Swedes occupied parts of the imperial dominions. Temporary or more permanent enemy occupation of some of his richest dominions was one of the problems the Emperor faced. The other was the somewhat old-fashioned taxation system, which had never been properly overhauled and which continued to be controlled by the Estates of the individual provinces. In a way, Ferdinand II had raised money in the Empire much more arbitrarily during the late 1620s and the early 1630s than he dared to do in his own dominions, in spite of the victory he had gained against the rebellious Estates of Bohemia in 1620.[32] Thus the imperial armies' ability to attack and to fight major campaigns was gradually reduced. The garrison troops under imperial command which were paid for out of local contributions could probably have gone on fighting indefinitely, like the garrisons of their enemies. But the fact that at the end of the Thirty Years War two-thirds of the cost of maintaining the imperial army were financed by taxes and contributions raised outside the hereditary lands meant that the Emperor had lost control over many of his regiments. These tended to comply with the wishes of their local paymasters much more often than with the orders of the Imperial War Council in Vienna.[33]

Of course, the financial problems which the imperial armies experienced in the 1640s were not unique to them; other armies faced similar difficulties. However, the Emperor's main oppenents, in particular the Swedes, were in a comparatively more advantageous position.[34] When Sweden had entered the war in Germany in 1630, a relatively high percentage of her army consisted of conscripts drawn from the Swedish peasant population. Conscripts had the advantage of being cheaper than mercenaries. They did not need to be persuaded by a special financial premium to take up service in a regiment, and later they could be paid less well than men serving exclusively for money and ever prepared to desert for better payment. During the years 1625–30 altogether about 50,000 men were conscripted in Sweden according to a rota system which ensured that every village provided a certain number of men – by no means all adult men had to serve. A further 25,000 were sent to Germany in 1630–31.[35]

Once Gustavus Adolphus began to operate in Germany, however, more and more mercenaries were recruited. As early as 1631, the year of the battle of Breitenfeld, no more than one-fifth of the soldiers fighting in Gustavus Adolphus's army were Swedes; later the figure dropped to about 10 per cent. Only during the difficult period after the battle of Nördlingen did the share of native Swedish troops increase; they may have provided about a third of Banér's 16,000 men at the battle of Wittstock in 1636.[36] But with the exception of this period, Swedish soldiers were mainly used for garrison duty along the Baltic coast or outside Germany – at home, or in Estonia and Livonia, for example. The concripts thus gave the Swedish army a relatively cheap core of reliable troops, which was important during the initial stages of the intervention in Germany when contributions from occupied territories were not yet available, and later, when the Swedes were forced to retreat to Pomerania for some time after the battle of Nördlingen.

However, for most of the period after 1630 mercenaries made up the bulk of the Swedish army in Germany. These mercenaries were paid for out of the contributions which the inhabitants of the occupied territories and Sweden's allies had to provide. In this respect, the structure of Swedish war finance was not that different from the system on which the imperial forces relied. In fact, taxes raised in Sweden supplied only a very limited amount of the sums necessary to finance the war in Germany. During the years 1630–34 they provided perhaps 14 per cent of the total costs (most of this sum during the first two years 1630–31), and later even less, so that during the last years of the war only 4 per cent of the Swedish crown's ordinary budget was spent on the war in Germany.[37] Admittedly, further funds were provided by loans from Swedish or foreign financiers, not to mention the fact that the Swedish crown owed huge sums to the officers and soldiers of the army at the end of the war (unpaid wages etc.), as well as to the contractors and merchants who had provided the army with provisions. This fact made the indemnity to be paid by the Empire so important for Sweden during the negotiations in Osnabrück.[38]

Nevertheless, during certain crucial phases of the war the Swedish armies had more money at their disposal than their imperial opponents. This was due to two factors: firstly, Swedish control of a large share of the trade in the Baltic and the concomitant income from customs, and secondly, French subsidies. Income from customs had been particularly high between 1629 and 1635 when Sweden controlled the harbours of Polish Prussia. In 1635 the right to raise customs duties in these harbours, which in the preceding years had been worth up to 800,000 Taler annually, had to be handed back to Poland.[39] At this critical moment, when mutinies among its German officers and mercenaries threatened to cripple the military power of the Swedish crown, the French resumed payment of their subsidies. In the years 1631–33 they had already supported Sweden financially to the tune of, on average, about 300,000 Taler per year. From 1638 until the end of the war Sweden received about 3.5 million Taler from the French.[40] This did not solve Sweden's financial problems altogether, and the danger of further mutinies – such mutinies had already occurred after Gustavus Adolphus's death and after the battle of Nördlingen – remained. This was to become apparent in 1641, when more than 20 colonels of the Swedish field army refused to obey orders unless their and their soldiers' arrears were paid promptly.[41] Furthermore, the income from contributions levied in Germany was, in purely quantitative terms,[42] much more important to Swedish war finances than the French subsidies. But these subsidies provided the Swedes with those essential central funds which the imperial armies increasingly lacked. And these funds kept the Swedish troops mobile, because they had not yet been assigned to maintain the garrisons.

Finance and Warfare outside Germany

Other participants in the Thirty Years War admittedly relied to a far smaller extent on contributions, but the only country successfully to draw on domestic taxation as the principal source of war finance *without* provoking major internal revolts, or facing the repeated or indeed permanent threat of financial collapse, was the United Provinces. However, as Marjolein 't Hart has recently shown, even the Netherlands occasionally found that attempts to raise taxes provoked revolts in the peripheral provinces (for example, Gelderland and Overijssel). As in other countries, these revolts had to be put down by troops. But the situation was different in the central provinces, in particular Holland. Holland's society was extremely urbanised and commercialised; it was one of the economically most advanced areas of Europe. Moreover, the biggest town in Holland, Amsterdam, was not only a focus of international trade but also the dominant centre of the European money market north of the Alps. The bankers of Amsterdam provided half of Europe with credit, and the Dutch state therefore found it easy to raise loans at fairly low rates of interest within Holland. The merchants, rentiers and financiers of Amsterdam were often only too glad to provide the Dutch Republic with funds. After all, the finances of the Republic were sound, and domestic creditors had the great advantage of being able to control the budget and policies of their debtor themselves through the Estates of Holland and the Dutch Estates General. Furthermore, there was a surplus of mobile capital in Holland and arable land, which would have been an alternative investment, was relatively scarce. Thus buying state loans was attractive. Moreover, the fact that so many leading Dutch families had a large share of their capital invested in government loans diminished their reluctance to pay taxes. After all, a high income for the state ensured the prompt payment of interest on loans. Finally, the Estates of Holland and to a lesser extent of the central provinces of Zeeland and Utrecht, too, were able to rely much more on indirect taxation, on excises of all sorts, than on direct taxation. Direct taxation tended to create the problem of how to assess the taxpayers' income or capital and estates, a problem which early modern states with their inadequate financial and other statistics often found impossible to solve in any satisfactory manner. Excises on food or luxury items, by contrast, were much easier to collect, at least in a commercialised market economy such as undoubtedly existed in Holland.[43]

The Dutch Republic's great antagonist, Spain, also largely relied on indirect taxation on trade and consumption in the most important kingdom of the monarchy, Castile, to finance her wars.[44] However, Spain's economy was dominated by agriculture, and a high percentage of agricultural produce never reached the market to be sold for cash because it was consumed by the producers, or because it remained part of a non-monetarised economy in other ways, for example as wages paid in kind to agricultural labourers. This system was therefore never ideally suited to tap the real wealth of the country. It became, however, ever more inadequate when the economy in general and trade and manufacturing in particular, expanding for most of the sixteenth century, were struck by a severe slump around 1590. This was an economic crisis which deepened from the 1620s onwards.[45]

However, until the 1620s the Spanish monarchy was able to finance major military campaigns surprisingly well. This was due to a number of factors. First – and here there is a parallel with the Dutch Republic after all – almost the whole 'political nation', most members of the political and social elite of Castile, had invested in state loans. As the King's creditors they had a vested interest in keeping the crown financially afloat; Philip II and his successors therefore quite often found the Estates of Castile, the Cortes, co-operative when they asked them to approve new taxes or raise the level of existing ones.

Apart from this domestic market for loans, the Spanish crown also had a vast network of international credit facilities at its disposal. Despite the repeated Spanish state bankruptcies, the great bankers and financiers of Europe were eager enough to lend money to the Spanish Habsburgs, partly perhaps because until the 1620s, and possibly until the more serious crisis of 1647, these bankruptcies were not as dramatic as the term suggests. They implied more a rescheduling of interest payments and a restructuring of debts than a genuine collapse of royal credit.[46] Even if full payment of interest and repayment of the capital were somewhat doubtful, the *potential* wealth of Spain's world-wide Empire was so great that it seemed well worth while to be the Spanish monarch's creditor. If the King could not pay his debts in cash, he could still grant profitable monopolies or economic concessions and privileges of the greatest value. Thus Spain was able to live for decades with an enormous structural deficit in her budget because there were always financiers willing to fill the widening gap between expenditure and income. At the beginning of the Thirty Years War financiers from Genoa were the Spanish crown's most important bankers. They mobilised the wealth of northern Italy, still one of the richest regions of Europe, for Spain.[47] It was no coincidence that the commander-in-chief of the army of Flanders, Ambrogio Spínola, was also the head of the richest Genoese banking family. Thus Spínola, like Wallenstein, though in a more limited and much more subtle way and without actually owning the army he commanded, combined the role of one of the crown's principal creditors with a position as commander of its armies.[48]

During the course of the 1620s, however, and in particular after the bankruptcy of 1627, the Genoese bankers were largely replaced by financiers from Lisbon in Portugal, mainly *conversos* (New Christians of Jewish descent). Until the early 1630s this system, in spite of its serious shortcomings, kept the crown financially afloat; as much as 45 per cent of the Spanish treasury's expenditure went into servicing debts during the period 1621–40 (47 per cent was needed to wage war whereas the costs of the court and the central administration amounted to only 8 per cent),[49] although interest to creditors was by no means fully paid. During the 1630s, however, the system gradually collapsed. The measures taken by the Inquisition against the *conversos*, including some of the royal bankers, certainly did not help. Olivares also attempted to raise more revenue in the traditionally undertaxed peripheral dominions of the Spanish monarchy, in particular in the provinces of the crown of Aragon and in Portugal (the Italian possessions of the Spanish crown and the Spanish Netherlands already made a substantial contribution to imperial defence and adminstration and this contribution could be further increased in the 1630s).[50] Olivares's attempts, however, resulted in revolt first in Catalonia and then Portugal, thus threatening Madrid's links with its Portuguese bankers.

Spain's financial problems were greatly exacerbated by the decline in royal income from imports of American silver (and to a lesser extent gold), although the quantitative importance of these imports has sometimes been overestimated. According to fairly reliable contemporary accounts, the crown derived only about 10 per cent of its income in Castile – all silver from America had to be landed in Seville, Castile's monopoly harbour for traffic with the Indies – from its share of bullion imports in the period 1620–40.[51] However, in the 1630s the amount of silver and gold belonging to merchants and other private importers was about three and a half times larger than the crown's share, and precious metal belonging to private parties was taxed by the crown, and could be borrowed and sometimes sequestered. Moreover, it was ready cash which, once it had arrived in Seville, required comparatively little administrative effort to collect and which had not been assigned beforehand to the crown's creditors like other revenues. The silver from America was therefore more important than its share of overall royal income would suggest.

According to the official figures on which Earl J. Hamilton based his seminal 1930s study, the total amount of bullion imported (both private and royal) had already declined from its peak in the 1590s (about 35 million pesos during a given period of five years, or more than 250 tons of silver per annum) to 27 million in the period 1621–25, and about 25 million pesos for the five years from 1626 to 1630. From 1630 on the decline accelerated. During the late 1640s (1646–50) imports amounted to no more than 12 million pesos. The royal share of these imports was a mere 1.7 million pesos, after it had been nearly 11 million pesos in the period 1596–1600. It had, in fact, declined steeply earlier than overall imports during the years 1615–20.[52] Admittedly, the figures on which these estimates are based are not beyond dispute and they have, in fact, been challenged. More recent estimates, taking into account the bullion which was smuggled into Spain and therefore not registered by customs officials, are more optimistic and suggest that as much as 68.8 million pesos worth of bullion were still imported as late as 1635–39 (the figure for 1595–99 is 78.4 million).[53] However, even if we assume that more and more silver was imported without being registered by royal customs officials, such smuggled bullion was unlikely to find its way into the royal coffers. Moreover, gradually more and more silver was diverted to Dutch or French and later also to English harbours, either because silver fleets were captured or, more importantly, because the Spanish monopoly on trade with the 'Indies' was broken. Thus trade between America and Seville decreased markedly in volume in the early seventeenth century.[54]

To a limited extent, the shortfall of income from the colonial empire and Castile itself could be compensated for by shifting the burden of war to the peripheral provinces of the Spanish monarchy, the Spanish Netherlands and the Italian dominions of the Spanish crown. This had been the intention behind Olivares's plans for mobilising the resources of the whole monarchy, a true 'union of arms' first developed in the mid-1620s.[55] But, with credit facilities and income from taxation in Castile drying up in the late 1630s, the Spanish crown was forced to fall back on expedients which other participants in the Thirty Years War had already employed earlier. When fighting started along the border between Spain and France after 1635, the frontier provinces were asked to contribute in cash and kind to the upkeep of the troops stationed in these areas. If they refused, the troops would be used to enforce compliance or let loose to plunder villages and towns. Such measures helped to provoke the Catalan revolt of 1640.[56] Nevertheless, with warfare concentrated on Spanish soil much more after 1640 than before – apart from the war in Catalonia Spanish troops were fighting against the Portuguse after 1640 – the system of raising contributions locally in or near the areas where troops were actually operating was maintained. It ensured that Spain could go on fighting (in the case of the war against Portugal, until 1668) despite the collapse of her finances and her credit system.

During the course of the war Spain underwent a gradual regression from a fairly sophisticated system of taxation and raising credit to comparatively more primitive forms of financing warfare – a regression exacerbated by the increasingly widespread devolution of formerly public rights and services, such as the recruiting of soldiers or the provisioning of troops, to great noble magnates and private contractors respectively.[57] The opposite holds true, though with major qualifications, for France. France, unlike Spain, had no colonies of economic significance in the 1630s, and far from receiving subsidies from other states she had to pay subsidies herself to her allies, such as Sweden and, at times, the Dutch and various German princes, like the Landgrave of Hesse-Kassel, for example. Nor was the French crown able to raise enough contributions to finance its armies; the areas under French occupation in the 1630s and early 1640s were too small and, like Lorraine, had repeatedly been ruined by undisciplined troops or deliberate destruction before 1635, when war against Spain was officially declared. Thus the only solution was to raise the level of taxation, and, in fact, the 1630s saw the biggest rise in French taxation since the fifteenth century.

During the 1620s, when royal income was already increasing, the central treasury in Paris received about 43 million livres tournois each year from revenues of all sorts; in the decade 1630–39 this figure went up to 92 million, and in the decade 1640–49 to 115 million livres (approximately the equivalent of 46 million Taler).[58] Even if we take account of the fact that the silver content of the livres tournois was decreasing, fairly reliable estimates assume that the French crown could dispose of a gross annual income of 770 tons of silver in 1645–46 as opposed to 470 tons in 1623, and 560 tons at the beginning of the 1630s. The reign of Louis XIV, after 1661, saw a further increase but it was not as dramatic as that of the 1630s and 1640s. Gross income in the 1680s amounted to as much as 1,000 tons of silver, but this represented a ceiling which would not be broken during the eighteenth century and was, in fact, not even reached for a long time after 1714.[59] Counted in grain equivalents, in order to assess the real value of this income, French taxes, direct and indirect, had brought in about 5 million hectoliters in 1620 and 9.2 million hectoliters in 1640. According to one estimate, a French peasant who had to work about 10–15 days per annum to pay his taxes before Richelieu became the King's first minister in 1624, had to work about 35 days in 1641 shortly before the Cardinal's death.[60]

All these figures show that the years of Richelieu's government and the subsequent years of the Thirty Years War until 1648, when the Peace of Westphalia was signed and the outbreak of the Fronde put paid to all attempts to increase the level of taxation even further, were a revolutionary period for French crown finances. Within two decades the income of the French crown doubled in real terms. In terms of monetary units the increase was even steeper. Of all European states participating in the Thirty Years War, France was probably most deeply transformed by the impact of the war. The French example shows what it meant to finance warfare for long periods of time primarily out of domestic taxation, without the benefit of a vast income from overseas colonies or the ability to transfer most of the costs of warfare to occupied enemy or neutral territories. What exacerbated French problems further was that the credit facilities of the French crown were far more limited than those of the Spanish Habsburgs (at the beginning of the war before they gradually deteriorated). Spain could always offer various economic concessions in her vast empire as security. Furthermore the crown could ask the Estates, in particular the Castilian Cortes, to guarantee loans. The French King had neither American silver mines nor a viable and effective assembly of Estates for the realm as a whole, and provincial assemblies of Estates had survived only in a limited number of peripheral provinces.[61]

Thus the only way to raise credit seemed to be to sell royal offices and regalian rights as security, like the right to retain a certain percentage or even all of the proceeds of newly introduced taxes. These surtaxes granted to officeholders in the financial administration were called *droits aliénés*.[62] During the war against the Huguenots, the Mantuan war, and the covert warfare against Spain in 1631–35, the French crown had, in fact, largely relied on this system to finance its policy. Income from the sale of offices and related regalian rights reached an all-time high, amounting to as much as 55 per cent of regular royal income, considerably more than the income from direct taxation during the years 1630–35. This is not to say that direct taxation did not increase from the late 1620s onwards, but a very considerable share, probably the greater part of the new taxes, went to officeholdes and owners of *droits aliénés*.[63]

In 1634, with open war against Spain imminent, however, the crown changed its policy: the surtaxes granted to private parties were now largely resumed. Those who had bought these rights were compensated but not at all adequately; that is, in effect the crown declared a partial bankruptcy in 1634. This policy did work to some extent. The level of taxation and, more importantly, the actual crown income from taxation could be raised even further. Statistics show that the *taille*, the most important direct tax, reached a maximum in about 1640, at a level which, in real terms, was never to be exceeded until the end of the *ancien régime* in 1789. But the new financial policy put considerable pressure on the peasant population, who had to pay the bulk of the taxes, and at the same time antagonised important vested interests, the (former) owners of the *droits aliénés* and hereditary officeholders in general. The result was stiff resistance to the increased taxation, often encouraged by the officeholders and regional elites. Not only did it become much more difficult to collect anything like the full amount of the official taxes in many regions after 1634, but the later 1630s also saw a series of provincial rebellions which threatened the foundations of the French monarchy and, of course, further reduced the amount of taxes actually collected. One of the most serious of these provincial risings was the revolt of the Nu-Pieds, in Normandy in 1639, which required 10,000 regular soldiers to put it down.[64]

In general, during the Thirty Years War the collection of direct taxes increasingly became the responsibility of the *intendants*, who largely replaced the older hereditary officeholders, the *élus* and *trésoriers*. The *intendants* were officials with short-term, revokable commissions who were sent into the provinces to supervise local law courts and administration. To facilitate their task the *intendants* had troops of horse at their disposal, the so-called *carabiniers* or *fusiliers de taille*. But the use of soldiers, whether *fusiliers de taille* or regular regiments, to collect taxes and irregular contributions always remained problematic. The destruction caused by such violent methods was as much of a disadvantage as the fact that a considerable amount of the taxes collected disappeared into the soldiers' pockets. There is, therefore, reason to believe that after 1640 any attempts to increase taxation further foundered on the resistance of the peasantry and the local elites. If open tax revolts became rarer after the early 1640s, this was because it was now sufficient just to refuse to pay taxes, except in frontier provinces, where regular troops forced the people to pay contributions.[65]

Thus French finances were by no means in a healthy state in the 1640s.The expansion of taxation in the preceding years had only been achieved at a high price, that of administrative reform.[66] The basic structures of the highly illogical and inefficient French taxation system, with its many exemptions for certain provinces and privileged social groups, had remained largely unchanged. Nor had the problem of venal officeholding been solved. The vast majority of all offices in the French royal administration remained venal or/and hereditary, despite the fact that special royal commissaries like the *intendants* had curtailed the power of the traditional bureaucracy in some areas.

Essentially, France, like Spain, was just muddling through in the 1640s as far as meeting the ever-increasing financial demands of warfare were concerned. Like Spain, she got by only by anticipating future income for several years to come. In fact, in 1648, the whole edifice of French state finance was about to collapse. The financiers who supplied the crown with loans were no longer able to borrow money themselves from private investors; distrust in the crown's financial policy was too great.[67] The crown had already tried to avoid the impending crisis by imposing new taxes on hitherto privileged groups. The result, however, was a general revolt, led, at first, by the *noblesse de robe* – those (generally hereditary) officeholders who claimed noble status. The Fronde, in which the crowds of Paris and other cities and many of the great noblemen of France, including some of the highest-ranking commanders of the French armies, later joined, paralysed France for nearly five years until the beginning of 1653. But it could not permanently undo the changes which Richelieu's and Mazarin's administration had brought about in raising the level of taxation and curtailing at least some of the privileges of the officeholders.[68]

Nevertheless, the question remains why France proved victorious in her fight against Spain, although she faced financial problems which were, *prima facie*, not altogether dissimilar. Basically, we must take account of the fact that France was a much richer country, not by comparison with the whole Spanish Empire, but certainly compared with Castile. This was of vital importance, as the Spanish Habsburgs never really managed to exploit the resources of their other kingdoms fully, despite Olivers's schemes for a union of arms. Furthermore, though rebellions struck France as well as Spain, none of the French provinces rising against the agents of the central administration in the late 1630s or during the Fronde seriously tried to break away from the kingdom to seek independence or a union with another monarchy. Even during the Fronde 'national' unity – and the word national is not entirely anachronistic in the context of seventeenth-century French politics – and loyalty to the reigning dynasty and its head, Louis XIV, then still under age, were not fundamentally called into question, whereas in the Spanish Empire 'national' sentiment concentrated on the individual kingdoms and provinces not the monarchy as a whole.[69] For France 'Vive le roi sans gabelle' was the characteristic slogan of popular rebellion,[70] while the Spanish Habsburgs lost one kingdom for ever in the 1640s, and only recovered another province (Catalonia), after 12 years of war, because the peripheral provinces saw further co-operation with the central institutions of the monarchy as incompatible with their own national or regional interests.[71]

In the end, the impact of the Thirty Years War was to strengthen royal authority in France; this was a slow and extremely tortuous process accomplished only at great political and social cost. All the same its consequences were momentous. In contrast to France, Spain (or rather, Castile) could go on fighting only by 'liquidating' the crown's sole remaining capital, its own authority, as I. A. A. Thompson has pointed out. Adminstrative tasks, especially in the military sphere, which had formerly been carried out by royal officials, were delegated to private contractors, noble magnates and local communities. Ultimately, royal authority was largely privatised and decentralised. This process may have ensured Spain's ability to go on fighting an essentially defensive war, but certainly from the 1640s onwards it entirely eroded her capacity to wage an offensive war in the manner France did then, and later.[72]

The Impact of Warfare on the Civilian Population

The preceding remarks have shown that of the major participants in the Thirty Years War only the Dutch Republic was
able to meet the costs of warfare out of the proceeds of taxation. Lack of supplies and of cash was therefore a problem
for all armies, and, in fact, it was this problem which was to a
large extent responsible for the undisciplined behaviour of
soldiers. At least from the later 1630s onwards, starved or half-
starved soldiers were quite a common sight, and undoubtedly
the desperate state of this *soldatesca* was largely responsible for
the atrocities which they committed when they encountered a
civilian population unable or unwilling to satisfy their
demands. Recent research, for example Myron Gutmann's
study of warfare in the Prince-Bishopric of Liége, has
confirmed that so long as soldiers were reasonably well paid,
they were unlikely to loot and burn the houses of civilians, or
indeed to kill them.[73]

Of course Gutmann's results cannot be generalised without
qualifications. During the Thirty Years War Spanish and Dutch
troops rarely, if ever, resorted to a deliberate scorched earth
strategy. The other side's opportunities to retaliate in kind
were too obvious and both sides tried to ensure that the
impact of the war on the civilian population was limited.[74]
This was not necessarily the case in other areas, where armies
sometimes deliberately destroyed all supplies which could
have been used by their enemy to feed and maintain his own
force. Such methods were employed, for example, during the
fighting in Lorraine in the 1630s, or when Swedish troops
invaded Bavaria in 1632. Fourteen years later in 1646, they
were used even more systematically and more recklessly
during another Swedish invasion of the same region.[75] Even
in these cases, however, the indiscriminate slaughter of civilians and the burning of villages and towns seems to have been
the exception rather than the rule. Soldiers did 'confiscate'
horses, cattle and all the stocks of grain they could find; sometimes the animals were then sold back to their original owners

or other peasants at prices which may have been moderate enough, but were still so high that the soldiers managed to extract most of the cash the peasants might possess. Torture, so often depicted in contemporary chronicles, novels or engravings was not necessary to achieve this, though it did, of course, occur in some cases.[76] On balance, however, the worst sufferings of the population during the war were not caused by the direct impact of military violence, massacres and atrocities, but by the scarcity of food and the spread of diseases, which were, admittedly, also to a large extent results of decades of warfare.

Although many smaller towns were burned down when taken by enemy forces, in particular when the garrison of the place refused to surrender and the town had to be taken by assault, the larger German towns were, as a rule, spared this fate; they were too valuable as fortresses but also as centres of commerce and trade. Moreover, they were normally able to pay such vast amounts of contributions that it would have been foolhardy to destroy them. Bernhard Kroener, one of the foremost experts on the military history of the period, has come to the conclusion that most of the large towns of the Holy Roman Empire did not even see any major military units within their walls during the war; soldiers were normally billeted in the suburbs, and only the officers were assigned quarters within the walls.[77] Thus the fate of Magdeburg, burned down by Tilly's soldiers in 1631 with a loss of nearly 20,000 lives – about 4,000 soldiers, the entire garrison, and up to 15,000 of the 20,000 civilian inhabitants – was exceptional, though similar events did occur frequently enough when smaller towns of 2,000 or 3,000 inhabitants were taken by assault.[78]

Nevertheless, despite the scepticism occasionally voiced by some historians, the losses which the civilians suffered were enormous.[79] But as has already been pointed out, they were due more to the scarcity of food and to the infectious diseases which the armies spread, and which found a fertile breeding ground among a half-starved and weakened population, than to direct acts of violence by the military. The worst years of the war for many German regions were undoubtedly the 1630s, and in particular the second half of this decade; during this period, large areas had already been devastated but the population had not yet been reduced to such an extent that the demand for food had diminished sufficiently to allow some sort of balance between supply and demand to be re-established at a lower level. In many areas grain prices reached their maximum during the years 1634–40 as several factors combined to reduce agricultural production: widespread destruction, unfavourable climatic conditions and fields neglected by a peasant population which had deserted the villages to seek refuge in towns and provinces or principalities less likely to be invaded by undisciplined soldiers. A similar rise in prices had occurred in some areas, but more briefly, in the late 1620s, and prices were to climb very steeply again at the very end of the war, in 1648–51.[80] Not only civilians, but also soldiers, suffered from malnutrition, if not starvation during the later phases of the war. According to some reports, it was not unusual for soldiers in the late 1630s to eat dead cats and other animal carcasses, or even to beg alms from the civilian population.[81] Other reports also claim that children were slaughtered and cooked, but these alleged cases of cannibalism are not confirmed by reliable evidence.

Nevertheless, the years 1634–40 certainly inflicted maximum hardship on many regions of the Holy Roman Empire, not least because the financial and logistical problems which all armies fighting in Germany experienced became more acute than ever. Compared with the chaotic lootings of these years, the contributions imposed in a relatively orderly manner by Wallenstein in the late 1620s were, by and large, less harmful. One of many contemporary accounts, Johann Daniel Minck's Chronicle of the Odenwald area (north of Heidelberg) confirms that many peopled suffered terrible hardships during the years 1635–38. They were so famished 'that they were nothing but skin and bone'. Most marriages became infertile. Whereas there were more than enough 'bastards' born to 'whores' (*Hurenkinder*), the affection of married couples for each other disappeared. Husbands and wives ceased to make love, families disintegrated and in the search for food and a livelihood, children left their parents never to see them again.[82]

As this testimony demonstrates, the disasters of the 1630s had social and psychological consequences as well as demographic ones. Family life was thrown into disarray and marriages broke up.[83] But once some sort of peaceful life was restored, mass weddings seem to have been a common phenomenon, as Minck also claims. Even people who would have stayed unmarried for social or economic reasons before the war now suddenly took a husband or wife.[84] The pattern of behaviour reported by Minck for the Odenwald seems to have been fairly typical. In Bavaria hardly any weddings were celebrated for about three years in the parishes struck by the Swedish invasion of 1632, and subsequently by famine and plague. Once the worst was over, in 1635, however, more weddings were celebrated than ever. In this as in other cases the resilience of the striken population is quite remarkable. Apparently even areas badly devastated and depopulated could regain their former economic, though hardly their demographic, strength quite rapidly. They could recover within a period of ten or twelve years, unless (and this is, of course, an important qualification) another disaster struck again in the form of occupation by large numbers of enemy or even 'friendly' troops during this time.[85]

It needs to be stressed that war did not only reduce the size of the population, it also affected social structures, for not all social groups were affected by the war in the same way. It is obvious that during an epidemic old people and small children were likely to be the worst affected, but the lower orders of society, the economically weak, were also much more vulnerable than the wealthier classes. When the price of grain went up, large landowners and wealthy peasants could possibly, unless their farms and granaries had already been looted and devastated, benefit by selling at premium prices the harvests and the grain they might have hoarded. Small tenants and cottagers were more likely to have to buy grain and other food at prices which they could not afford; after a short time they succumbed to starvation or malnutrition. But even when troops occupied an area, those with cash to spare were in a much better position to survive, or even to benefit. During an occupation it was customary for the officeholders of the territorial prince and the local noblemen to buy a *salva guardia* (a *sauvegarde* or letter of safe conduct and protection) from the commanding officers for their seats of office and castles. That is, the officers issued a declaration that the buildings in question were under their protection and should remain unmolested. Of course, such agreements could only be effective if the occupying army was still reasonably disciplined. If the soldiers had received neither pay nor regular provisions for weeks or months on end, they were likely to loot every building in sight, whatever their officers told them.

However, more often than not the buying of such a *salva guardia* did work,[86] and fortified towns were even more likely to be able to buy off troops occupying the villages beyond their walls. If, however, the peasant population wanted to seek protection, they had to take refuge in or near a castle which possessed a *salva guardia*, or in a similarly privileged town. Frequently this sort of asylum was costly. To pay the special taxes or charges which noblemen and officeholders sometimes and towns nearly always demanded, the peasants had to sell their cattle or other goods. Often those with cash to spare bought the cattle and later re-sold them at much higher prices to the soldiers of the occupying army. When the peasants returned to their fields after the danger was over, they had to borrow money from the same merchants to whom they had earlier sold their cattle at discount prices.[87] By such and similar mechanisms, a vast redistribution of capital and wealth was accomplished during the war.

In general, small landowners, rural and urban labourers and their families were likely to succumb to the war, while the better-off managed to survive. Some, though by no means all, were even able to strengthen their economic position. Thus Christopher Friedrichs comes to the conclusion for the imperial city of Nördlingen: 'Although all groups suffered financial losses during the war, in relative terms the burden of military taxation must have fallen much more heavily on the lower and middle groups than on the rich.'[88] However, if a town was looted once or twice or occupied for several years by troops, the well-to-do could also find it difficult to maintain their status. Bernd Roeck's findings for Augsburg show that the highest and the lowest income groups were hardest hit by the war. After 1648 a significant number of patricians, the old-established elite of the town, had to be counted – for purposes of taxation at least – among the 'habnit' (the have-nots), and there were few patricians left among the richest families in Augsburg.

The picture which emerges for other towns is similar. The poorest strata of society were decimated by epidemics and famine, and made up a much smaller proportion of the total population after 1648 than before 1618. The very rich, however, though much more likely to survive physically, suffered heavy financial losses, not only through contributions and pillage, but because the interest on the loans and bonds they had invested their money in before 1618 was no longer paid. Indeed, it was not unlikely for them to lose the entire capital itself.[89] If certain occupational groups did benefit from the war in a town like Augsburg, it was the brewers and keepers of great taverns and alehouses who tended to reap profits from the presence of soldiers and officers.[90]

By and large, it was not the old-established urban and rural elites who prospered most during the turmoil of the war. Large-scale contractors providing troops with supplies were often in a more favourable position,[91] and to some extent military entrepreneurs and high-ranking officers were also able to accumulate vast fortunes. This was, of course, a risky business, as Wallenstein's fate or that of the many other generals and colonels who fell in battle showed. Nevertheless, a number of commanders, including some of non-noble or even peasant origin, did manage to survive long enough to build up vast fortunes through the spoils of war, the share of the contributions paid by civilians which they pocketed, or because they received large donations of land from the princes they served as compensation for the money they had invested in their regiments and armies.[92]

For the simple soldier, in particular the foot-soldier (the better paid horsemen were in a slightly more advantageous position), any chances for social betterment were very limited indeed.[93] In fact, the ordinary soldier's life was in every respect 'nasty, brutish and short'. Hated by the peasants, though often himself the son of a peasant or a former tenant farmer or cottager ruined by the war, his chances of survival were slim.[94] The French army, for example, seems to have lost at least half a million soldiers (not counting deserters) during the years 1635–59, and most of the Swedish regiments fighting in Germany from 1631 to 1633 seem to have lost about two-thirds of their original strength within two years. Indeed losses of about 30 per cent annually were quite common for a given unit of soldiers during the war as a whole.

Thus the adult male population of whole villages in Sweden was all but wiped out between 1617, when war with Poland had been resumed, and 1648. This was despite the fact that the Swedish regiments were, after the initial invasion, primarily used for garrison duties in Germany, though the same may not have been true for the regiments fighting against Denmark, in the Baltic provinces and in Poland.[95] For the common soldiers, the most common cause of death was not to be killed or fatally wounded in action – though given the lack of any medical facilities worth speaking of in the armies, even light injuries, in particular from bullets, could prove fatal. For them the most common cause of death was disease, contracted in unsanitary lodgings or because their resistance to an epidemic had been undermined by forced marches and mal-nutrition. Only for the officers, better fed and better housed, was death in battle – or as a result of wounds received in action – the most common form of death.[96]

Nevertheless, the armies of the Thirty Years War had no problems in recruiting soldiers, at least in Germany. This was partly due to the fact that soldiers, when they actually received their pay, were paid much better than unskilled day-labourers (though not as well as skilled craftsmen, especially those who had attained the status of master). Once the war had destroyed the normal structures of life, many young and not-so-young men saw service in the army as one of the few oppor-tunities open to them in a world where famine and plague were ever-present and where the normal patterns of life had been upset. This explains to some extent why recruiting captains and colonels could even reduce the pay of ordinary soldiers during the later phases of the war.[97] There was now a surplus of men whose economic existence had been so thoroughly destroyed that a company of soldiers seemed the only refuge left to them. Thus in the area of recruitment as much as in questions of finance the dictum *bellum se ipsum alit* (the war feeds itself) proved to be true.

Epilogue: Germany After 1648

The first signs of economic recovery were already visible in some regions of Germany in the 1640s, even where the 1620s and 1630s had brought widespread devastation. Demographic recovery, however, took several decades and even longer in many particularly badly hit areas where the population levels of 1618 were not reached again until 1750. If we assume that Germany – within the borders of 1871 – had about 18 million inhabitants in 1618, this population had been reduced by about a third to less than 12 million in 1650. If we take the historical borders of the seventeenth-century Empire as a statistical starting point the result is only slightly less drastic, for then the population can be assumed to have declined from about 21 million to about 16 million people. All these figures are only estimates, but in general there can be little doubt that the war had reduced the population of Germany by at least 25 per cent according to the most conservative estimates, but much more likely by 35 or even 40 per cent.[1] Losses may have been exaggerated by some contemporary and later accounts, but the scepticism of those historians who want to confine one of the greatest demographic disasters in German history to the realm of myth is nevertheless unwarranted.[2]

Of course, the various regions were affected very unequally. North-western Germany between the river Elbe and the Dutch border had suffered comparatively little or not at all. This was also true for Austria (the German-speaking Habsburg hereditary lands) and partly true for a number of districts along the lower Rhine. In other areas, however, the devastation assumed truly apocalyptic proportions. This was the case in north-eastern Germany, where Mecklenburg and Pomerania

(Hinterpommern, the area east of the river Oder more so than Vorpommern) were worst hit with losses of probably more than 60 per cent of their pre-war population. Brandenburg did not fare much better, with losses of about 50 per cent. The Palatinate – to the left and right of the river Rhine – Alsace, and most of Württemberg, as well as the area between Ulm and Nördlingen, were also totally devastated with losses of between 50 and 70 per cent;[3] Nördlingen, for example, did not regain its pre-war population level until the twentieth century.[4] Bavaria may have 'escaped' with losses of between 30 and 40 per cent, and Saxony suffered an even lower decline in its population (perhaps not more than 20 per cent).

It is self-evident that such colossal losses affecting not just one or two regions, but altogether more than two-thirds of the Holy Roman Empire, had grave economic and social consequences. Economically they greatly reduced the demand for agricultural products which, unlike the demand for manufactured goods, is normally directly related to the size of the population. Of course, the volume of agricultural production declined too, but not to the same extent, for the surviving farmers tended to abandon the least fertile fields first. By working only on the fields with the best soil they could achieve higher average yields per acre, or at least prevent the decline in the yield per acre which would otherwise have been caused by the lack of manure, in itself a result of the reduced number of animals owned by farmers, or by the lack of capital and farm tools. Thus the price of grain plummeted after about 1650–51 in Germany, and in areas not too severely affected by the war up to ten years earlier. This trend was not reversed until the end of the seventeenth century; in fact, in some regions it was more than a century before the downward trend was really broken and a lasting recovery set in.[5]

On the other hand, real wages recovered compared to their long-term decline before 1618; in particular, masons and other craftsmen in construction-related occupations now earned much more than before the war. In Württemberg, for example, their wages seem to have been three or four times higher in real terms in the 1650s than in the 1620s.[6]

Agricultural day-labourers also benefited, even in those areas where the landowning nobility, with the co-operation of the territorial ruler, forced peasants to provide unpaid labour services (*Gesindedienste*) and tried to impose regulations intended to keep wage levels stable. In Brandenburg, wages for agricultural labourers continued to rise, in real terms, at least until the 1680s, for example.[7] Urban craftsmen may not have been quite so lucky. Low agricultural prices meant that the purchasing power of the rural population was limited and this was bound to have an adverse effect on the demand for the goods craftsmen produced. This trend was exacerbated by the fact that with the huge armies and their hangers-on gone, so many consumers of manufactured goods had also disappeared.

Nevertheless, not all was bleak in economic terms after 1648. One historian, Rudolf Schlögl, who has studied rural society in Bavaria, has even spoken of the period 1640–80 as witnessing an 'economic miracle' as far as agricultural production is concerned.[8] Not only did production recover comparatively quickly, but smallholders and cottagers also benefited greatly from higher wages and lower prices. With a surplus of arable land available, the younger sons of farmers were also in a more advantageous position than before the war (in areas where impartible inheritance favouring the eldest son prevailed); they were now much more likely to acquire their own farm. Better economic prospects also meant that men and women could marry younger, or that those who would have remained unmarried before 1618 had a chance to marry after all. The result was that the fertility of the population increased. In Württemberg children and young people under the age of 15 may have made up as much as 50 per cent of the population in the first two or three decades after the war.[9]

But the 'economic miracle', if such it was, had its drawbacks too. As Schlögl argues, the decline in population and the undoubtedly much improved situation of the surviving smallholders and cottagers – a great many of this particular group of rural society had of course died during the war – meant that the pressure for economic change which had existed before 1618 was now gone. Once the balance between agricultural production and population had been re-established, a return to traditional agricultural techniques and economic patterns of behaviour was possible, and with these patterns of behaviour traditional rural society was preserved too. In other European countries which had not suffered such a steep demographic decline as Germany, such as England – though population growth may have halted there too between 1650 and 1700 – economic structures and society had to change to avoid disaster. Germany, however, could afford to stay 'backward' and 'underdeveloped'.[10]

It is certainly true that many German regions *were* underdeveloped economically and, though here a judgement is much more difficult, socially backward by comparison with England and France, let alone the Dutch Republic, in the later seventeenth century. This is true in particular for north-eastern Germany – Mecklenburg, Pomerania and Brandenburg – all areas which had suffered particularly badly during the war. More difficult is to spell out to what extent the Thirty Years War directly caused this backwardness. In the areas mentioned most of the peasants were personally unfree in the later seventeenth century. This meant that they had to provide the lord of the manor, whose tenants they were, with labour services free of charge (either in person or, more frequently, through members of their family or labourers they employed). Nor could they leave their farm or even marry without the local squire's permission. However, the trend towards establishing this form of 'serfdom', more properly called *Erbuntertänigkeit* (hereditary status as an unfree tenant) was well under way before 1618. In the areas east of the Elbe the nobility often farmed in person quite a large proportion of the land they owned (*Eigenwirtschaft*). The rye or other grain they harvested was shipped down the rivers and sold to merchants who transported it to Amsterdam and other harbours in populous western Europe. The legal status of the leases peasants held in north-eastern Germany – areas colonised in the Middle Ages – was particularly vulnerable and thus the lords of the manor (*Gutsherren*) could either transform peasant land into demesne, or force their tenants to farm their land under increasingly unfavourable conditions.

However, as recent research shows, the crucial developments laying the foundations for *Gutsherrschaft* (the economic,
social and jurisdictional structures which enabled a nobleman,
as lord of the manor, to control not only the economic activities but the entire lives of his tenants) and *Erbuntertänigkeit*
mostly antedated the war.[11] After 1648 the nobility persuaded
the territorial princes to confirm existing arrangements including encroachments on the rights of peasants, but it was
difficult if not impossible for them to improve their position
any further. In fact, their situation was often quite desperate as
the devastations of the war, the extreme lack of manpower and
the agricultural depression all worked to their disadvantage.
It is therefore no surprise that a ruler determined to increase
his authority such as Friedrich Wilhelm the 'Great Elector' of
Brandenburg (1640–88) exploited this situation and gradually
transformed the Brandenburg *Junker* (squires) into a service
nobility.

Those wealthy families which had dominated the Estates of
Brandenburg in the sixteenth century and managed to maintain their economic status nevertheless often preferred to stay
away from the Elector's court. Their members sought employ-
ment outside Brandenburg instead of serving as officers in the
Hohenzollern army or accepting positions as officeholders.[12]
Most noble landowners in the Kurmark could not, however,
afford the luxury of such independent behaviour. In fact, the
developments in Brandenburg are not unique in this respect.
Elsewhere the social and political elite, and in particular the
nobility, also became more dependent on the prince's favour.

The fact that the money market and the credit system had
been thrown into disarray undoubtedly favoured the princes.
Within the framework devised by the Imperial Diet after 1648,
their councillors decided which loans from before 1618 and
which debts incurred during the war were to be repaid and
under what conditions. This was of crucial importance to most
noble families, for they had nearly all either invested money in
loans before the war or incurred vast debts. By regulating the
repayment or permitting the partial cancellation of outstanding debts and interest payments, the territorial goverment

could make or unmake the fortunes of entire families among the nobility and the urban elite. If the relationship between territorial princes and the nobility remained a partnership based on mutual interest, it nevertheless holds true that the nobility, acting as the prince's partner, was now increasingly defined in terms of membership and internal hierarchy by the prince himself.[13]

In this respect the Habsburg monarchy is an extreme example. The assemblies of Estates continued to exert considerable influence at regional level but they were dominated by families who owed their status to the ruling dynasty much more than was the case for their sixteenth-century predecessors. The 1620s had, after all, seen a vast process of social selection, not only in Bohemia and Moravia, whereby families which, for religious and political reasons, were regarded as disloyal were expropriated and sent into exile. Elsewhere measures taken were less drastic, but there was, nevertheless, a similar process of selection operating through the grant of offices, pensions much needed by noblemen whose income from peasant rents and agriculture had declined, and letters of protection against creditors.[14]

Did all this amount to a victory of 'absolutism' after 1648? To be sure, the scope of government activity was greatly increased after, or in fact even during the war. Although 'the war had corroded the traditional legitimacy of *Herrschaft* [lordship and government] the confusion and desperation underscored the necessity of some kind of protection and thus provided the basis for the revival of *Herrschaft* after the war'.[15] With the traditional economic and social order certainly thrown out of balance, if not destroyed, there was a clear need for an economic policy and measures to re-establish some sort of social equilibrium. Contemporaries employed the catchword *Polizey* to describe this area of policy. *Polizey* in this sense was much more than, and in fact not even primarily, the maintenance of public order and security. Rather it signified all administrative measures designed to promote the public welfare of a principality and the orderly behaviour, well-being and prosperity of its subjects.[16]

The territorial states of the later seventeenth century were not only more ambitious in their policy than the states of the preceding century which had concentrated mostly on providing 'good justice' and maintaining peace – though ecclesiastical policy had, of course, loomed large as well – they also had more resources with which to implement these policies. Nearly everywhere the level of taxation had gone up enormously during the war and at least in the larger and more powerful principalities it was to continue to rise for a considerable time after 1648.[17] The armies, often foreign, occupying entire principalities had achieved in Germany what Richelieu's *intendants* with their *fusiliers de taille* had accomplished in France during the 1630s: they had broken a threshold of taxation. Once this barrier had been breached, Estates and taxpayers in general tended to accept a much higher level of tax extraction, even if this meant that landlords found it more difficult to raise their tenants' rents because they already had to pay a large percentage of their income in taxes to the prince.[18]

Thus the German states of the later seventeenth century were more intensively governed and their rulers had more money available for these purposes. Nevertheless, the tendency towards the sort of strengthening of princely authority which is traditionally called 'absolutism' should not be exaggerated. The Peace of Westphalia had reaffirmed the ideal of the rule of law as the foundation for the very existence of the Empire. Even those rulers who were either not at all, or only partially, subject to the jurisdiction of the Empire's law courts (the Aulic Council and the Empire's Chamber Court), such as the prince electors and of course the Emperor himself, could ill afford to ignore well established privileges and legal traditions, given an all-pervading political culture in which this sort of limitation on monarchical power remained self-evident and supremely important. Moreover, even where the full assemblies of the provincial Estates were no longer convened after 1648, standing committees often continued to exert considerable influence, if not at the level of high politics then at least on regional and local affairs. If the members of these committees now tended to see themselves more as princely officeholders than as the ruler's born opponents,[19] this can be taken as a proof of their terminal decline only by those who wrongly think that the natural, and indeed the only, function of the Estates, their representatives and their assemblies, was to oppose the monarch and his councillors and thwart his purposes.[20]

A final point needs to be made: the driving force behind 'absolutism' in France, the classic early modern 'absolute' monarchy, as in many other European countries, was the perceived need to improve the standing of one's own state in competition with other powers, and in particular to increase its ability to win large-scale wars. It is undoubtedly true that a number of German rulers initially saw the order created in Münster and Osnabrück as giving them an opportunity to pursue their own foreign policy and achieve for their own principality the status of a European power. Within a few decades, if not earlier, however, most had to recognise that their resources were by no means sufficient to obtain such objectives, and returned to less ambitious policies.[21]

Others refused to abandon their hopes of matching the prestige of the great European dynasties, the Bourbons and the Habsburgs. The Welfen Dukes of Hanover did, indeed, manage to gain the English crown (1714) while the Wettins from Dresden became Kings of Poland for a while (c.1697–1763). But these foreign realms absorbed so much of their attention and energy that they tended to treat their own German principalities with benign neglect, glad enough to leave the traditional power of the Estates intact. Thus in most cases the driving force for far-reaching constitutional and political changes was simply no longer there in the eighteenth century. Prussia remained an exception in this as in other respects, but even the Hohenzollern found it extremely difficult to establish their monarchy as a major European power.

Thus the 'absolutism' of the German princes after 1648 must be regarded with a high degree of scepticism. There was one area, however, where their authority was on balance further increased in spite of the limitations imposed on the *ius reformandi* by the Peace of Westphalia: in ecclesiastical matters. The churches and their clergy, which even in Protestant areas had maintained a residual autonomy in the age of the Reformation and Counter-Reformation, were now subjected more completely to state control.[22] On the other hand, we should not overemphasise the tendency towards secularisation which this increased state control implied. Although 1648 is conventionally assumed to be the end of the 'Confessional Age', this does not mean that society and culture were de-confessionalised. In the Habsburg dominions, for example, Counter-Reformation and Catholic reform certainly did not end in 1648, but continued and completed what had been begun in the 1620s and earlier. Moreover, rulers continued to legitimate their authority in religious terms and the Habsburgs, in particular, took great pride in their publicly acclaimed Catholic piety.[23]

It is certainly true that the constitution of the Empire was secularised in 1648, a process which had implicitly already started in 1555, but whose full implications Protestants as well as Catholics had long refused to recognise. At the same time, reason of state, as opposed to religious allegiance, was much more openly acknowledged as the basis of high politics governing European power politics as well as relations between the princes of the Empire.[24] Survivors from an earlier age, such as the Lutheran lawyer and political theorist Theodor Reinking, protested in vain against the 'godless and Machiavellian' principles which the catchword *Staatsräson* (reason of state) embodied; their ideal of a princely government inspired primarily by religious and confessional principles, which had never been entirely realistic even before 1618, was now definitely *passé*.[25] Nevertheless, even in the realm of high politics and diplomacy, religious considerations never entirely lost their influence, and important sections of the general public (though probably not the leading politicians themselves) continued to regard the major political and military conflicts of the next century (such as, for example, the Seven Years War of 1756–63) as in some way religious or confessional wars.[26]

In religious matters, as in other areas, the Peace of Münster and Osnabrück defused the conflicts of the preceding century but also kept them alive, albeit in a more muted form. By confirming the existing status, rights and privileges of the confessional churches, the peace of 1648 to some extent perpetuated the religious divisions of the sixteenth century. Thus the confessional antagonisms of the Age of the Reformation, incorporated into the legal order created in 1648 and thereby in a manner of speaking cast in stone, continued to haunt Germany, in a subtler and more subdued manner than before 1618, until the end of the Empire in 1806. Here, as in other areas, the price which the Empire had to pay for a lasting peace, so enthusiastically welcomed nearly everywhere in Germany in 1648, after 30 years of warfare, was a certain inflexibility. The constitutional framework of the Empire, redesigned in Münster and Osnabrück to deal with the problems of the preceding century, proved largely resistant to any attempts at reform thereafter. During the course of the eighteenth century it therefore gradually but inexorably became less and less able to deal with the problems of a different age.

NOTES

Summary citations are given of all works which appear in the select bibliography. Other works are cited in full once in a chapter, and are given a summary citation if mentioned again in the same chapter.

Introduction

1. Edmund Calamy, *England's Looking Glass* (London, 1641), p. 33.
2. Samuel Hartlib and John Durie, *Clavis Apocalyptica or a Prophetical Key Written by a German D. and now translated out of High-Dutch* (London, 1651). For the eschatological interpretation of the war, cf. Tschopp, *Deutungsmuster*, in particular pp. 191–228.
3. For Richelieu's policy, cf. pp. 117–26.
4. N. M. Sutherland, 'The Origins of the Thirty Years War and the Structure of European Politics', *EHR* 107 (1992), pp. 587–625, at p. 587. For a similar approach see Steinberg, *War*, who argues that the decisive contest between France and Spain really began in 1609 and lasted until 1659, and Engel, 'Respublica christiana', pp. 316–17, as well as pp. 340 and 346–7, note 11. Engel argues, somewhat more cautiously than Sutherland, that the so-called Thirty Years War was just one stage in a wider European conflict which had begun in the 1580s and was not to end until 1659–61. He does, in fact, reject the term 'Thirty Years War' as an invention of anti-French 'patriotic' German propaganda of the later seventeenth century.
5. See in particular K. Repgen, 'Über die Geschichtsschreibung des Dreißigjährigen Krieges: Begriff und Konzeption', in idem, *Krieg und Politik*, pp. 1–84; cf. idem, 'Seit wann gibt es den Begriff "Dreißigjähriger Krieg"', in H. Dollinger *et al.* (eds), *Weltpolitik, Europagedanke, Regionalismus* (Münster, 1982), pp. 59–70.

6. Burkhardt, *Krieg,* pp. 63–128, and idem, 'Der Dreißigjährige Krieg als frühmoderner Staatsbildungskrieg', *Geschichte in Wissenschaft und Unterricht* 45 (1994), pp. 487–99.

Chapter 1

1. For the legal aspects of the Peace of Augsburg see M. Heckel: 'Autonomia und Pacis Compositio. Der Augsburger Religionsfrieden in der Deutung der Gegenreformation', in idem, *Gesammelte Schriften,* i, pp. 1–81; and idem 'Die reichsrechtliche Bedeutung der Bekenntnisse', as well as 'Die Krise der Religionsverfassung des Reiches und die Anfänge des Dreißigjährigen Krieges', ibid. ii, pp. 737–72 and pp. 970–98. The text of the Peace of Augsburg is printed in Buschmann, *Kaiser und Reich,* pp. 215–83, and in Hofmann, *Quellen,* pp. 98–128.

2. M. Heckel, *Staat und Kirche nach den Lehren der evangelischen Juristen Deutschlands in der ersten Hälfte des 17. Jahrhunderts* (Munich, 1968), p. 168.

3. The Treaty of Passau was an agreement between Ferdinand (I) representing his brother, the Emperor Charles V, and a number of Protestant princes who had risen against the Emperor in 1551–52 in the so-called Conspiracy of Princes (Fürstenverschwörung) to reject the high-handed measures which Charles V had introduced after his victory in the war against the League of Schmalkalden (1546–47).

4. M. Heckel, 'Die Reformationsprozesse im Spannungsfeld des Reichskirchensystems', in B. Diestelkamp (ed.), *Die politische Funktion des Reichskammergerichts* (Cologne, 1993), pp. 9–40, at p. 28.

5. For the consolidation of Lutheran churches see H.-C. Rublack (ed.), *Die lutherische Konfessionalisierung in Deutschland* (Gütersloh, 1992).

6. On Calvinism in Germany before 1618 see M. Schaab (ed.), *Territorialstaat und Calvinismus* (Stuttgart, 1993); H. Schilling (ed.), *Die reformierte Konfessionalisierung in Deutschland – Das Problem der Zweiten Reformation* (Gütersloh, 1986); G. Schmidt, *Der Wetterauer Grafenverein* (Marburg, 1989), pp. 273–338; and H. J. Cohn, 'The Territorial Princes in Germany's Second Reformation, 1559–1622', in M. Prestwich (ed.), *International Calvinism 1541–1715* (Oxford, 1985), pp. 135–65.

7. For the different notions of Catholic reform and Counter-Reformation see Schmidt, *Konfessionalisierung*, pp. 67–8. Cf. further W. Reinhard, 'Reformation, Counter-Reformation and the Early Modern State. A Reassessment', *Catholic History Review* 75 (1989), pp. 383–404, as well as idem, 'Gegenreformation als Modernisierung? Prolegomena zu einer Theorie des konfessionellen Zeitalters', *Archiv für Reformationsgeschichte* 68 (1977), pp. 226–52, and most recently idem and H. Schilling (eds), *Die Katholische Konfessionalisierung* (Münster, 1995).

8. Peace of Augsburg §§ 9, 10 and 139, 140.

9. For Maximilian see F. Edelmayer and A. Kohler (eds), *Kaiser Maximilian II. Kultur und Politik im 16. Jahrhundert* (Munich, 1992), and M. Lanzinner, *Friedenssicherung und politische Einheit des Reiches unter Kaiser Maximilian II. (1564–1576)* (Göttingen, 1993).

10. H. Schilling, 'Confessionalization in the Empire: Religious and Societal Change in Germany between 1555 and 1620', in idem, *Religion, Political Culture and the Emergence of Early Modern Society: Essays in German and Dutch History* (Leiden, 1992), pp. 247–301; cf. idem, 'Die Konfessionalisierung von Kirche, Staat und Gesellschaft – Profil, Leistung, Defizite und Perspektiven eines geschichtswissenschaftlichen Paradigmas', in Reinhard/Schilling, *Katholische Konfessionalisierung*, pp. 1–49; and further Schmidt, *Konfessionalisierung*, pp. 86–110; as well as the articles by W. Reinhard, quoted above n. 7.

11. For Rudolf see the biography by R. J. W. Evans, *Rudolf II and his World. A Study in Intellectual History, 1576–1612* (Oxford, 1973, repr. 1984).

12. For the constitutional problems of the Empire in the later sixteenth century see Duchhardt, *Verfassungsgeschichte*, pp. 143–70.

13. H. Duchhardt (ed.), *Politische Testamente und andere Quellen zum Fürstenethos der frühen Neuzeit* (Darmstadt, 1987), p. 34. The Landgrave of Hesse-Darmstadt had appealed against his cousin in Kassel to the Emperor in a conflict over an inheritance and so his loyalty was not entirely uninterested. For similar attitudes in Saxony cf. A. Gotthard, '"Politice seint wir bäpstisch"', p. 315, quoting the last will of the Prince Elector Johann Georg of Saxony (1652).

14. J. H. Franklin, 'Sovereignty and the Mixed Constitution: Bodin and his Critics', in J. H. Burns (ed.), *The Cambridge History of Political Thought 1450–1700* (Cambridge, 1991), pp. 298–328, see in particular pp. 309–24; Stolleis, *Geschichte des öffentlichen Rechts*, i, pp. 174–85; and N. Hammerstein,

'"Imperium Romanum cum omnibus suis qualitatibus ad Germanos est translatum". Das vierte Weltreich in der Lehre der Reichsjuristen', in Kunisch, *Neue Studien*, pp. 187–202.

15. Theodor Reinking, *Tractatus de Regimine Saeculari et Ecclesiastico* (Marburg, 1641 [first edition 1619]), Lib I. Chapter v, §43. For theories of resistance and the idea of a mixed or limited monarchy in Germany in the early seventeenth century see H. Dreitzel, *Monarchiebegriffe in der Fürstengesellschaft*, 2 vols (Cologne, 1991), ii, pp. 492–4, cf. 529–34.

16. M. Stolleis, 'Glaubensspaltung und öffentliches Recht in Deutschland', in idem, *Staat und Staatsräson in der frühen Neuzeit* (Frankfurt/M., 1990), pp. 268–98; cf. H. Gross, *Empire and Sovereignty. A History of the Public Law Literature in the Holy Roman Empire, 1599–1804* (Chicago, 1973)

17. W. Schulze, *Bäuerlicher Widerstand und feudale Herrschaft in der frühen Neuzeit* (Stuttgart, 1980), pp. 76ff; idem, *Einführung in die Neuere Geschichte* (Stuttgart, 1987), pp. 61–66; and Stolleis, *Geschichte des öffentlichen Rechts*, i, pp. 127ff, 209–12, 401–4. Cf. also the works by M. Heckel quoted above n. 1.

18. J. G. A. Pocock, *The Ancient Constitution and the Feudal Law. A Study of English Historical Thought in the Seventeenth Century*, 2nd edn (Cambridge, 1987); Glenn Burgess, *The Politics of the Ancient Constitution. An Introduction to English Political Thought 1603–1642* (London, 1992).

19. For the legal arguments of Catholic authors see, Heckel, 'Autonomia'.

20. Of course, Catholic lawyers were more inclined to see the settlement of 1555 as only a temporary compromise and some polemical tracts even declared the settlement invalid because it was incompatible with the canon law. However, the strongest attack on the position of the Protestants ever undertaken during the war, the Edict of Restitution of 1629, was justified as the authentic interpretation of the Peace of Augsburg, not as its abrogation or suspension (see pp. 94–7).

21. For the following remarks cf. V. Press, 'Die Territorialstruktur des Reiches und die Reformation', in R. Postel and F. Kopitzsch (eds), *Reformation und Revolution, Festschrift Rainer Wohlfeil* (Stuttgart, 1989), pp. 239–68.

22. For Bavaria and Duke/Elector Maximilian cf. Glaser, *Um Glauben und Reich*; Altmann, *Reichspolitik*; and further H. Dollinger, *Studien zur Finanzreform Maximilians I. von Bayern in den Jahren 1598–1618* (Göttingen, 1968).

23. Press, *Kriege und Krisen* , pp. 107–8; idem, *Calvinismus und Territorialstaat. Regierung und Zentralbehörden der Kurpfalz 1559–1619* (Stuttgart, 1970); and C. P. Clasen, *The Palatinate in European History 1559–1660* (London, 1963).

24. Saxony had played a leading role even before the 1550s, when the electoral title had still belonged to the ill-fated Ernestine branch of the Wettin Dynasty. In 1547 Charles V had transferred the title from the rebellious Ernestine to the more loyal Albertine branch together with about half of the Ernestine territories; this was in many ways a precedent for the transfer of the Palatine electoral dignity to Bavaria in the 1620s.

25. This is a point much stressed by Georg Schmidt, in his *Der Dreißigjährige Krieg*. Cf. also his important article 'Integration und Konfessionalisierung. Die Region zwischen Weser und Ems im Deutschland des 16. Jahrhunderts', *ZHF* 21 (1994), pp. 1–36.

26. For the problem of the respective status of *states* and *Estates* see Burkhardt, *Krieg*, pp. 63–128.

27. For contributions to the debate about the so-called crisis of the seventeenth century see T. Aston (ed.), *Crisis in Europe, 1560–1660* (London, 1965); G. Parker and L. M. Smith (eds), *The General Crisis of the Seventeenth Century* (London, 1978); H. G. Koenigsberger, 'The Crisis of the Seventeenth Century: A Farewell?', in idem, *Politicians and Virtuosi* (London, 1986), pp. 149–68; and Ogilvie, 'Germany and the Seventeenth-Century Crisis'; see also Haan, 'Prosperität'.

28. Dipper, *Deutsche Geschichte*, p. 44; Schulze, *Deutsche Geschichte*, pp. 23–4; C. M. Cipolla (ed.), *Europäische Wirtschaftsgeschichte*, ii (Stuttgart, 1983), p. 20.

29. Henning, *Wirtschafts- und Sozialgeschichte*, i, pp. 542–5; Kriedte, *Spätfeudalismus*, pp. 67–8. H. Kamen, *European Society 1500–1700* (London, 1984), pp. 52–62.

30. W. Achilles, *Landwirtschaft in der Frühen Neuzeit* (*EDG* 10, Munich, 1991), pp. 28–40, 91ff. For the tendency to demand higher rents during the decades before 1618 cf. Schlögl, *Bauern, Krieg und Staat*, pp. 265–9 (on Bavaria).

31. For Austria see the case studies by G. Grüll, *Der Bauer im Land ob der Enns am Ausgang des 16. Jahrhunderts* (Vienna, 1969), and H. Rebel, *Peasant Classes. The Bureaucratization of Property and Family Relations under Early Habsburg Absolutism 1511–1636* (Princeton, N.J., 1983), in particular pp. 132–3. Cf. E. Bruckmüller, *Sozialgeschichte Österreichs* (Vienna, 1988),

pp. 186–215, in particular pp. 191–5, and for the other provinces of the monarchy Evans, *Habsburg Monarchy*, pp. 87–91, 97–9, and further K. Bosl (ed.), *Handbuch der Geschichte der Böhmischen Länder*, ii (Stuttgart, 1974), pp. 219–20.

32. Schilling, *Aufbruch*, p. 381; cf. idem, 'The European Crisis of the 1590s: the Situation in German Towns', in P. Clark (ed.), *The European Crisis of the 1590s* (London, 1985), pp. 135–56. For the general context of these revolts see also C. R. Friedrichs, 'Urban Politics and Urban Social Structure in Seventeenth-Century Germany', *European History Quarterly* 22 (1992), pp. 187–216.

33. Dipper, *Geschichte*, p. 187; Kriedte, *Spätfeudalismus*, p. 11. For the thesis of general downward trend in European economic development since about 1620 see also J. de Vries, *The Economy of Europe in an Age of Crisis 1600–1750* (Cambridge, 1976), in particular pp. 17ff.

34. F. Mathis strikes a note of caution in his *Die deutsche Wirtschaft im 16. Jahrhundert (EDG* 11, Munich, 1992), pp. 93–111. Cf., however, Schilling, *Aufbruch*, pp. 372–81, for an approach which broadly accepts the thesis of a general crisis.

35. Haan' s attempt to do so (Haan, 'Prosperität') is not very convincing.

36. Ogilvie, 'Germany and the Seventeenth-Century Crisis', p. 441.

37. See most recently D. Kratzsch, *Justiz – Religion – Politik. Das Reichskammergericht und die Klosterprozesse im ausgehenden sechzehnten Jahrhundert* (Tübingen, 1990), and B. Ruthmann, *Die Religionsprozesse am Reichskammergericht nach dem Augsburger Religionsfrieden von 1555* (Cologne, 1996).

38. On the Union most recently A. Gotthard, 'Protestantische "Union" und Katholische "Liga" – Subsidiäre Strukturelemente oder Alternativentwürfe', in V. Press and D. Stievermann (eds), *Alternativen zur Reichsverfassung in der Frühen Neuzeit?* (Munich, 1995), pp. 81–112; cf. idem, *Konfession*, pp. 28–49; for the policy of electoral Saxony see idem,'"Politice seint wir bäpstisch"'.

39. See W. Schulze, 'Concordia, Discordia, Tolerantia. Deutsche Politik im konfessionellen Zeitalter', in Kunisch, *Neue Studien*, pp. 43–80, at pp. 59–69; idem, 'Majority Decisions in the Imperial Diets of the Sixteenth and Seventeenth Centuries', *JMH* 58, supplement (1986), pp. S.46–S.63; K. Schlaich, 'Die Mehrheitsabstimmungen im Reichstag zwischen 1495 und 1613', *ZHF* 10 (1983), pp. 299–340.

40. For the internal problems of the Habsburg monarchy see pp. 47–56. Because of their very close connection with the immediate outbreak of the war in 1618 they will be treated in a later chapter.

41. Press, *Kriege*, pp. 186–90; cf. J. Rainer, 'Kardinal Melchior Klesl (1552–1630). Vom "Generalreformator" zum "Ausgleichspolitiker"', *Römische Quartalsschrift* 59 (1964), pp. 14–35.

42. H. Schmidt, 'Pfalz-Neuburgs Sprung zum Niederrhein. Wolfgang Wilhelm von Pfalz-Neuburg und der Jülisch-Klevische Erbfolgestreit', in Glaser, *Um Glauben und Reich*, pp. 77–89.

43. B. Nischan, *Prince, People and Confession: The Second Reformation in Brandenburg* (Philadelphia, 1994).

44. F. Neuer-Landfried, *Die Katholische Liga, Gründung, Neugründung und Organisation eines Sonderbundes*, 1608–1620 (Kallmünz, 1968), pp. 102–5, 108–25; A. Litzenburger, *Kurfürst Johann Schweikard von Kronberg als Erzkanzler. Mainzer Reichspolitik am Vorabend des Dreißigjährigen Krieges (1604–1619)* (Stuttgart, 1985), pp. 245–61, 279; cf. further Altmann, *Reichspolitik*, pp. 8, 13.

45. Though he later turned against him in 1551, in the so-called 'Fürstenverschwörung' ('Conspiracy of Princes').

46. Such solidarity was also rejected because it seemed to endanger the pre-eminence of the prince electors over 'simple' princes. Gotthard, '"Politice seint wir bäpstisch"', pp. 315–18.

47. Christian's chancellor Nicolaus Krell was indicted for high treason by the Estates of the Electorate and Christian's successor, and condemned to death by the Supreme Court of the Kingdom of Bohemia, which had been asked for a sentence by the Saxon authorities, in 1601; T. Klein, *Der Kampf um die Zweite Reformation in Kursachsen 1586–1591* (Cologne, 1962).

48. Gotthard, *Konfession*, pp. 228–9.

49. Caspar Schoppius, *Classicum Belli Sacri* [Trumpet Call to Holy War] (Ticini, 1619), praefatio, p. 8: 'adversus Calvini sectatores res omnis est integra' (we are under no obligation whatsoever to the Calvinists). For Schoppe see Bireley, *Religion and Politics*, pp. 115–16, and M. d'Addio, *Il Pensiero politico de Gaspare Scioppio e il Machiavellismo del Seicento* (Milan, 1962).

50. For this interpretation see for example Engel, 'Respublica christiana', pp. 316–17; cf. pp. 2–4 and Introduction n. 4.

51. As a *procurador* in the Cortes of Castile, calling for an end to the war in the Netherlands, put it in 1593: 'if they want to be damned, let them!' (Kamen, *Spain*, p. 139).

52. Israel, *Dutch Republic*, pp. 28–42, in particular pp. 29–30.

53. For the controversy about the *monarchia universalis*, see F. Bosbach, *Monarchia universalis: Ein politischer Leitbegriff der frühen Neuzeit* (Göttingen, 1988).

54. See Elliott, *Olivares*, and cf. J. I. Israel, 'Olivares and the Government of the Spanish Netherlands, 1621–1643', in idem, *Empires and Entrepots* (London, 1990), pp. 163–88.

55. Burkhardt, *Krieg*, in particular pp. 32 and 39–40.

56. See pp. 94–100, 115.

57. For the notion of the composite monarchy see H. G. Koenigsberger, 'Dominium Regale or Dominium Politicum et Regale? Monarchies and Parliaments in Early Modern Europe', in idem, *Politicians and Vituosi*, pp. 1–26; J. H. Elliott, 'A Europe of Composite Monarchies', *Past and Present* 137 (1992), pp. 48–71. See further M. Greengrass (ed.), *Conquest and Coalescence. The Shaping of the State in Early Modern Europe* (London, 1991).

58. On Henry IV's foreign policy see M. Greengrass, *France in the Age of Henry IV*, 2nd edn (London, 1995), pp. 241–50; cf. J. M. Hayden, 'Continuity in the France of Henry IV and Louis XIII, French Foreign Policy 1598–1615', *JMH* 45 (1973), pp. 1–23.

59. See p. 30.

60. Jenny Wormald, 'Gunpowder, Treason and Scots', *Journal of British Studies* 24 (1985), pp. 141–68.

61. For James's foreign policy see S. Adams, 'Spain or the Netherlands? The Dilemmas of Early Stuart Foreign Policy', in H. Tomlinson (ed.), *Before the Civil War* (London, 1983), pp. 79–102; and M. Lee, *Great Britain's Solomon* (Urbana, Ill., 1990), pp. 261–93.

62. Cf. K. Fincham and P. Lake, 'The Ecclesiastical Policy of James I', *Journal of British Studies* 24 (1985), pp. 169–207, at p. 185; Lee, *Solomon*, pp. 164–95.

63. For the affinities between the three religious movements see J. H. M. Salmon, 'Gallicanism and Anglicanism in the Age of the Counter-Reformation', in idem, *Renaissance and Revolt, Essays in the Intellectual and Social History of Early Modern France* (Cambridge, 1987), pp. 155–91; H. Trevor-Roper, *Catholics, Anglicans and Puritans. Seventeenth Century Essays* (London, 1987), pp. 100–1; W. Lamont, 'Arminianism, the Controversy

that never was', in N. Phillipson and Q. Skinner (eds), *Political Discourse in Early Modern Britain* (Cambridge, 1993), pp. 45–66; and, most recently, A. Milton, *Catholic and Reformed. The Roman and Protestant Churches in English Protestant Thought, 1600–1640* (Cambridge, 1995), pp. 264–8.

64. Y.-M. Bercé, *La Naissance dramatique de l'absolutisme, 1598–1661* (Paris, 1992), pp. 64–7; cf. J. M. Hayden, *France and the Estates General of 1614* (Cambridge, 1974), pp. 131–48. There was a clear parallel between this projected oath and the English Oath of Allegiance of 1606 which also denied the deposing power of the Pope (for the Oath of Allegiance see below n. 67). James I did in fact defend the resolution of the French Estates General in his *Remonstrance for the Right of Kings and the Independence of their Crowns, against an Oration of the Most Illustrious Cardinal of Perron* published in 1615, first in French then in English.

65. For the rise of Arminianism in the Dutch Republic see Israel, *Rise, Greatness and Fall*, pp. 422–49; on James's attitude which is not easy to elucidate see Fincham/Lake, 'Policy', pp. 199–202.

66. Adams, 'Spain or the Netherlands?', pp. 80–97, in particular p. 94.

67. James's policy found its expression in particular during the so-called Oath of Allegiance controversy in 1608–10 and the following years, in which James appealed to the solidarity of European monarchs against the Pope's claim to be entitled to depose heretical monarchs. See L. F. Solt, *Church and State in Early Modern England 1509–1640* (Oxford, 1990), pp. 150–1; Milton, *Catholic and Reformed*, pp. 255–62.

68. C. Hermann and J. Marcadé, *La Péninsule Ibérique au XVIIe siècle* (Paris, 1989), p. 36, give the following figures: 6,610,000 for Castile in 1590 plus 350,000 for Navarra and the Basque country. The provinces of the crown of Aragon had about 1.5 million inhabitants.

69. For this problem see pp. 129, 171.

70. For a sceptical view of the correlation between economic resources and political power in the case of Spain see, however, R. A. Stradling, 'Seventeenth Century Spain: Decline or Survival?', *ESR* 9 (1979), pp. 157–94, and idem, *Europe and the Decline*. For Spain's decline cf. further I. A. A. Thompson and B. Yun Casalilla (eds), *The Castilian Crisis of the Seventeenth Century: New Perspectives on the Economic and Social History of Seventeenth-Century Spain* (Cambridge, 1994).

71. Israel, *Dutch Republic,* pp. 53–5, 25–8 and 66–74. For Spanish political options after 1609 cf. P. Brightwell, 'The Spanish System and the Twelve Years' Truce', *EHR* 89 (1974), pp. 270–92.
72. Israel, 'Olivares', pp. 165–7.
73. Brightwell, 'Spanish Origins', and idem, 'Spain and Bohemia'; cf. Ernst, *Madrid und Wien,* pp. 14–5.
74. Israel, *Dutch Republic,* pp. 49–63; cf. idem, *Rise, Greatness, and Fall,* pp. 433–49.
75. Stressed by Israel, *Dutch Republic,* pp. 63–4.

Chapter 2

1. G. Schramm, 'Armed Conflict in East-Central Europe, Protestant Noble Opposition and Catholic Royalist Factions 1604–20', in Evans/Thomas, *Crown, Church and Estates,* pp. 176–95, at pp. 191–2.
2. J. Pánek, 'The Religious Question and the Political System of Bohemia before and after the Battle of the White Mountain', in Evans/Thomas, *Crown, Church and Estates,* pp. 129–48, at p. 133.
3. In the Utraquist Church laymen were allowed to partake of the wine as well as of the bread in mass (to receive the sacrament *sub utraque*), hence the name.
4. For Bohemia and Moravia see the brief survey: F. Machilek, 'Böhmen', in A. Schindling and W. Ziegler (eds), *Die Territorien des Reichs im Zeitalter der Reformation und Konfessionalisierung. Land und Konfession 1500–1650,* i, *Der Südosten* (Münster, 1989), pp. 135–52; cf. J. Bahlke, *Regionalismus und Staatintegration im Widerstreit. Die Länder der Böhmischen Krone im ersten Jahrhundert der Habsburgerherrschaft (1526–1619)* (Munich, 1994), pp. 127–48, 227–59; and T. Winkelbauer, 'Wandlungen des mährischen Adels um 1600', in K. Mack (ed.), *Jan Amos Comenius und die Politik seiner Zeit* (Vienna, 1992), pp. 16–36, in particular pp. 27–35.
5. W. Ziegler, 'Nieder- und Oberösterreich', in Schindling/Ziegler, *Die Territorien des Reichs,* i, *Der Südosten,* pp. 118–33, at p. 126.
6. J. Loserth, *Die Reformation und Gegenreformation in den innerösterreichischen Ländern im XVI. Jahrhundert* (Stuttgart, 1898), p. 276.

7. Evans, *Rudolf II*, pp. 64, 68. For the war against the Turks see J. P. Niederkorn, *Die europäischen Mächte und der 'Lange Türkenkrieg' Kaiser Rudolfs II. (1593–1606)* (Vienna, 1993).

8. K. J. MacHardy, 'Der Einfluß von Status, Konfession und Besitz auf das politische Verhalten des Niederösterreichischen Ritterstandes 1580–1620', in G. Klingenstein and H. Lutz (eds), *Spezialforschung und "Gesamtgeschichte" (Wiener Beiträge zur Geschichte der Neuzeit* 8, Munich, 1982), pp. 56–83; cf. eadem, 'The Rise of Absolutism and Nobel Rebellion in Early Modern Habsburg Austria, 1570–1620' *Comparative Studies in Society and History* 34 (1992), pp. 411–27, and G. Heilingsetzer, 'The Austrian Nobility, 1600–1650: Between Court and Estates', in Evans/Thomas, *Crown, Church and Estates*, pp. 245–60.

9. Bahlke, *Regionalismus*, pp. 430–45.

10. G. Grüll, *Der Bauer im Land ob der Enns am Ausgang des 16. Jahrhunderts* (Vienna, 1969), p. 39: 'Daß die Bauern ums Leben bisher niemand gebracht, hindert nicht, daß sie das Leben verwirkt' [the fact that the peasants have not killed anybody so far, is not a sufficient reason not to punish them by imposing the death penalty]. Cf. H. Sturmberger, *Erasmus Tschernembl. Ein Beitrag zur Geschichte der Gegenreformation und des Landes ob der Enns* (Graz, 1953). Tschernembl later recognised that concessions to the peasantry – an abolition of serfdom, *Leibeigenschaft*, for example – were inevitable if the struggle against the Habsburgs was to be successful, but he was an exception in this respect.

11. Cf. above ch. 1, n. 31.

12. Ritter, *Geschichte*, iii, p. 50.

13. Gindely, *Geschichte*, part i, p. 99; cf. Lorenz, *Quellen zur Vorgeschichte*, p. 327 (report by Doncaster, 19 July 1619).

14. See the short biographical sketch: D. Albrecht, 'Ferdinand II (1619–1637)', in A. Schindling and W. Ziegler (eds), *Die Kaiser der Neuzeit 1519–1918* (Munich, 1990), pp. 125–41; cf. H. Sturmberger, *Kaiser Ferdinand II. und das Problem des Absolutismus* (Munich, 1957).

15. R. Bireley, 'Ferdinand II, Founder of the Habsburg Monarchy', in Evans/Thomas, *Crown, Church and Estates*, pp. 226–44, at p. 229; cf. idem, 'Confessional Absolutism in the Habsburg Lands in the Seventeenth Century', in C. Ingrao (ed.), *State and Society in Early Modern Austria* (West Lafayette, Ind., 1994), pp. 36–53.

16. See Brightwell, 'Spanish Origins', and idem, 'Spain and Bohemia'. Ferdinand had already received the considerable sum of 3.4 million Taler from Spain in July 1619, and in May 1619 7,000 Spanish or Spanish-paid soldiers were sent from

Flanders to Vienna to help the German Habsburgs. Further reinforcements came from northern Italy, and later other troops attacked the Palatinate. In July 1620 Ferdinand had altogether about 12,000 Spanish soldiers at his disposal in Austria and Bohemia. (Parker, *War*, p. 50; Ernst, *Madrid und Wien*, p. 18).

17. See for example Parker, *War*, p. 50.

18. Michael Londorp (ed.), *Acta Publica ... von 1617 biß 1641*, 4 vols (Frankfurt, 1641), i, lib. vi, ch. 391, p. 431.

19. For French policy during these years see V. L. Tapié, *La politique étrangère de la France et le début de la Guerre de Trente Ans 1616–21* (Paris, 1934). For the Treaty of Ulm cf. Gotthard, *Konfession*, pp. 302–19.

20. The so called Bataille de Ponts-de-Cé, in August 1620.

21. C. Desplat, 'Louis XIII and the Union of Béarn to France', in M. Greengrass (ed.), *Conquest and Coalescence. The Shaping of the State in Early Modern Europe* (London, 1991), pp. 68–83.

22. For James I's policy cf. Elmar Weiss, *Die Unterstützung Friedrichs V. von der Pfalz durch Jakob I. und Karl I. von England im Dreißigjährigen Krieg (1618–1632)* (Stuttgart, 1966).

23. For the dissolution of the Union see Gotthard, *Konfession*, pp. 341–9, Gotthard has also emphasised that the Rhine valley was seen as the most likely focus of an armed conflict until 1618. Here the construction of a new fortress at Udenheim by the warlike Bishop of Speyer, Philip Christoph von Sötern, during the years 1616–18 – destroyed by Palatine troops in 1618 – seemed to make an armed confrontation inevitable (ibid., pp. 235–41.)

24. Gindely, *Geschichte*, part i, p. 210; cf. J. Kocc, 'Die Klassenkämpfe der Untertanen in den böhmischen Ländern während des Dreißigjährigen Krieges', in G. Heckenast (ed.), *Aus der Geschichte der europäischen Bauernbewegungen im 16. und 17. Jahrhundert* (Budapest, 1977), pp. 341–9, and Polišenský, *War and Society*, pp. 63–4.

25. C. van Eickels, *Schlesien im Böhmischen Ständestaat. Voraussetzungen und Verlauf der böhmischen Revolution von 1618 in Schlesien* (Cologne, 1994), pp. 438–65.

26. In June 1620 Ferdinand II had reassured Johann Georg that the freedom of worship which the Lutherans enjoyed in Bohemia would be respected. Only Calvinism was to be eliminated (Londorp, *Acta Publica*, i, p. 436). Later Johann Georg tried to insist that these promises were kept, especially as far as the German Protestants in Bohemia were concerned, but with

no success. (Johann Georg to Ferdinand II, 19 November 1622, ibid. p. 437, cf. Ferdinand's reply 25 January 1623, ibid. pp. 438–40).

27. T. Winkelbauer, 'Krise der Aristokratie? Zum Strukturwandel des Adels in den böhmischen und niederösterreichischen Ländern im 16. und 17. Jahrhundert', *Mitteilungen des Instituts für österreichische Geschichtsforschung* 100 (1992), pp. 328–53; Evans, *Making*, pp. 201–13, cf. pp. 169–80.

28. C. Kampmann, *Reichsrebellion und kaiserliche Acht. Politische Strafjustiz im Dreißigjährigen Krieg und das Verfahren gegen Wallenstein 1634* (Münster, 1992), pp. 47–100.

29. Ritter, *Geschichte*, iii, p. 190, and Heckel, *Deutschland im konfessionellen Zeitalter*, p. 130. The transfer of the electoral dignity of Saxony to a different branch of the Saxon dynasty in 1547 can be considered a precedent for this measure (see above ch. 1, n. 24).

30. For Spanish opposition to the transfer of the electoral dignity see Straub, *Pax et Imperium*, pp. 188 and 161–2, cf. pp. 181–4.

Chapter 3

1. Elliott, *Olivares*, pp. 326–38.

2. The crucial importance of Olivares's decision to intervene in northern Italy in order to deny Nevers's claim to Mantua has been underlined by Stradling, 'Olivares and the Origins', pp. 72–94.

3. See Straub, *Pax et Imperium*, pp. 188 and 161–2, cf. pp. 181–4

4. Sir Edward Conway, James's Secretary of State, summed up the objectives of a future war against Spain after Prince Charles's return to England in these terms: 'a warr for the stoppinge of that threateninge monarchie [Spain], for the generall and intire peace of Germanie, for the recoverie of the Pallatinatt and for the perpetuall sueritie of his [James's] friends and Allies' (quoted by T. Cogswell, *The Blessed Revolution, English Politics and the Coming of War, 1621–24*, Cambridge, 1989, p. 70).

5. Cogswell, *Revolution*, pp. 137–54, 268–72; cf. Russell, *Parliaments*, pp. 198–202, for the impeachment against Cranfield.

6. On anti-Popery see P. Lake, 'Anti-popery: The Structure of a Prejudice', in R. Cust and A. Hughes (eds), *Conflict in Early Stuart England. Studies in Religion and Politics 1603–42* (London, 1989), pp. 72–106.

7. On the problems of the English Church in the early seventeenth century see K. Fincham (ed.) *The Early Stuart Church* (London, 1993); C. Russell, *The Causes of the English Civil War* (Oxford, 1990), pp. 83–109; and, most recently, A. Milton, *Catholic and Reformed. The Roman and Protestant Churches in English Protestant Thought, 1600–1640* (Cambridge, 1995).

8. See K. Fincham and P. Lake, 'The Ecclesiastical Policy of James I', *Journal of British Studies* 24 (1985), pp. 169–207, in particular pp. 198–202.

9. It was significant that the commentary on the Letter to the Romans by one of the leading Heidelberg theologians, David Pareus, was burned in England in 1622 on James's order, because Pareus had defended the right of subjects to resist tyrannical rulers. See S. R. Gardiner, *History of England from the Accession of James I to the Outbreak of the Civil War, 1603–1642*, 10 vols (London, 1883/84), iv, pp. 297–9, and Milton, *Catholic and Reformed*, p. 519.

10. For the Mansfeld expedition see R. Lockyer, *Buckingham. The Life and Political Career of George Villiers, First Duke of Buckingham 1592–1628* (London, 1981), pp. 222–9; Gardiner, *History*, v, pp. 280–90; Cogswell, *Revolution*, pp. 239–45.

11. On the forced loan see R. Cust, *The Forced Loan and English Politics 1626–1628* (Oxford, 1987).

12. Thus the Earl of Clare in 1627, who also argued, 'The Duke ... indevors to strengthen himself in the military, having lost the civil part of our estate, ... by pulling on more necessities, to iustify the rather whatsoever shall be taken from us by prerogative ways.' Earl of Clare to Earl of Somerset, 2 August 1627, *The Letters of John Holles 1587–1637*, ed. P. R. Seddon, 3 vols (*Thoroton Record Series* 31, 35, 36, Nottingham, 1975–1986), ii, no. 482, pp. 359–60.

13. Cf. B. Donagan, 'Halcyon Days and the Literature of War: England's Military Education before 1642', *Past and Present* 147 (1995), pp. 65–100. The author argues that the news about the war on the Continent, the military literature instructing Englishmen in the new techniques of warfare and the professional experience which English, Scottish and Irish officers had acquired in foreign armies in the 1630s prepared England mentally for the Civil War and provided English soldiers with models for action in this war.

14. Details according to E. Ladewig Petersen, 'The Danish Intermezzo', in Parker, *War*, pp. 71–82, at p. 80; idem,

'Defence, War and Finance: Christian IV and the Council of the Realm 1596-1629', *Scandinavian Journal of History* 7 (1982), pp. 277–313, at pp. 303 and 307; and Krüger, 'Dänische und schwedische Kriegsfinanzierung', pp. 280–1.

15. Khevenhiller *Annales*, xi, col. 82, Protest of the Mecklenburg Estates, 27 April 1628. The Dukes of Mecklenburg were the descendants of Niklot (died 1160) Prince of the Abodrites, a Slav chieftain. Reinstated in the 1630s they were to rule the Duchy until 1918.

16. Cf. C. Kampmann, *Reichsrebellion und Kaiserliche Acht. Politische Strafjustiz im Dreißigjährigen Krieg und das Verfahren gegen Wallenstein 1634* (Münster, 1992), pp. 90–7.

17. Israel, *Dutch Republic*, p. 162.

18. For Spanish naval strategy relating to northern Germany during these years see Straub, *Pax et Imperium*, pp. 288–314; cf. M. Hroch, 'Wallensteins Beziehungen zu den wendischen Hansestädten', in *Hansische Studien* (Berlin, 1961), pp. 135–61; J. I. Israel, 'The Politics of International Trade Rivalry during the Thirty Years' War: Gabriel de Roy and Olivares' Mercantilist Projects 1621–45', in idem, *Empires and Entrepots* (London, 1990), pp. 213–46, in particular pp. 224-32; and J. Alcalá-Zamora y Queipo de Llano, *España, Flandes y el Mar del Norte 1618–1639* (Barcelona, 1975), pp. 229–42. For Spanish naval strategy during the war cf. further R. A. Stradling, *The Armada of Flanders: Spanish Maritime Policy and the European War, 1568–1668* (Cambridge, 1992).

19. On the deterioration of the Spanish position in 1629 and 1630 see Elliott, *Olivares*, pp. 372ff, and Stradling, 'Olivares and the Origins', pp. 77–9.

20. For the character of the Edict see H. Ströle-Bühler, *Das Restitutionsedikt von 1629 im Spannungsfeld zwischen Augsburger Religionsfrieden 1555 und dem Westfälischen Frieden 1648* (Regensburg, 1991), and M. Frisch, *Das Restitutionsedikt Kaiser Ferdinands II. vom 6. März 1629. Eine rechtsgeschichtliche Untersuchung* (Tübingen, 1993). Cf. further H. Urban, *Das Restitutionsedikt* (Munich, 1966). The edict is printed by Schulz, *Krieg*, i, pp. 60–78.

21. For the process leading to the ratification of the Edict of Restitution see Bireley, *Maximilian von Bayern*, pp. 73–107, and idem, *Religion and Politics*, pp. 75–84, as well as Frisch, *Restitutionsedikt*, in particular pp. 90ff.

22. Memorandum by imperial councillors, *BA* NS, part ii, 3, no. 272, pp. 338–45, [*c.*October 1626]. Particularly important

was the argument that the imperial army with so many Protestant soldiers and officers would hardly be a reliable instrument in a religious war (p. 341). Cf. the advice by Count Collalto *BA* NS, ii, 4, no. 191, p. 202, and on relations with Bavaria the anonymous notes *BA* NS, ii, 4, no. 209, p. 219, 1 January 1629.

23. W. Seibrich, *Gegenreformation als Restauration. Die restaurativen Bemühungen der alten Orden im Deutschen Reich von 1580 bis 1648* (Münster, 1991), pp. 219–34, cf. pp. 170ff.

24. See p. 62.

25. See for example Johann Georg's letter to the Archbishop of Mainz, *BA* NS, ii, 4, no. 226, p. 231, January 1629.

26. Frisch, *Restitutionsedikt*, pp. 91, 97.

27. For the strength of Wallenstein's army see Parker, *War*, p. 100.

28. For war finance and its implications see below, ch. 6.

29. Maximilian of Bavaria saw the danger of an imperial 'plenarium dominium' and a Habsburg universal monarchy built on the ruins of the ancient German liberty ('soll also die liga zergeen, sei es umb die libertet getan und die monarchia stabiliert': 'should the Liga fall apart, liberty will be destroyed and the foundations of monarchy [in the sense of absolute monarchy] be laid', *BA* NS, ii, 4, no. 252, p. 325, post 17 March 1629, and cf. ibid. no. 232, p. 238, 29 January 1629.)

30. Cf. J. Kessel, *Spanien und die geistlichen Kurstaaten am Rhein während der Regierungszeit der Infantin Isabella 1621–33* (Frankfurt/M., 1979).

31. Ritter, *Geschichte*, iii, pp. 457–60.

32. See the memorandum quoted above n. 22. In 1628 Ferdinand had been told by his councillors that even a strict Counter-Reformation in his own dominions – in this case Lower Austria – was too risky given the high percentage (more than half of the officers and soldiers) of Protestants in the imperial army under Wallenstein's command (Khevenhiller, *Annales*, xi, col. 305). For the circumstances of Wallenstein's dismissal see Mann, *Wallenstein*, pp. 677–728; Diwald, *Wallenstein*, pp. 417–34; and Lorenz, *Quellen zur Geschichte Wallensteins*, pp. 211–19. Cf. further D. Albrecht, 'Der Regensburger Kurfürstentag 1630 und die Entlassung Wallensteins', in *Regensburg, Stadt der Reichstage* (Regensburg, 1980), pp. 51–71.

Chapter 4

1. S. Lundkvist, 'Die schwedischen Kriegs- und Friedensziele 1632–1648', in Repgen, *Krieg und Politik*, pp. 219–41, at p. 223; Roberts, *Gustavus Adolphus*, pp. 59–72.

2. However, cf. the sceptical assessment of the significance of economic motives for Swedish foreign policy by Roberts, *Imperial Experience*, pp. 28–36. K. Zernack, 'Schweden als europäische Großmacht in der frühen Neuzeit', *HZ* 232 (1981), pp. 327–57, at pp. 333–43, following an influential school of post-war Swedish historians, on the other hand, considers economic interests as one of the decisive factors fuelling Swedish expansion in the late sixteenth and the early seventeenth centuries.

3. Cf. pp. 164–6.

4. For a survey of recent research see W. Buchholz, 'Der Eintritt Schwedens in den Dreissigjährigen Krieg in der schwedischen und deutschen Historiographie des 19. und 20. Jahrhunderts', *HZ* 245 (1987), pp. 291–314, in particular pp. 301–8.

5. Cf. M. Roberts, *The Early Vasas. A History of Sweden 1523–1611* (Cambridge, 1968), pp. 394–7, 467–8, and idem, *Gustavus Adolphus. A History*, pp. 101–11 and 216–20 for Popish or Polish plots in Sweden and Polish plans for an invasion during Gustav Adolphus's reign.

6. See G. Barudio, *Gustav Adolf der Große* (Frankfurt/M., 1982). This approach also informs Barudio's more comprehensive history of the war (Barudio, *Teutsche Krieg*).

7. Roberts, *Gustavus Adolphus*, pp. 26–8.

8. Parker, *War*, pp. 116–18.

9. 'O Schmach und Schande, Kaiser dir, daß, du es konntest dulden was deutschen Landes Edelzier erlitten ohn verschulden', Ditfurth/Bartsch, *Volkslieder*, 'Ein Trauerlied', 1631, no. 57, p. 136.

10. 'Wack up, o dütsches Land! Lat Jesuiten buten, … Din Freiheit defendere, … Dat men nicht körtlich höre dat dütsche Riek si ut!', Ditfurth/Bartsch, *Volkslieder*, no. 61, pp. 159–63, at p. 163.

11. Tschopp, *Heilsgeschichtliche Deutungsmuster*, pp. 229–47. It is, admittedly, not always easy to distinguish between Swedish propaganda depicting the King as a liberator and spontaneous manifestations of sympathy for Gustavus Adolphus. But at least between Breitenfeld and Lützen the King's popularity in the Imperial Free Cities, for example, seems to have been

considerable as French envoys found to their chagrin in Strassburg in 1632 (Weber, *Frankreich, Kurtrier*, p. 223). After his death, however, enthusiasm for the alliance with Sweden evaporated (D. Böttcher, 'Propaganda und öffentliche Meinung im Protestantischen Deutschland 1628–1636', in Rudolf, *Krieg*, pp. 325–66, at pp. 348–9, 358); cf. S. Oredsson, *Geschichtsschreibung und Kult. Gustav Adolf, Schweden und der Dreißigjährige Krieg* (Berlin, 1994).

12. J. Kretschmar, *Der Heilbronner Bund (1632–1635)*, 3 vols (Lübeck, 1922).

13. Roberts, 'Oxenstierna in Germany', in idem, *From Oxenstierna to Charles XII. Four Studies* (Cambridge, 1991), pp. 6–54, at pp. 42–3.

14. Parker, *War*, pp. 158–9.

15. Roberts, 'Oxenstierna in Germany', p. 26, cf. S. Goetze, *Die Politik des schwedischen Reichskanzlers Oxenstierna gegenüber Kaiser und Reich* (Kiel, 1971), p. 103.

16. Straub, *Pax et Imperium*, p. 456.

17. A. Wandruszka, *Reichspatriotismus und Reichspolitik zur Zeit des Prager Friedens von 1635* (Graz/Cologne, 1955); cf. Schmidt, *Krieg*, p. 59.

18. For the situation at the imperial court see Bireley, *Religion and Politics*, pp. 208–27.

19. Haan, *Kurfürstentag*, p. 243, n. 86, quoting a statement by Maximilian, July 1636: 'Hierauf wolt ich den Radolt [the imperial diplomatic agent in England] mit seiner politica gern hören, was er thet, wann er an des Khöniges statt were, ob er lieber … ein rechter absolutus rex sein wolte, … ober aber ob er sich lieber seines parlamentes tutel und praescriptis underwerffen wollte, damit er sich mit andern conjungieren und khrieg fieren khönde. Und ob der Khönig lieber den Pfaltzgrafen zu einem churfürsten als sich zu einem rechten herren und khönig sehen werde.'

20. V. Press, 'Hessen im Zeitalter der Landesteilung (1567–1655)', in W. Heinemeyer (ed.), *Das Werden Hessens* (Marburg, 1986), pp. 267–331, at pp. 310–11.

21. For the problem of Württemberg see Haan, *Kurfürstentag*, pp. 176–81, and Bierther, *Der Regensburger Reichstag*, pp. 147–50.

22. For a discussion of this problem see Schmidt, *Krieg*, pp. 57–61; Burkhardt, *Krieg*, pp. 96–9, and Haan, 'Reichsabsolutismus'.

23. This clause of the treaty was apparently not enforced among Protestant troops, and Maximilian later managed to have the troops under his command excepted from this new oath of

fealty and allegiance as well (Haan, 'Reichsabsolutismus', pp. 255–7; cf. A. Kraus, 'Zur Vorgeschichte des Friedens von Prag 1635. Die Entstehung der Kommandoregelung nach Art. 24', in H. Dickerhof *et al.* (eds), *Festgabe Heinz Hürten zum 60. Geburtstag* (Frankfurt/M., 1988), pp. 265–99.

24. For the opposition to Richelieu in France see J. M. Constant, *Les conjurateurs, le premier libéralisme politique sous Richelieu* (Paris, 1987).

25. J. Russell Major, *From Renaissance Monarchy to Absolute Monarchy: French Kings, Nobles and Estates* (Baltimore, 1994), p. 293.

26. See, for example, C. J. Burckhardt, *Richelieu and his Age*, 3 vols (London, 1971), or more recently M. Carmona, *Richelieu, L'Ambition et le pouvoir* (Paris, 1983). For a recent survey of research on Richelieu see also R. J. Knecht, *Richelieu* (London, 1991).

27. F. Dickmann, 'Rechtsgedanke und Machtpolitik bei Richelieu', *HZ* (1963), pp. 5–32; Weber, *Frankreich, Kurtrier*, idem, 'Vom verdeckten zum offenen Krieg. Richelieus Kriegsgründe und Kriegsziele 1634/35', in Repgen, *Krieg und Politik*, pp. 203–18; idem, 'Une paix sûre et prompte. Die Friedenspolitik Richelieus', in H. Duchhardt (ed.), *Zwischenstaatliche Friedenswahrung in Mittelalter und Früher Neuzeit* (Cologne, 1991), pp. 111–30; and idem, '"Une Bonne Paix"'. For an assessment of Richelieu's ideas and principles cf. further W. F. Church, *Richelieu and Reason of State* (Princeton, N.J.,1972), and J. Wollenberg, *Richelieu, Staatsräson und Kircheninteresse* (Bielefeld, 1977).

28. Weber, '"Une Bonne Paix"', p. 68.

29. J. Bergin, *Cardinal Richelieu. Power and the Pursuit of Wealth* (New Haven, Conn., 1985); and Parrott, 'Richelieu, the *Grands* and the French Army'; idem, 'Causes'.

30. Parrott, 'Causes', p. 87.

31. For Lorraine: R. Babel, *Zwischen Habsburg und Bourbon Außenpolitik und europäische Stellung Herzog Karls IV von Lothringen und Bar 1624–1634* (Sigmaringen, 1989).

32. Cf. W. H. Stein, *Protection Royale. Eine Untersuchung zur den Protektionsverhältnissen im Elsaß zu Zeit Richelieus, 1622–1643* (Münster, 1978), and Weber, *Frankreich, Kurtrier*.

33. For this policy see Richelieu's famous memorandum (*advis*) of January 1629. Grillon, *Papiers*, iv, pp. 24–47, at p. 25: France should acquire 'portes pour entrer dans tous les estats des ses voisins'.

34. For Olivares's plans, see Stradling, 'Olivares and the Origins', pp. 83–91.
35. Ernst, *Madrid und Wien*, pp. 40–1, 81–5, 130–1. According to Ernst (p. 81) Olivares thought on the one hand that Spain was too weak to attack France, and on the other that once the Emperor had declared war on France, a lasting peace with the Bourbons, under conditions which were favourable to Spain, might be possible after all.
36. Ernst, *Madrid und Wien*, p. 83.
37. The point is emphasised by Weber, 'Vom verdeckten zum offenen Krieg', pp. 208–9.
38. Parrott, 'Causes', p. 95 n. 87
39. Cf. Ernst, *Madrid und Wien*, pp. 65–7.
40. For Spain's own vision of peace see Straub, *Pax et Imperium*, pp. 44–78 and 109–29.

Chapter 5

1. Israel, *Greatness and Fall*, pp. 516–23; idem, *Dutch Republic*, p. 251.
2. Israel, *Dutch Republic*, p. 260.
3. J. H. Elliott, *The Revolt of the Catalans* (Cambridge, 1963); Lynch, *Hispanic World*, pp. 140–9.
4. Ibid., pp. 149–57; C. Hermann and J. Marcadé, *La Péninsule Ibérique au XVIIᵉ siècle* (Paris, 1989), pp. 249–65.
5. Roberts in Parker, *War*, pp. 158–9, cf. idem, 'Oxenstierna in Germany', in *From Oxenstierna to Charles XII. Four Studies* (Cambridge, 1991), pp. 45–54.
6. Bierther, *Reichstag*, pp. 230–1, 243.
7. For Bavarian policy during the last years of the war see G. Immler, *Kurfürst Maximilian I. und der Westfälische Friedenskongreß. Die bayerische auswärtige Politik von 1644 bis zum Ulmer Waffenstillstand* (Münster, 1992). Maximilian eventually signed a ceasefire with France in March 1648 in Ulm.
8. F. Wolff, *Corpus Evangelicorum und Corpus Catholicorum auf dem Westfälischen Friedenskongreß* (Münster, 1966).
9. Secret imperial instruction 16 October 1645, *APW*, i, 1, pp. 440–52, at p. 450.
10. Cf. e.g. *APW*, ii, B 2, p. 274, against a separate peace with the Emperor (15 April 1645).

11. For French policy see M. Laurain-Portemer, 'Question européennes et diplomatie mazarine', *XVIIe Siècle* 42 (1990), pp. 17–55, in particular pp. 35–7; for Spanish policy cf. M. Fernandez Álvarèz, 'El fracaso de la hegemonía española', in F. Tomas y Valente (ed.), *La España de Felipe IV* (*Historia de España* t. xv, Madrid, 1982), pp. 764ff. For the outbreak of the Fronde in France cf. p. 175.

12. Cf. Weber, '"Une Bonne Paix"', p. 49: 'The Most Christian King was to be not only the supreme arbiter in Christendom but above all its protector, and for Richelieu this function as protector was sufficient to justify all possible kinds of political and military intervention on the part of France.'

13. *APW*, i, 1, p. 71: 'Pour l'establissement de cette seureté il faut faire deux ligues, l'une en Italie, l'autre en Allemagne, en vertu desquelles touts les Princes, Potentatz et Communautéz de ces provinces soient garendz du Traitté qui se fera, et obligéz à s'opposer à touts ceux qui y voudront contrevenir.'

14. *APW*, ii, B 2, pp. 298–9, 22 April 1648.

15. *APW*, ii, B 2, p. 51, 14 January 1645.

16. Ruppert, *Die kaiserliche Politik*, pp. 112–19.

17. The treaty of Osnabrück eventually granted Sweden the sum of 5 million Taler to pay off her soldiers (Parker, *War*, p. 186).

18. For the negotiations about the principle of religious toleration in Osnabrück see G. May, 'Die Entstehung der hauptsächlichen Bestimmungen über das ius emigrandi (Art. V §§ 30-43 IPO) auf dem Westfälischen Friedenskongreß', *Zeitschrift für Rechtsgeschichte. Kan. Abt.* 74 (1988), pp. 436–94; Dickmann, *Frieden*, pp. 365, 462–3.

19. Dickmann, *Frieden*, pp. 333–4.

20. *APW*, i, 1, pp. 132–6 (no. 8), *ante* 22 July 1642, supplement to instruction for French envoys, not incorporated into final version, at p. 135: 'Si les Espagnolz veulent ensuite se mesler des affaires de quelques uns des mescontents de France, il faut faire connoistre aux Entremetteurs que leur prétention est tellement contre le droict des gens, qu'elle mérite plustost une risée qu'une response'; cf. pp. 128–38 on Catalonia and the French Queen Mother (supported by the Spanish).

21. Dickmann, *Frieden*, pp. 332–43, 490–3.

22. For the *ius foederis* and *ius superioritatis* conceded to the individual Estates of the Empire in 1648 cf. Schilling, *Höfe*, pp. 131–3. Schilling sees the arrangements of 1648 as leading to full

territorial sovereignty at least for the larger principalities in spite of the Empire's theoretical suzerainty.

23. H. Duchhardt, *Gleichgewicht der Kräfte, Convenance, Europäisches Konzert*, (Darmstadt, 1976), pp. 35–40.

24. Osiander, *States System*, pp. 16–89, in particular pp. 43–8, 73; H. Duchhardt, 'Westfälischer Friede und Internationales System im Ancien Régime', *HZ* 249 (1989), pp. 529–43.

25. Stressed by Duchhardt, *Verfassungsgeschichte*, p. 159, cf. p. 180.

26. Press, *Kriege und Krisen*, pp. 267, 379–84.

27. For these questions see Oschmann, *Exekutionstag*.

28. Against this traditional interpretation of the peace see now Schmidt, *Krieg*, pp. 94–8, and idem, 'Der Westfälische Friede – eine neue Ordnung für das Alte Reich?', in *Wendemarken in der deutschen Verfassungsgeschichte* (*Der Staat*, supplement 10, Berlin, 1993), pp. 45–72.

29. Cf. Repgen, *Kurie*.

Chapter 6

1. P. Sörensson, 'Das Kriegswesen während der letzten Periode des Dreißigjährigen Krieges', in Rudolf, *Krieg*, pp. 431–57, in particular pp. 452–3.

2. More troops were concentrated in the encounter between Gustavus Adolphus and Wallenstein near Nuremberg in 1632 but this was not a pitched battle (see below n. 23).

3. For the size of armies, see Tallett, *War and Society*, pp. 5–6; for Rocroi see Bély, *Les relations*, pp. 142–3.

4. Salm, *Armeefinanzierung*, p. 42, n. 34.

5. B. Kroener, 'Die Entwicklung der Truppenstärken in den französischen Armeen zwischen 1635 und 1661', in Repgen, *Forschungen*, pp. 163–220, at pp. 203–5 and 171–5. Cf. the cautionary remarks by A. Corvisier, *La France de Louis XIV* (Paris, 1979), p. 61, who estimates that at the death of Louis XIII not more than 100,000 Frenchmen were serving in the royal armies, and that on average the size of the royal armies varied from 80,000 to 120,000 men between 1635 and 1659 (p. 124). Cf. further J. A. Lynn, 'Recalculating French Army Growth during the *Grand Siècle*, 1610–1715', in Rogers, *Military Revolution Debate*, pp. 117–47. Lynn puts the maximum strength of the French forces (for 1639) at 125,000 men (p. 130).

6. For the inadequacy of finance and supply in the Thirty Years War see D. A. Parrott, 'Strategy and Tactics in the Thirty Years' War: The Military Revolution', *Militärgeschichtliche Mitteilungen* 38 (1985), pp. 7–25 [reprinted in Rogers, *Military Revolution Debate*, pp. 227–52], in particular pp. 17–22.

7. Tallett, *War and Society*, p. 62, and in general pp. 55–68.

8. Parker, *The Army of Flanders*, pp. 87–101.

9. Kroener, *Les routes*. Cf. Corvisier, *La France*, pp. 107–12; J. A. Lynn, 'How War Fed War: the Tax of Violence and Contributions during the *Grand Siècle*', *JMH* 65 (1993), pp. 286–310; and M. van Creveld, *Supplying War: Logistics from Wallenstein to Patton* (Cambridge, 1977), pp. 19–26.

10. The imperial general Gallas, for example, when fighting the Swedes in northern Germany in 1644, had 11,500 horse and 10,000 foot-soldiers under his command. Of the cavalry about two-thirds survived the campaign; of the foot only about 50 per cent (Salm, *Armeefinanzierung*, p. 43).

11. For the debate on the military revolution see M. Roberts, 'The Military Revolution', in idem, *Essays in Swedish History* (London, 1967), pp. 195–225, reprinted in Rogers, *Military Revolution Debate*, pp. 13–35, and the other essays in the collection edited by Rogers. See further Parker, *The Military Revolution*, pp. 6–44, and J. Black, *European Warfare 1660–1815* (London, 1994), pp. 3–33, with further references.

12. Roberts, *Gustavus Adolphus. A History*, ii, pp. 245–64, in particular pp. 255–6; also G. E. Rothenberg, 'Maurice of Nassau, Gustavus Adolphus, Raimondo Montecuccoli and the "Military Revolution" of the Seventeenth Century', in P. Paret (ed.), *Makers of Modern Strategy from Machiavelli to the Nuclear Age* (Oxford, 1986), pp. 32–63, at pp. 45–9.

13. A. Åberg, 'The Swedish Army from Lützen to Narva', in Roberts, *Sweden's Age of Greatness*, pp. 265–87, at p. 283; see also Roberts, *Gustavus Adolphus*, p. 106, and M. Junkelmann, *Gustav Adolf* (Regensburg, 1993), pp. 208–59.

14. M. Junkelmann, 'Feldherr Maximilians: Johann Tserclaes Graf von Tilly', in Glaser, *Um Glauben und Reich*, pp. 377–99, at pp. 385–6.

15. H. Dollinger, *Studien zur Finanzreform Maximilians I. von Bayern in den Jahren 1598–1618* (Göttingen, 1968); Junkelmann, 'Tilly', pp. 377–9.

16. For Spanish subsidies after 1618 see Parker, *War*, p. 50; for papal subsidies see D. Albrecht, 'Zur Finanzierung des

Dreißigjährigen Krieges. Die Subsidien der Kurie für Kaiser und Liga 1618–1635', in Rudolf, *Krieg*, pp. 368–412.

17. For these coinage manipulations and the Kipper- und Wipperzeit in general see Mann, *Wallenstein*, pp. 237–45; Ernstberger, *De Witte*, pp. 86ff; H. C. Altmann, *Die Kipper- und Wipperinflation in Bayern 1620–23. Ein Beitrag zur Strukturanalyse des frühabsolutistischen Staates* (Munich, 1976); F. Redlich, *Die deutsche Inflation des frühen 17. Jahrhunderts in der zeitgenössischen Literatur: Die Kipper und Wipper* (Cologne, 1972).

18. For de Witte see the biography by Ernstberger.

19. Redlich, *Enterpriser*, i, pp. 292–5, cf. pp. 84–5, 88–90.

20. Schormann, *Krieg*, pp. 85–91, with further references.

21. Lorenz, *Quellen zur Geschichte Wallensteins*, pp. 111–14, report of Imperial Treasury to Council of War, November 1626, which states that Wallenstein had promised in 1625 to finance his army without the Treasury's help. Cf. however, Diwald, *Wallenstein*, pp. 271–85, in particular pp. 274–5.

22. Ernstberger, *De Witte*, p. 194.

23. For the strength of armies see B. Sicken, 'Die Schlacht bei Nördlingen', in *Frieden ernährt* (*Historischer Verein für Nördlingen und das Ries, Jahrbuch* 27, Nördlingen, 1985), pp. 175–220, at pp. 188–9. The greatest concentration of troops during the war – at least in Germany – was the confrontation between the imperialists and the Swedish army near Nuremberg in 1632. Gustavus Adolphus had about 40,000 and Wallenstein nearly 50,000 men (ibid., p. 189).

24. Ernstberger, *De Witte*, pp. 200, 246.

25. For the role of the Duchy of Friedland see A. Ernstberger, *Wallenstein als Volkswirt im Herzogtum Friedland* (Reichenberg i. B., 1929), in particular p. 10, on the legal autonomy of the Duchy and idem, 'Wallensteins Heeressabotage und die Breitenfelder Schlacht (1631)', in idem, *Franken-Böhmen-Europa. Gesammelte Aufsätze*, i (Kallmünz, 1959), pp. 294–326.

26. Redlich, *Enterpriser*, i, pp. 234–5; cf. Gustav Droysen, *Bernhard von Weimar* (Leipzig, 1885).

27. A. Corvisier, *Louvois* (Paris, 1983), p. 80, cf. pp. 81 and 103; cf. further idem, *La France*, pp. 178–81. Le Tellier's statement is borne out by the facts as D. Parrott has shown (Parrott, 'Richelieu, the *Grands* and the French Army').

28. Thus an imperial field marshal (the third rank in the military hierarchy) was worth 20,000 florins and a lieutenant general (the second after the generallissimus) fetched 30,000 florins

according to the *cartel* between the Emperor and Sweden signed in 1645. Redlich, *Enterpriser*, i, pp. 365–8, 398–9.

29. Magen, 'Die Reichskreise'; Salm, *Armeefinanzierung*, pp. 11–26.

30. Ibid., pp. 45–6, 172–6. Between 1632 and 1640 Spain had paid on average between 300,000 and 500,000 florins each year in subsidies to the Emperor (Ernst, *Madrid und Wien*, p. 279).

31. Salm, *Armeefinanzierung*, pp. 43–4. The imperial cavalry lost about 35 per cent through desertion, illness, etc.; the infantry as much as 50 per cent.

32. J. Bérenger, *Finances et absolutisme autrichién dans la second moitié du XVIIe siècle* (Paris, 1975). Cf. the complaints of the Protestant princes of the Empire (Khevenhiller, *Annales*, xi, 8 February 1631, col. 1540ff, in particular 1543–5), who argued that the liberties of the Estates in the imperial hereditary lands were respected, whereas the old privileges of the German princes were ignored.

33. Salm, *Armeefinanzierung*, p. 176.

34. Swedish war finance is here analysed in the section on military finance in Germany as after 1631 most of the money for the Swedish forces came from German sources.

35. Krüger, 'Kriegsfinanzierung', pp. 283–5; Tallett, *War and Society*, p. 83; Roberts, *Gustavus Adolphus*, p. 124.

36. Roberts, *Imperial Experience*, p. 44; idem, *Gustavus Adolphus: A History*, ii, p. 207.

37. Krüger, 'Kriegsfinanzierung', pp. 288–9; Roberts, *Imperial Experience*, p. 53.

38. S. A. Nilsson, *De Stora krigens tid. Om Sverige som militärstaat och bondesamhället* (Uppsala, 1990), pp. 284–7.

39. The 800,000 Taler were a maximum reached only in 1634; in 1630 the income had been less than half that sum. See Krüger, 'Kriegsfinanzierung', p. 288; *New Cambridge Modern History*, iv, p. 401; cf. K. R. Böhme, *Die schwedische Besetzung des Weichsellandes 1626–1636* (Würzburg, 1963); S. E. Åstrom, 'The Swedish Economy and Sweden's Role as a Great Power', in Roberts, *Sweden's Age of Greatness*, pp. 58–101; and generally L. Ekholm, *Svensk Kreigsfinansiering 1630–1681* (Uppsala, 1974).

40. G. Lorenz, 'Schweden und die französischen Hilfsgelder', in Repgen, *Forschungen und Quellen*, pp. 98–148, in particular p. 100, n. 6.

41. T. Lorentzen, *Die schwedische Armee im Dreißigjährigen Krieg und ihre Abdankung* (Leipzig, 1894), pp. 91–105. This mutiny, however, was one of the main reasons for the extension of the

Franco-Swedish alliance in 1641 on terms favourable to France.

42. The prince-bishoprics of Bremen and Verden in north-western Germany, which remained under Swedish administration after 1648 and which had admittedly not suffered all that badly from the effects of warfare, alone yielded more than 200,000 Taler each year from 1646 to 1648; see K. R. Böhme, 'Geld für die schwedischen Armeen nach 1640', *Scandia* 33 (1967), pp. 54–95, at pp. 80–1.

43. M. C. 't Hart, *The Making of a Bourgeois State: War, Politics and Finance during the Dutch Revolt* (Manchester, 1993), pp. 118–57 and 173–84. The Dutch army consisted of about 130,000 men at its strongest, during the late 1620s; 70,000 of these soldiers belonged to the Dutch standing army. The remainder were recruited by hired military entrepreneurs (ibid., p. 45). Thus the Dutch forces were as strong as the largest armies of the major European powers during the period, even on land, quite apart from the powerful Dutch navy.

44. The following remarks are based mainly on I. A. A. Thompson, 'Castile: Polity, Fiscality and Fiscal Crisis', in P. T. Hoffman and K. Norberg (eds), *Fiscal Crises, Liberty and Representative Government* (Stanford, Calif., 1994), pp. 140–80.

45. Kamen, *Spain*, pp. 222–30; cf. I. A. A. Thompson and B. Yun Casalilla (eds), *The Castilian Crisis of the Seventeenth Century: New Perspectives on the Economic and Social History of Seventeenth-Century Spain* (Cambridge, 1994).

46. Thompson, 'Castile', pp. 160–3. On state finance in Spain cf. Lynch, *Hispanic World*, pp. 110–21; A. Domínguez Ortiz, *Política y Hacienda de Felipe IV* (Madrid, 1960); F. Ruiz Martín, *Las finanzas de la monarquía hispaníca en tiempos de Felipe IV, 1621–1665* (Madrid, 1990); J. E. Gelabert, 'El impacto de la guerra y del fiscalismo en Castilla', in Elliott/Sanz, *La España*, pp. 555–73, as well as the contribution of the same author to the forthcoming collection of essays edited by R. Bonney, *The Rise of the Fiscal State in Europe, c. 1200–1815* (Oxford, 1996).

47. For Genoa's role in international finance see F. Braudel, *Civilization and Capitalism 15th–18th Century*, iii, *The Perspective of the World* (New York, 1982), pp. 157–70, and G. Muto, 'The Spanish System: Centre and Periphery', in R. Bonney (ed.), *Economic Systems and State Finance* (Oxford, 1995), pp. 231–260, at pp. 245–51.

48. For Spínola see R. A. Stradling, *Philip IV and the Government of Spain, 1621–1665* (Cambridge, 1988), pp. 70–2.

49. C. Boyajian, *Portuguese Bankers at the Court of Spain 1626–1650* (New Brunswick, N.J., 1983);.Thompson, 'Castile', p. 156, cf. pp. 158–9.

50. Cf. Parker, *Army of Flanders*, p. 157, for Italian contributions to the Spanish military effort in the Netherlands.

51. Kamen, *Spain*, pp. 217–8. For the political impact of the rise and fall in bullion imports see A. Domínguez Ortiz, 'Los caudales de Indias y la política exterior de Felipe IV', *Anuario de Estudios Americanos* 13 (1956), pp. 311–83.

52. D. Flynn, 'Fiscal Crisis and the Decline of Spain', *Journal of Economic History* 42 (1982), pp. 139–47, in particular p. 142. Cf. E. J. Hamilton, *American Treasure and the Price Revolution in Spain, 1501–1650*, 2nd edn (1st edn 1934; Cambridge, Mass., 1965), in particular p. 34.

53. Lynch, *Hispanic World*, p. 241; M. Morineau, 'Gazettes hollandaises et trésors américains', *Anuario de Historia Económica y Social* 2 (1969), pp. 289–347 and 3 (1970), pp. 139–209; cf. idem, *Incroyables gazettes et fabuleux métaux. Les retours des trésors américains d'après les gazettes hollandaises* (Cambridge, 1985), esp. pp. 77–83, 247–50. See further A. García-Baquero González, 'Andalusia and the Crisis of the Indies Trade, 1610–1720', in Thompson/Casalilla, *The Castilian Crisis of the Seventeenth Century*, pp. 115–35, at pp. 118–23.

54. R. Pieper, 'The Volume of African and American Exports of Precious Metals and its Effects in Europe, 1500–1800', in H. Pohl (ed.), *The European Discovery of the World and its Economic Effects on Pre-Industrial Society 1500–1800* (Stuttgart, 1990), pp. 97–121; Lynch, *Hispanic World*, pp. 235–40; Bonney, *European Dynastic States*, pp. 215, 445.

55. For the Union of Arms, Elliott, *Olivares*, pp. 244–77, 553ff; Lynch, *Hispanic World*, pp. 131–40.

56. Thompson, 'Castile', pp. 173–4; Kamen, *Spain*, pp. 236–8; cf. J. H. Elliott, *The Revolt of the Catalans* (Cambridge, 1963), and I. A. A. Thompson, *War and Government in Habsburg Spain 1560–1620* (London, 1976), pp. 33–45.

57. For general administrative developments in Spain and, in particular, decentralisation and fragmentation of administrative responsibilities, see Thompson, *War and Government*, and idem, 'The Government of Spain in the Reign of Philip IV', in idem, *Crown and Cortes: Government, Institutions and Representation in*

Early-Modern Castile (Aldershot, 1993), ch. 4, esp. pp. 27ff, for the role of the nobility in recruiting soldiers. In the sixteenth century volunteers had been recruited by captains appointed by royal commission; now the magnates sent their tenants to war.

58. P. T. Hoffman, 'Early Modern France, 1450–1700', in Hoffman/Norberg, *Fiscal Crises*, pp. 226–52, at p. 238.

59. W. Mager, *Frankreich vom Ancien Régime zur Moderne 1630–1830* (Stuttgart, 1980), pp. 112–3, cf. P. Goubert and D. Roche, *Les Français et l'ancien régime*, 2 vols (Paris, 1984), i, p. 335, who put the annual *expenses* of the French monarchy at 192 tons of silver for the decade 1600–09, and at 810 tons for the two first decades of Louis XIV's independent rule (after 1661). This remained the normal level of expenditure for the first half of the eighteenth century, though it had been exceeded during the War of the Spanish Succession.

60. Hoffman, 'France', p. 239, and Mager, *Frankreich*, p. 114, the latter quoting F. Braudel and E. Labrousse (eds), *Histoire économique et sociale de la France*, i, 2 (Paris, 1977), p. 980, giving the equivalent in labour days of the tax burden for each head of a family in France. If the whole adult population, including women and unmarried men, were counted, the burden would, of course, be lower.

61. For the French Estates and their assemblies see J. Russell Major, *From Renaissance Monarchy to Absolute Monarchy: French Kings, Nobles and Estates* (Baltimore, 1994), esp. pp. 236–60, and J. M. Hayden, *France and the Estates General of 1614* (Cambridge, 1974).

62. Hoffman, 'France', pp. 232–5; Collins, *Fiscal Limits*, pp. 98–107. For the sale of offices as a means of raising credit cf. W. Reinhard, 'Staatsmacht als Kreditproblem. Zur Struktur und Funktion des frühneuzeitlichen Ämterhandels', *VSWG* 61 (1974), pp. 289–319.

63. R. Bonney, 'Louis XIII, Richelieu and the Royal Finances', in Bergin/Brockliss, *Richelieu and his Age*, pp. 99–135, at pp. 108–10; Collins, *Fiscal Limits*, pp. 135–65. Collins states that in 1633 about 46 per cent of all direct taxes went to holders of *droits aliénés*, not to the King (p. 164).

64. Collins, *Fiscal Limits*, pp. 141, 215 and 200–13, 219; Hoffman, 'France', p. 244; Bonney, 'Royal Finances', p. 119; idem, *Political Change*, pp. 214–37.

65. Collins, *Fiscal Limits*, p. 209; for the intendants: Bonney, *Political Change*, pp. 29–56 and 163–90.

66. Elliott, *Richelieu and Olivares*, pp. 138–42, and Bonney, 'Royal Finances'; but cf. R. Briggs, 'Richelieu and Reform: Rhetoric and Political Reality', in Bergin/Brockliss, *Richelieu and his Age*, pp. 71–98.

67. R. Bonney, *The King's Debts: Finance and Politics in France 1589–1661* (Oxford, 1981), pp. 204–5.

68. For the Fronde see A. L. Moote, *The Revolt of the Judges: The Parlement of Paris and the Fronde* (Princeton, N.J., 1971), O. Ranum, *The Fronde: A French Revolution 1648–1652* (New York, 1993), and Le Roy Ladurie, *L'Ancien régime*, i, pp. 168–75; cf. P. Goubert, *Mazarin* (Paris, 1990).

69. For Olivares's rejection of national, i.e. Castilian, Portuguese or Neapolitan etc. sentiment see Elliott, *Olivares*, p. 564.

70. The *Gabelle* was the unpopular tax on salt.

71. Cf. Kamen, *Spain*, pp. 239–40; cf. further J. H. Elliott, R. Villari and A. M. Hespanha (eds), *1640: La Monarquía hispánica en crisis* (Barcelona, 1992), and J.-F. Schaub, 'La crise hispanique de 1640. Le modèle des "révolutions périphériques" en question (note critique)', *Annales ESC* 49 (1994), pp. 219–39.

72. Thompson, 'The Government of Spain in the Reign of Philip IV', in particular p. 79; cf. idem, 'War and Institutionalization: the Military-Administrative Bureaucracy of Spain in the Sixteenth and Seventeenth Centuries', in idem, *Crown and Cortes*, ch. 3, esp. pp. 36–7.

73. M. P. Gutmann, *War and Rural Life in the Early Modern Low Countries* (Assen, 1980), esp. pp. 163–4; cf. P. Burschel, *Söldner im Nordwestdeutschland des 16. und 17. Jahrhunderts* (Göttingen, 1994), pp. 195–8.

74. Israel, *Dutch Republic*, p. 97.

75. S. Gaber, *La Lorraine meurtrie* (Nancy, 1979), in particular pp. 26–9, 69–70; G. Rystad, 'Die Schweden in Bayern während des Dreißigjährigen Krieges', in Glaser, *Um Glauben und Reich*, pp. 424–36, in particular pp. 426, 433.

76. Schlögl, *Bauern, Krieg und Staat*, pp. 64–70.

77. Kroener, 'Soldat oder Soldateska?', p. 111.

78. Junkelmann, 'Tilly', p. 384 and n. 65.

79. See pp. 185–6.

80. Henning, *Wirtschafts- und Sozialgeschichte*, i, p. 745; Abel, *Massenarmut*, pp. 148–51. In Hamburg, which did not suffer directly from the war and which was an important harbour, prices reached their highest level in about 1623, 1630 and at the end of the war in 1649–50. In Leipzig the years 1637–38

were the worst and in Würzburg 1633–35 (ibid.). Unfavourable climatic conditions exacerbated the problems of agricultural production during this period. As John Theibault has pointed out 'The "Little Ice Age" of the seventeenth century was at its worst during the war' (Theibault, *German Villages*, p. 183).

81. F. Schröer, *Das Havelland im Dreißigjährigen Krieg* (Cologne, 1966), p. 94–5, on events during the late 1630s in the Mark Brandenburg, in particular in 1639; cf. L. Enders, *Die Uckermark. Geschichte einer kurmärkischen Landschaft vom 12. bis zum 18. Jahrhundert* (Weimar, 1992), pp. 314–51.

82. G. Franz (ed.), *Quellen zur Geschichte des deutschen Bauernstandes in der Neuzeit* (Darmstadt, 1963), no. 52, 'Der Odenwald im Dreißigjährigen Krieg nach den Aufzeichnungen des Pfarrers M. Jh. Daniel Minck in Großbieberau', p. 122. Cf. also the edition of the same chronicle in R. Kunz and W. Lizalek (eds), *Südhessische Chroniken aus der Zeit des Dreißigjährigen Krieges* (Heppenheim, 1983), pp. 229–86.

83. For the trauma caused by the death of so many men and women within a short time cf., however, the sceptical remarks by Roeck, *Eine Stadt*, ii, pp. 779–82.

84. Franz, *Quellen*, p. 122 (Minck's chronicle).

85. Schlögl, *Bauern, Krieg und Staat*, pp. 75–6, and 67–8; cf. Schröer, *Das Havelland*, pp. 131ff, and von Hippel, 'Bevölkerung und Wirtschaft', pp. 436–9.

86. I. Bog, *Die bäuerliche Wirtschaft im Zeitalter des Dreißigjährigen Krieges. Die Bewegungsvorgänge in der Kriegswirtschaft nach den Quellen des Klosterverwalteramtes Heilsbronn* (Coburg, 1952), in particular pp. 109ff; cf. Theibault, *German Villages*, p. 143.

87. Kroener, 'Soldat oder Soldateska?', p. 110.

88. Friedrichs, *Nördlingen*, p. 123; cf. pp. 121–5, where Friedrichs stresses, however, that after the war the lower income groups could make good some of their losses, partly apparently because of declining prices for bread and agricultural products in general and a corresponding rise of wages in real terms – itself a result of the lack of manpower caused by the demographic decline.

89. Roeck, *Eine Stadt*, ii, pp. 905ff, 945–6, 948–9; cf. idem, 'Bayern und der Dreißigjährige Krieg. Demographische, wirtschaftliche und soziale Auswirkungen am Beispiel Münchens', *Geschichte und Gesellschaft* 17 (1991), pp. 434–58, at p. 444, with similar findings for Munich, and Dipper, *Deutsche Geschichte*, p. 276, quoting G. Wunder, *Die Bürger von Hall. Sozialgeschichte einer Reichsstadt* (Sigmaringen, 1980).

90. Roeck, *Eine Stadt*, ii, p. 907, cf. pp. 925–30; somewhat different findings for Nördlingen, Friedrichs, *Nördlingen*, pp. 133–5.
91. Schröer, *Havelland*, pp. 189–91.
92. Redlich, *Enterpriser*, i, pp. 306ff and 408–34.
93. Burschel, *Söldner*, pp. 201–5. For the life of the ordinary soldier cf. further R. Baumann, *Landsknechte. Ihre Geschichte und Kultur vom späten Mittelalter bis zum Dreißigjährigen Krieg* (Munich, 1994). See also G. Parker, 'The Soldiers of the Thirty Years' War', in Repgen, *Krieg und Politik*, pp. 303–16.
94. For the hatred between peasants and soldiers see Peters, *Söldnerleben*, pp. 173–5, where the author of the diary relates how he was given a thorough beating and robbed by three peasants who suddenly appeared from behind a hedge, when he, incautiously, followed his regiment at a couple of hundred yards distance one day because he felt sick.
95. Corvisier, *La France*, p. 124, Parker, *War*, p. 193, Tallett, *War and Society*, p. 218.
96. Burschel, *Söldner*, pp. 258–73, Krüger, 'Kriegsfinanzierung', p. 296.
97. For the soldiers' pay see Kroener, *Routes*, p. 97; Redlich, *Enterpriser*, i, pp. 484–93; and Burschel, *Söldner*, pp. 165–94.

Epilogue

1. For population losses during the war see Dipper, *Deutsche Geschichte*, pp. 44, 266–72. G. Franz, *Der Dreißigjährige Krieg und das deutsche Volk*, 4th edn (1st edn 1940; Stuttgart, 1979), remains of fundamental importance.
2. Steinberg, *Krieg*, pp. 128–32, assumes that the war had little impact on demographic development; H.-U. Wehler, *Deutsche Gesellschaftsgeschichte*, i, *Vom Feudalismus des Alten Reiches bis zur defensiven Modernisierung der Reformära 1700–1815* (Munich, 1987), p. 54, accepts Steinberg's figures.
3. Von Hippel, 'Bevölkerung und Wirtschaft', p. 438, puts the losses for Württemberg at 57 per cent with a top figure of 71 per cent for the worst hit districts, and hardly any district with losses below 30 per cent.
4. Dipper, *Deutsche Geschichte*, p. 272.
5. bid., p. 187.
6. Von Hippel, 'Bevölkerung und Wirtschaft', p. 439.

7. W. W. Hagen, 'Seventeenth-Century Crisis in Brandenburg: The Thirty Years' War, The Destabilization of Serfdom, and the Rise of Absolutism', *American Historical Review* 94 (1989), pp. 302–35, at p. 327.

8. Abel, *Massenarmut*, pp. 154–5; Schlögl, *Bauern, Krieg und Staat*, p. 360.

9. Von Hippel, 'Bevölkerung und Wirtschaft', p. 446.

10. Schlögl, *Bauern, Krieg und Staat*, p. 367; For the 'Malthusian crisis' before the war – which clearly no longer existed in 1650 – see also Henning, *Wirtschafts- und Sozialgeschichte*, i, pp. 729–32.

11. H. Harnisch, 'Grundherrschaft oder Gutsherrschaft. Zu den wirtschaftlichen Grundlagen des niederen Adels in Norddeutschland zwischen spätmittelalterlicher Agrarkrise und Dreißigjährigem Krieg', in R. Endres (ed.), *Adel in der Frühneuzeit. Ein regionaler Vergleich* (Cologne, 1991), pp. 73–98 (with further references); J. Peters (ed.), *Gutsherrschaft als soziales Modell* (*HZ*, supplement 18; Munich, 1995).

12. P.-M. Hahn, 'Aristokratisierung und Professionalisierung. Der Aufstieg der Obristen zu einer militärischen und höfischen Elite in Brandenburg-Preu·en von 1650 bis 1725', *Forschungen zur Brandenburgischen und Preußischen Geschichte*, New Series 1 (1991), pp. 161–208, in particular pp. 194, 197; cf. idem, 'Landesstaat und Ständetum im Kurfürstentum Brandenburg während des 16. und 17. Jahrhunderts', in P. Baumgart (ed.), *Ständetum und Staatsbildung in Brandenburg-Preußen* (Berlin, 1983), pp. 41–79, in particular p. 67. Cf. further Hagen, 'Crisis'.

13. R. Schlögl, 'Absolutismus im 17. Jahrhundert – Bayerischer Adel zwischen Disziplinierung und Integration. Das Beispiel der Entschuldungspolitik nach dem Dreißigjährigen Krieg', *ZHF* 15 (1988), pp. 151–86; for the nobility after 1648 cf. V. Press, 'Soziale Folgen', pp. 245–52.

14. For the nobility of Bohemia and Austria see most recently J. Van Horn Melton, 'The Nobility in the Bohemian and Austrian Lands, 1620–1780', in H. M. Scott (ed.), *The European Nobilities in the Seventeenth and Eighteenth Centuries*, 2 vols (London, 1995), ii, pp. 110–43; cf. T. Winkelbauer, 'Krise der Aristokratie? Zum Strukturwandel des Adels in den böhmischen und niederösterreichischen Ländern im 16. und 17. Jahrhundert', *Mitteilungen des Instituts für österreichische Geschichtsforschung* 100 (1992), pp. 328–53. For similar develop-

ments, that is, a stricter definition of noble status according to criteria imposed by the state, in France in the seventeenth century see J. Meyer, *La Noblesse française á l'époque moderne (XVIe–XVIIIe siècles)* (Paris, 1991), pp. 61–74.

15. Theibault, *German Villages*, p. 195.

16. Dipper, *Deutsche Geschichte*, pp. 231–41; cf. Stolleis, *Geschichte des öffentlichen Rechts*, i, pp. 334–93, and H. Maier, *Die ältere deutsche Staats- und Verwaltungslehre*, 2nd edn (Munich, 1980).

17. Schlögl, *Bauern, Krieg und Staat*, p. 261; cf. Von Hippel, 'Bevölkerung und Wirtschaft', pp. 444–5, for Württemberg, where the level of per capita taxation was four times higher after 1648 than before the war.

18. Thus Hagen, 'Crisis', pp. 332–3; cf. Schlögl, *Bauern, Krieg und Staat*, pp. 265–73.

19. Duchhardt, *Verfassungsgeschichte*, pp.180–7; Asch, 'Estates and Princes'; Schlögl, 'Absolutismus', p. 174.

20. For a powerful polemic against the traditional idea that the relationship between rulers and Estates was a sort of 'zero-sum game' see N. Henshall, *The Myth of Absolutism: Change and Continuity in Early Modern European Monarchy* (London, 1992), pp. 182–91.

21. This point is rightly stressed by Duchhardt, *Verfassungsgeschichte*, pp. 185–7.

22. K. Schlaich, 'Der rationale Territorialismus. Die Kirche unter dem staatsrechtlichen Absolutismus um die Wende vom 17. zum 18. Jahrhundert', in *Zeitschrift für Rechtsgeschichte, Kan. Abt.* 85 (1968), pp. 269–340. Cf. W. Sommer, *Gottesfurcht und Fürstenherrschaft. Studien zum Obrigkeitsverständnis Johann Arndts und lutherischer Hofprediger zur Zeit der altprotestantischen Orthodoxie* (Göttingen, 1988).

23. A. Coreth, *Pietas Austriaca. Ursprung und Entwicklung barocker Frömmigkeit in Österreich* (Munich, 1959).

24. G. Schmid, 'Konfessionspolitik und Staatsraison bei den Verhandlungen des Westfälischen Friedenskongresses über die Gravamina Ecclesiastica', *Archiv für Reformationsgeschichte* 44 (1953), pp. 203–23; U. Scheuner, 'Staatsräson und religiöse Einheit des Staates. Zur Religionspolitik in Deutschland im Zeitalter der Glaubensspaltung', in R. Schnur (ed.), *Staatsräson. Studien zur Geschichte eines politischen Begriffs* (Berlin, 1975), pp. 363–405, esp. pp. 401–5.

25. Maier, *Staats- und Verwaltungslehre*, pp. 131–9; cf. Sommer, *Gottesfurcht und Fürstenherrschaft*, pp. 296–312.

26. Dipper, *Deutsche Geschichte*, pp. 306–7. For the renewed importance of religious arguments in the politics of the Empire in the eighteenth century see D. Stievermann, 'Politik und Konfession im 18. Jahrhundert', *ZHF* 18 (1991), pp. 177–99; G. Haug-Moritz, 'Kaisertum und Parität. Reichspolitik und Konfessionen nach dem Westfälischen Frieden', *ZHF* 19 (1992), pp. 445–82, at pp. 472–81, and eadem, *Württembergischer Ständekonflikt und deutscher Dualismus. Ein Beitrag zur Geschichte des Reichsverbandes in der Mitte des 18. Jahrhunderts* (Stuttgart, 1992), pp. 138–71.

SELECT BIBLIOGRAPHY

The bibliography aims to provide the reader with a number of titles, in English as well as in German, and, in some cases, in other languages, which are either general surveys or, alternatively, special studies published principally during the last two decades. However, some books which are important for the general history of the early seventeenth century without necessarily treating the Thirty Years War itself extensively have also been included.

The modern standard account in English is G. Parker *et al.*, *The Thirty Years War* (London, 1984). Among works published in Germany the most substantial recent book about the war is by J. Burkhardt, but the short introductions by Limm (in English), Schormann and Schmidt (the latter two in German) can also be recommended. For an exhaustive and reliable narrative account one has to go back to Moriz Ritter, whose *Deutsche Geschichte im Zeitalter der Gegenreformation und des Dreißigjährigen Krieges* remains unsurpassed in its richness of detail and balanced assessment of political events, although it does not cover the last 13 years of the conflict. The most important collections of essays on the war have been edited by K. Repgen and H. U. Rudolf.

Printed Sources and Selections of Documents

Acta Pacis Westphalicae, ed. M. Braubach and K. Repgen for the Rheinische-Westfälische Akademie der Wissenschaften and the Vereinigung zur Erforschung der Neueren Geschichte; Series I, *Instruktionen*; Series II, *Korrespondenzen*; Series III, *Protokolle, Verhandlungsakten, Diarien, Varia* (Münster, 1962–).

G. Benecke (ed.), *Germany in the Thirty Years War* (London, 1978).

Briefe und Akten zur Geschichte des Dreißigjährigen Krieges, Neue Folge, Die Politik Maximilians von Baiern und seiner Verbündeten 1618–1651, Part I, vol. i and ii, ed. G. Franz and A. Duch; Part II, vol. i–v, viii and ix, ed. W. Goetz, D. Albrecht and K. Bierther (Leipzig, Munich, Vienna, 1907–82).

A. Buschmann (ed.), *Kaiser und Reich. Klassische Texte und Dokumente zur Verfassungsgeschichte des Heiligen Römischen Reiches Deutscher Nation* (Munich, 1984).

F. W. von Ditfurth and K. Bartsch (eds), *Die historisch-politischen Volkslieder des Dreißigjährigen Krieges* (Heidelberg, 1882).

Documenta Bohemica Bellum Tricennale Illustrantia, ed. J. Kocí *et al.,* 7 vols (Prague, 1971–81).

H. H. Hofmann (ed.), *Quellen zum Verfassungsorganismus des Heiligen Römischen Reiches Deutscher Nation 1495–1815* (Darmstadt, 1976).

F. C. Khevenhiller, *Annales Ferdinandei ... von Anfang des 1578. biß auf das 1637. Jahr,* 2nd edn, 12 parts (Leipzig, 1721–26).

G. Lorenz (ed.), *Quellen zur Geschichte Wallensteins* (Darmstadt, 1987).

G. Lorenz (ed.), *Quellen zur Vorgeschichte und zu den Anfängen des Dreißigjährigen Krieges* (Darmstadt, 1991).

Axel Oxenstierna, *Rikskansleren Axel Oxenstiernas Skrifter och Brefvexling,* ed. C. G. Styffe, P. Sondén *et al.,* Section I, vol. i–xv; Section II, vol. i–xii (Stockholm, 1888–1977).

J. Peters (ed.), *Ein Söldnerleben im Dreißigjährigen Krieg* (Berlin, 1993).

Cardinal Richelieu, *Les Papiers de Richelieu,* ed. P. Grillon, *Section politique intérieure,* vol. i–vi (Paris, 1975–85); *Section politique extérieure,* vol. i (Paris, 1982).

Cardinal Richelieu, *Lettres, Instructions diplomatiques et papiers d'état du Cardinal de Richelieu,* ed. D. L. M. Avenel, 8 vols (Paris, 1853–77).

H. Schulz (ed.), *Der Dreißigjährige Krieg,* Part i (Leipzig, 1917).

G. Zillhardt (ed.), *Der Dreißigjährige Krieg in zeitgenössischer Darstellung. Hans Heberles 'Zeitregister' (1618–1672). Aufzeichnungen aus dem Ulmer Territorium* (Ulm, 1975).

Secondary Literature

Books (including chapters in textbooks and in works of reference)

W. Abel, *Massenarmut und Hungerkrisen im vorindustriellen Europa* (Hamburg, 1974).

D. Albrecht, *Die auswärtige Politik Maximilians von Bayern 1618–1635* (Göttingen, 1962).

J. Alcalá-Zamora y Queipo de Llano, *Razon y crisis de la política exterior de España en el reinado de Felipe IV* (Madrid, 1977).

H. Altmann, *Die Reichspolitik Maximilians von Bayern 1613–1618* (*Briefe und Akten zur Geschichte des Dreißigjährigen Krieges* 12, Munich, 1978).

G. Barudio, *Der Teutsche Krieg 1618–1648* (Frankfurt/M., 1985).

W. Becker, *Der Kurfürstenrat, Grundzüge seiner Entwicklung in der Reichsverfassung und seine Stellung auf dem Westfälischen Friedenskongreß* (Münster, 1973).

J. Bély, *Les relations internationales en Europe, xviie–xviiie siècles* (Paris, 1992).

J. Bergin and L. Brockliss (eds), *Richelieu and his Age* (Oxford, 1992).

K. Bierther, *Der Regensburger Reichstag von 1640/1641* (Kallmünz, 1971).

R. Bireley, SJ, *Maximilian von Bayern, Adam Contzen S. J. und die Gegenreformation in Deutschland 1624–1635* (Göttingen, 1975).

R. Bireley, SJ, *Religion and Politics in the Age of the Counterreformation: Emperor Ferdinand II, William Lamormaini, S. J., and the Formation of Imperial Policy* (Chapel Hill, N. C., 1981).

R. Bonney, *Political Change in France under Richelieu and Mazarin 1624–1661* (Oxford, 1978).

R. Bonney, *The European Dynastic States 1494–1660* (Oxford, 1991).

J. Burkhardt, *Der Dreißigjährige Krieg* (Frankfurt/M., 1992).

J. Collins, *Fiscal Limits of Absolutism: Direct Taxation in Early Seventeenth-Century France* (Berkeley, Calif., 1988).

J. Cooper (ed.), *The New Cambridge Modern History*, vol. iv: *The Decline of Spain and the Thirty Years War 1609–48/59* (Cambridge, 1970).

A. Corvisier, 'Renouveau militaire et misères de la guerre, 1635–1659', in idem (ed.), *Histoire militaire de la France*, vol. i: *Des origines à 1715* (Paris, 1992), pp 353–82.

F. Dickmann, *Der Westfälische Frieden*, 2nd edn (Münster, 1965); additional bibliography in 5th edn, 1985.

C. Dipper, *Deutsche Geschichte 1648–1789* (Frankfurt/M., 1991).

H. Diwald, *Wallenstein* (Munich, 1969).

H. Duchhardt, *Deutsche Verfassungsgeschichte 1495–1806* (Stuttgart, 1991).

J. H. Elliott, *Richelieu and Olivares* (Cambridge, 1984).

J. H. Elliott, *The Count-Duke of Olivares: The Statesman in an Age of Decline* (New Haven and London, 1986).

J. H. Elliott and A. García Sanz (eds), *La España del Conde Duque de Olivares*, (Valladolid, 1990).

J. Engel, 'Von der spätmittelalterlichen respublica christiana zum Mächte-Europa der Neuzeit', in idem (ed.), *Handbuch der europäischen Geschichte*, vol. iii: *Die Entstehung des neuzeitlichen Europa* (Stuttgart, 1971), pp. 1–443.

H. Ernst, *Madrid und Wien 1632–37. Politik und Finanzen in den Beziehungen zwischen Philipp IV. und Ferdinand II* (Münster, 1991).

A. Ernstberger, *Hans de Witte, Finanzmann Wallensteins* (Wiesbaden, 1954).

R. J. W. Evans, *Rudolf II and his World* (Oxford, 1973).

R. J. W. Evans, *The Making of the Habsburg Monarchy* (Oxford, 1979).

R. J. W. Evans and T. V. Thomas (eds), *Crown, Church and Estates: Central European Politics in the Sixteenth and Seventeenth Centuries* (London, 1991).

C. R. Friedrichs, *Urban Society in an Age of War, Nördlingen 1580–1720* (Princeton, N. J., 1979).

A. Gindely, *Geschichte des Dreißigjährigen Krieges*, 3 parts (Leipzig, 1882; translated as *History of the Thirty Years War*, 2 vols, London, 1885).

H. Glaser, (ed.), *Wittelsbach und Bayern*, vol. ii: *Um Glauben und Reich. Beiträge zur bayerischen Geschichte und Kunst 1573–1657* (Munich, 1980).

A. Gotthard, *Konfession und Staatsräson. Die Außenpolitik Württembergs unter Herzog Johann Friedrich (1608–1628)* (Stuttgart, 1992).

H. Haan, *Der Regensburger Kurfürstentag von 1636/37* (Münster, 1967).

M. Heckel, *Deutschland im konfessionellen Zeitalter* (Göttingen, 1983).

M. Heckel, *Gesammelte Schriften. Staat, Kirche, Recht, Geschichte*, ed. K. Schlaich, 2 vols (Tübingen, 1989).

F.-W. Henning, *Handbuch der Wirtschafts- und Sozialgeschichte Deutschlands*, vol. i: *Deutsche Wirtschafts- und Sozialgeschichte im Mittelalter und in der frühen Neuzeit* (Paderborn, 1991).

M. Hughes, *Early Modern Germany 1477–1806* (London, 1992).

J. I. Israel, *The Dutch Republic and the Hispanic World 1606–1661* (Oxford, 1982) (quoted Israel, *Dutch Republic*).

J. I. Israel, *The Dutch Republic: Its Rise, Greatness, and Fall 1477–1806* (Oxford, 1995) (quoted Israel, *Greatness and Fall*).

H. Kamen, *Spain 1469–1714: A Society of Conflict* (London, 1983).

P. Kriedte, *Spätfeudalismus und Handelskapital* (Göttingen, 1980; English translation: *Peasants, Landlords and Merchant Capitalists*, Cambridge, 1983).

B. Kroener, *Les routes et les étapes. Die Versorgung der französischen Armeen in Nordostfrankreich (1635–1661)* (Münster, 1980).

J. Kunisch (ed.), *Neue Studien zur frühneuzeitlichen Reichsgeschichte* (*ZHF*, supplement 3, Berlin, 1987).

H. Langer, *The Thirty Years War* (New York, 1980).

E. Le Roy Ladurie, *L'Ancien régime*, vol. i: *L'Absolutisme en vraie grandeur 1610–1715* (Paris, 1991).

P. Limm, *The Thirty Years War* (London, 1984).

G. Livet, *La Guerre de trente ans*, 3rd edn (Paris, 1972).

J. Lynch, *The Hispanic World in Crisis and Change 1598–1700* (Oxford, 1992).

D. Maland, *Europe at War 1600–1650* (London, 1980).

G. Mann, *Wallenstein* (Frankfurt/M., 1971; English translation London, 1976).

T. Munck, *Seventeenth-Century Europe* (London, 1990).

A. Oschmann, *Der Nürnberger Exekutionstag 1649–1650* (Münster, 1991).

A. Osiander, *The States System of Europe 1640–1990* (Oxford, 1994).

G. Pagès, *The Thirty Years War* (London, 1971; original French edition Paris 1949).

G. Parker, *The Army of Flanders and the Spanish Road 1567–1659* (Cambridge, 1972).

G. Parker, *Europe in Crisis 1598–1648* (London, 1979).

G. Parker et al., *The Thirty Years War* (London, 1984; revised edn 1987).

G. Parker, *The Military Revolution: Military Innovation and the Rise of the West 1500–1800* (Cambridge, 1988).

J. Polišenský, *The Thirty Years War* (London, 1971).

J. Polišenský, *War and Society in Europe 1618–1648* (Cambridge, 1978).

V. Press, *Kriege und Krisen. Deutschland 1600–1715* (Munich, 1991).

T. K. Rabb (ed.), *The Thirty Years' War*, 2nd edn (Lexington, Mass., 1972).

F. Redlich, *The German Military Enterpriser and his Workforce: A Study in European Economic and Social History*, 2 vols (Wiesbaden, 1964–65).

K. Repgen, *Die römische Kurie und der Westfälische Friede*, vol. i, parts 1 and 2 (Tübingen, 1962/65).

K. Repgen (ed.), *Forschungen und Quellen zur Geschichte des Dreißigjährigen Krieges* (Münster, 1981).

K. Repgen, 'Dreißigjähriger Krieg', in G. Krause and K. Müller (eds), *Theologische Realenzyklopädie*, vol. ix (Berlin, 1982), pp. 169–88.

K. Repgen (ed.), *Krieg und Politik 1618–1648. Europäische Probleme und Perspektiven* (Munich, 1988).

M. Ritter, *Deutsche Geschichte im Zeitalter der Gegenreformation und des Dreißigjährigen Krieges*, vols ii and iii (Stuttgart, 1895, 1908; reprint Darmstadt, 1962).

M. Roberts, *Gustavus Adolphus: A History of Sweden 1611–1632*, 2 vols (London, 1953–58) (quoted Roberts, *Gustavus Adolphus: A History*).

M. Roberts (ed.), *Sweden's Age of Greatness* (London, 1973).

M. Roberts, *The Swedish Imperial Experience* (Cambridge, 1979).

M. Roberts, *Gustavus Adolphus* (London, 1992) (quoted Roberts, *Gustavus Adolphus*).

B. Roeck, *Eine Stadt in Krieg und Frieden. Studien zur Geschichte der Reichsstadt Augsburg zwischen Kalenderstreit und Parität*, 2 vols (Göttingen, 1989).

C. J. Rogers (ed.), *The Military Revolution Debate: Readings on the Military Transformation of Early Modern Europe* (Boulder, Colo., 1995).

H. U. Rudolf (ed.), *Der Dreißigjährige Krieg* (Darmstadt, 1977).

K. Ruppert, *Die kaiserliche Politik auf dem westfälischen Friedenskongreß* (Münster, 1979).

C. Russell, *Parliaments and English Politics 1621–1629* (Oxford, 1979).

G. Rystad, *Kriegsnachrichten und Propaganda während des Dreißigjährigen Krieges* (Lund, 1960).

H. Salm, *Armeefinanzierung im Dreißigjährigen Krieg. Der Niederrheinisch-Westfälische Reichskreis 1635–1650* (Münster, 1990).

H. Schilling, *Aufbruch und Krise. Deutschland 1517–1648* (Berlin, 1988).

H. Schilling, *Höfe und Allianzen. Deutschland 1648–1763* (Berlin, 1989).

R. Schlögl, *Bauern, Krieg und Staat. Oberbayerische Bauernwirtschaft und frühmoderner Staat* (Göttingen, 1988).

G. Schmidt, *Der Dreißigjährige Krieg* (Munich, 1995).

H. R. Schmidt, *Konfessionalisierung im 16. Jahrhundert* (*EDG* 12; Munich, 1992).

G. Schormann, *Der Dreißigjährige Krieg*, 2nd edn (Göttingen, 1993).

W. Schulze, *Deutsche Geschichte im 16. Jahrhundert* (Frankfurt/M., 1987).

S. H. Steinberg, *The Thirty Years War and the Conflict for European Hegemony* (New York, 1966).

S. H. Steinberg, *Der Dreißigjährige Krieg und der Kampf um die Vorherrschaft in Europa 1600–1660* (Göttingen, 1967; German translation of Steinberg, *The Thirty Years War*).

B. Stier and W. von Hippel, 'War, Economy and Society', in S. Ogilvie (ed.), *Germany: A New Economic and Social History*, vol. ii: *1630–1800* (London, 1996), pp. 233–62.

M. Stolleis, *Geschichte des öffentlichen Rechts in Deutschland,* vol. i: *Reichspublizistik und Policeywissenschaft 1600–1800* (Munich, 1988).

R. A. Stradling, *Europe and the Decline of Spain: A Study of the Spanish System 1580–1720* (London, 1981).

E. Straub, *Pax et Imperium. Spaniens Kampf um seine Friedensordnung in Europa zwischen 1617 und 1653* (Paderborn, 1980).

F. Tallett, *War and Society in Early Modern Europe 1495–1715* (London, 1992).

J. C. Theibault, *German Villages in Crisis. Rural Life in Hesse-Kassel and the Thirty Years' War, 1580–1720* (Atlantic Highlands, N. J., 1995).

S. S. Tschopp, *Heilsgeschichtliche Deutungsmuster in der Publizistik des Dreißigjährigen Krieges* (Frankfurt/M., 1991).

R. R. Vilar, *La Política Europea de España durante la Guerra de Trente Años 1624–30* (Madrid, 1967).

H. Weber, *Frankreich, Kurtrier, der Rhein und das Reich 1623–1635* (Bonn, 1969).

C. V. Wedgwood, *The Thirty Years War* (London, 1938).

G. Zeller, *La Guerre de Trente Ans et les relations internationales* (Paris, 1948).

Articles

R. G. Asch, 'Estates and Princes after 1648: The Consequences of the Thirty Years War', *German History* 6 (1988), pp. 113–32.

G. Benecke, 'The Problem of Death and Destruction in Germany during the Thirty Years War', *ESR* 2 (1972), pp. 239–53.

P. Brightwell, 'The Spanish Origins of the Thirty Years' War', *ESR* 9 (1979), pp. 409–31.

P. Brightwell, Spain and Bohemia: the Decision to Intervene, 1619, *ESR* 12 (1982), pp. 117–41.

A. Gotthard, '"Politice seint wir bäpstisch". Kursachsen und der deutsche Protestantismus im frühen 17. Jahrhundert', *ZHF* 20 (1993), pp. 275–320.

H. Haan, 'Kaiser Ferdinand II. und das Problem des Reichsabsolutismus', in Rudolf, *Krieg*, pp. 208–64.

H. Haan, 'Prosperität und Dreißigjähriger Krieg', *Geschichte und Gesellschaft* 7 (1981), pp. 91–118.

W. von Hippel, 'Bevölkerung und Wirtschaft im Zeitalter des Dreißigjährigen Krieges. Das Beispiel Württemberg', *ZHF* 4 (1978), pp. 413–48.

H. Kamen, 'The Economic and Social Consequences of the Thirty Years War', *Past and Present* 39 (1968), pp. 44–61.

B. Kroener, 'Soldat oder Soldateska, Programmatischer Aufriß einer Sozialgeschichte militärischer Unterschichten in der ersten Hälfte des 17. Jahrhunderts', in M. Messerschmidt *et al.* (eds), *Militärgeschichte Probleme, Thesen, Wege* (Frankfurt/M., 1982), pp. 100–23.

K. Krüger, 'Dänische und schwedische Kriegsfinanzierung im Dreißigjährigen Krieg bis 1635', in Repgen, *Krieg und Politik*, pp. 275–98.

F. Magen, 'Die Reichskreise in der Epoche des Dreißigjährigen Krieges', *ZHF* 9 (1982), pp. 408–60.

S. C. Ogilvie, 'Germany and the Seventeenth-Century Crisis', *Historical Journal* 35 (1992), pp. 417–41.

D. Parrott, 'Richelieu, the *Grands* and the French Army', in Bergin/ Brockliss, *Richelieu*, pp. 135–74.

D. Parrott, 'The Causes of the Franco-Spanish War of 1635–59', in J. Black (ed.), *The Origins of War in Early Modern Europe* (Edinburgh, 1987), pp. 72–111.

J. Polišenský, 'The Thirty Years War and the Crises and Revolutions in Seventeenth Century Europe', in *Past and Present* 39 (1968), pp. 34–43.

V. Press, 'Soziale Folgen des Dreißigjährigen Krieges', in W. Schulze (ed.), *Ständische Gesellschaft und soziale Mobilität* (Munich, 1988), pp. 239–69.

R. A. Stradling, 'Olivares and the Origins of the Franco-Spanish War, 1627–1635', *EHR* 101 (1986), pp. 68–94.

H. Weber, '"Une Bonne Paix": Richelieu's Foreign Policy and the Peace of Christendom', in Bergin/Brockliss, *Richelieu*, pp. 45–69.

INDEX